The British Press and Broadcasting since 1945

Colin Seymour-Ure

Basil Blackwell

First published 1991

Basil Blackwell Ltd
108 Cowley Road, Oxford, OX4 1JF, UK

Basil Blackwell, Inc.
3 Cambridge Center
Cambridge, Massachusetts 02142, USA

British Library Cataloguing in Publication Data

A CIP catalogue record for this book is available from the British Library.

Library of Congress Cataloging in Publication Data

Seymour-Ure, Colin, 1938
    The British Press and Broadcasting since 1945/Colin Seymour-Ure.
        p. cm. − (Making Contemporary Britain)
    Includes bibliographical references and index.
    ISBN 0-631-16443-X: ISBN 0-631-16444-8 (pbk.)
    1. Press − Great Britain 2. Broadcasting − Great Britain. 3. Mass
      media − Political aspects − Great Britain. I. Title. II. Series.
    PN5118.S39 1991
    302.23′0941−dc20   90-45110
                                                    CIP

Typeset in 11 on 13 pt Ehrhardt
by Setrite Typesetters Ltd
Printed in Great Britain by Billing and Sons Ltd

The British Press and
Broadcasting since 1945

Making Contemporary Britain

General Editor: Anthony Seldon
Consultant Editor: Peter Hennessy

Books in the series

Institute of Contemporary British History
34 Tavistock Square, London WC1H 9EZ

Contents

For N. G. S-U.

List of Tables

General Editor's Preface

The Institute of Contemporary British History's series *Making Contemporary Britain* is aimed directly at students in schools and universities and at others interested in learning more about topics in post-war British history. In the series, authors are less attempting to break new ground than presenting clear and balanced overviews of the state of knowledge on each of the topics.

The ICBH was founded in October 1986 with the objective of promoting the study of British history since 1945 at every level. To that end, it publishes books and a quarterly journal, *Contemporary Record*; it organizes seminars and conferences for school students, undergraduates, researchers and teachers of post-war history; and it runs a number of research programmes and other activities.

A central theme of the ICBH's work is that post-war history is too often neglected in British schools, institutes of higher education and beyond. The ICBH acknowledges the validity of the arguments against the study of recent history, notably the problems of bias, of overly subjective teaching and writing, and the difficulties of perspective. But it believes that the values of studying post-war history outweigh the drawbacks, and that the health and future of a liberal democracy require that its citizens know more about the most recent past of their country than the limited knowledge possessed by British citizens, young and old, today. Indeed, the ICBH believes that the dangers of political indoctrination are higher where the young are *not* informed of the recent past. There are many books on the contemporary media in Britain, examining its ownership, structure, influences and importance. Many excellent autobiographical accounts have also been written by those who worked in the rapidly developing media since the war.

But no book has appeared until now describing and analysing the revolution that has occurred in the British media over the last forty-five years. Television and other new outlets have started up and radio and the printed media have changed beyond recognition. Without some knowledge of these developments, it is impossible to gain a full understanding of the media today.

Colin Seymour-Ure's book should be read with profit by all students, practitioners and observers of the rich and diverse media in Britain.

Anthony Seldon

Preface

This book is mainly about the press and broadcasting – who controlled them, what was available and how they related to one another – in the years 1945–90. It tries to be more than a contemporary look with glances backward, but it is not resolutely chronological. It avoids many issues that get intense scrutiny at particular moments: 'bias' of various kinds; influence on violence; 'effects' in general. There is ample literature about these and an historical account would be too much like an ancient map of the world: large wastes of conjecture punctuated by occasional islands of knowledge.

The scope of the subject makes the book necessarily selective and impressionistic. Its general focus, in the second half, is on the theme of media accountability, and in particular upon the see-saw of influence between media and government. Who is accountable to whom? As TV has spread into our lives, embracing (sometimes suffocating) other media, this theme is more important than ever.

I am most grateful for the help given by Andrew Cree in the early stages of preparing the book, and for enjoyable discussions with students taking the political communications option at the University of Kent. I owe special thanks to Nicola Kerry for her speed and skill in typing the manuscript and tables.

Colin Seymour-Ure

1 Snapshot: 1945/1990

British media changed so much between 1945 and 1990 that it may be best to begin with contrasting snapshots of these two years.

1945

There was no television. About ten million households had a radio set and most were run off the mains, not off a battery. The compulsory annual licence fee cost ten shillings (50p). You had a choice of two BBC stations. One was 'serious'; the other broadcast light music and entertainment. The nine o'clock evening news had an audience of half the population during the war, but this fell quickly in 1945. The BBC had its own foreign correspondents but none yet for domestic news. Quite a lot of people listened to light music on Radio Luxembourg. You could also hear music at home on a wind-up gramophone with ten- or twelve-inch 78 r.p.m. bakelite records. These played for only a few minutes at a time.

Most people read one of nine London-edited, 'national' morning newspapers, delivered through the letter-box. If it was the *Daily Mirror* or *Daily Sketch*, it was tabloid. If not — and those papers had less than a quarter of the total circulation — it was broadsheet. Because of paper rationing it had only four to eight pages, unless it was *The Times*, which averaged nine. Most of the contents were news, not features. One person in five, mainly in the big cities, bought a locally published morning paper as well or instead. Local evening papers were smaller but more numerous (76 compared with 29). Londoners had a choice of three evening papers. Even more people read a Sunday paper than a daily, often for the sport. Nearly 750 towns had weekly papers.

The national dailies differed sharply in style between the low-circulation 'qualities' and the mass-circulation 'populars'. All nine were separately owned, mainly by elderly barons (barons in fact and in managerial style), such as Lord Beaverbrook and Lord Kemsley. They also owned Sunday papers. Lord Kemsley and Lord Rothermere owned chains of provincial dailies too. The barons were politically partisan − mostly Conservative − and you expected your paper to play a vigorous part for or against Mr Churchill in the 1945 general election campaign. The BBC did not report the election at all until polling day, but it provided time for nightly talks by party leaders, up to half-an-hour in length.

On the news-stands, there were several popular illustrated weekly news and feature magazines: *Everybody's*, *Illustrated*, *Picture Post*. There were numerous general magazines and a growing market in women's weeklies and monthlies. Colour was limited. The brightest splash in the newsagent was probably the display of orange and green Penguin paperbacks − the main paperbacks available. 6,747 book titles were published. Boots and W.H. Smith ran cheap circulating libraries, supplementing the public libraries.

Regularly you went to the cinema. Thirty million cinema tickets a week were sold in 1945. *The Times* still listed cinemas as 'Picture Theatres'. The short weekly 'newsreels', a mixture of news and feature stories, gave a foretaste of TV news. Hollywood products dominated. In addition to the feature film, you saw a shorter, low budget, 'B movie'. Films were censored for decency by Local Authorities, with the aid of an independent board.

In the press, 'taste' was largely a matter of editorial discretion. Four-letter words and topless girls were taboo. Tasteful, airbrushed nudes appeared in light monthly magazines such as *Lilliput* and *Men Only*.

1990

There was almost no escape from television. Three homes out of five had two TV sets and one person in six had three. ITV broadcast round the clock. Viewers had a choice of four channels. Between them, BBC1, BBC2, ITV and Channel 4 provided some 450 hours of programmes a week. The licence fee was £71, all of which went to the BBC. ITV was paid for by advertisements, carefully regulated by the Independent Broadcasting Authority.

If your town was cabled and you were one of 80,000 householders who paid a subscription, you could get a variety of extra specialized channels such as sport and movies. Rupert Murdoch's Sky satellite channel had 600,000 subscribers and the rival BSB satellite service was just entering the market. A quarter of us had Teletext on our TV. Ten percent used the set for video games. More than half of us used it with a video-recorder, chiefly for films and soap operas taped from broadcasts. Nearly everyone had colour.

We spent twenty-six hours a week watching TV: news, soap operas, films, the House of Commons, endless studio discussion among politicians. Snooker was the most popular televised sport: only one team game (football) was among the TV top ten. TV was the nation's main evening activity.

We spent eight hours a week listening to the radio — but mainly while doing something else. The BBC had four national stations and 32 locals. There was also a commercial station near most people, licensed by the IBA, and any number of overseas stations. Stations mostly broadcast music and 'chat'. BBC Radio 4 was for news and talk; Radio 3, for classical music. You could listen almost any time, anywhere — especially with your Walkman headset that filtered nothing but a mildly irritating hiss to passengers in your bus, say, or your train compartment. As much as 85 per cent of cars had a radio, and over half were used whenever the car was driven. Half had a cassette player too. A quarter of us had four radio sets or more.

Music of high technical quality was available in the home through CDs, cassette tapes, LPs and pop videos. Older members of a family did not go out of the house in search of music but to get away from it.

Despite TV, most people still read a daily newspaper. The dominance of the national press had increased. Of eleven main dailies, six were tabloids with 80 per cent of the circulation. Your paper had 30−40 pages or more; a large proportion of features; pages of small ads (if it was a broadsheet); regular colour. Your Sunday paper very likely came in sections, some of which you were still reading the following week. If you wanted an illustrated weekly magazine, you could get one free, in excellent colour, with a Saturday or Sunday paper. Fewer people now read an evening paper: if they did, it was primarily to see what was on TV. Only eighteen provincial morning papers survived, so there was less opportunity to read one anyway. Thirteen towns outside London had a choice of local dailies. Half of us bought a local weekly paper, and three-quarters received an unsolicited 'free weekly', financed by advertising. Many of these contained little editorial copy. Their total circulation was 37 million. In London, only one evening paper survived, despite an unsuccessful attempt by Robert Maxwell to establish a new one in 1987.

The national dailies were bunched into eight ownership groups, headed by Rupert Murdoch, Robert Maxwell, the latest Lord Rothermere and others. More than in 1945, they controlled multimedia organizations, with interests in TV, radio, film, video, recorded music and book publishing, as well as news-papers and magazines. Moreover their interests were inter-national, and they generally included non-media businesses too. In the 1987 general election they presented you with a partisan newspaper, as in 1945: nearly all were rooting for Mrs Thatcher.

The news-stands were a blaze of glossy colour. In London's Victoria Station, a kiosk displayed over 700 magazines − 40 on computing, 75 on music and hi-fi, others on skateboarding, home freezers, body-building, and many other categories (including soft porn) that in 1945 did not exist. The traditional women's magazines, hugely successful in the 1950s, had slumped. Penguin books had changed their distinctive format. Paperbacks in general had pushed aside the hardback, except for the specialized and coffee table markets. The commercial lending libraries had disappeared. Book publishing had soared to more than 55,000 new titles and reprints.

You very rarely went to the cinema, unless you were young and middle class. Attendances were down to one million per week. If you did, you saw one main film and had ample opportunity to buy ice cream. Film was still censored, but by more liberal standards than in 1945.

Could you be more easily shocked by media in 1990 than in 1945? It is difficult to know. If you were, there was certainly more scope to complain. The Press Council, Broadcasting Complaints Commission and Advertising Standards Authority were at your disposal, though only the latter had teeth.

2 Which Media? What History?

How much of those snapshots might a history of mass media study? The term 'mass media' itself was not widely used until the 1960s. (Its first appearance in the index to *The Times*, not a bad indicator, was in 1965.) A history of mass media from 1945 must thus impose a common character upon a set of — what? Organizations? Technologies? Information sources? — which either went by a different name or was not recognised at that time.

Everyone agrees that newspapers and TV are mass media. Indeed the history of this period could be seen very largely as a process of adjustment by and to TV. But what about books — and cinema? Or is film, not cinema, the mass medium? What is 'TV', anyway? In 1946, when post-war service began, the TV set sat in the corner for most of the time, as the service lasted for only about four hours a day. Early TV sets sometimes had doors, which you folded back to reveal the screen when it was time to watch. ITV was allowed about seven hours a day when it started in 1955; and long before the growth of home computers, VCRs and video games in the 1980s, of course, the TV set had become a main focus (often *the* focus) of the living room. But with the growth of these other uses, what exactly did it mean by 1990 to say that 'TV' was a mass medium? Was a TV programme the same thing whether it came to your set by satellite, by cable, by terrestrial transmitter or by videotape?

'Mass medium' thus turns out to be one of those terms, apparently simple, that grow more elusive upon analysis. Partly this may be because the term gained currency precisely in response to the proliferation of media and the lack of a suitable umbrella word to cover them. Beyond that, uncertainty is caused by the fact that different media commonly take their names from different elements in the communication process. Any completed act of communication, from a conversation between two people to a summit communiqué beamed by world leaders round the globe, involves (to quote an old formulation) 'a sender, message, medium and receiver'. A further source of names is the purpose for which the communication takes place, such as advertising or news.

If we say the *Sun* is a mass medium we name a news organization (a 'sender') and a technology for distributing 'messages' (a 'medium'). If we say *newspapers* are a mass medium, we refer to a particular kind of 'message' – news. (Contrast the name 'magazine', using the same technology but suggesting a less news-based idea.) If we call *the press* a mass medium, we refer, strictly, to an ancient technology (a 'medium') of pressing sheets of paper against inked type – dominant, in 1945, in the ultimate guise of hot metal typesetting machines, which by 1990 were on the scrap-heap. If we call *the popular press* a mass medium, as we might when distinguishing the *Sun* from *The Times*, we refer to circulation numbers (the 'receivers'). The same product, the *Sun*, can thus be described in several different ways as a mass medium.

The same game can be played with radio and TV. We might apply the term 'mass medium' to *the BBC* ('sender'), or *broadcasting* ('medium'), or *News at Ten* ('message'). There is no broadcast equivalent to 'popular press', though the term 'pop radio' was current for a time in the 1970s. Compared with the press and broadcasting, other media have generally been named by reference to fewer elements of the communication process. 'Film' and 'movie' refer to a technology and 'cinema', by connoting a location, to 'receivers'. 'Records', 'CDs' and 'tapes' (audio and video) describe a 'medium'; 'pop' (records, videos) describes a kind of 'message'.

How then can the term 'mass medium' be pinned down for the period 1945–90? Those two words emphasize the key importance of the technology and the 'receivers'. Media qualify as mass media if they are good at conveying complex 'messages' fast, clearly and simultaneously to large numbers of people. The 'senders' and 'messages' are the least distinctive parts. No mass medium can yet serve mass 'senders' on the scale of mass audiences; and the 'messages' delivered in a daily paper could be conveyed in identical terms by typed letter through the mail. The mass audiences and the technology for reaching them are what give the press and electronic media their character as mass media.

Even so, the term is always flexible because it is relative. A 'mass' audience is large in relation to a maximum. New technology changes the maximum. Daily newspapers became increasingly possible on a national, not a London or a regional scale, as railways and faster presses made daily printing and distribution more practical in the late nineteenth century. The *Manchester Guardian* was a mass medium in Manchester from its foundation in 1821. As a mass medium nationally it achieved full status only in 1959 when it started printing in London, dropped Manchester from the mast-head and was distributed nationally like the other Fleet Street dailies.

'Fast' and 'simultaneous' distribution, again, are defined by the purposes of the 'sender' and the speed of alternative technologies. Until the 1950s, the news in daily papers had only limited competition from radio and virtually none from TV. But soon the big stories were written in the knowledge that readers would know at least the bare bones from a news bulletin, and the 24-hour cycle of the daily paper lost much of its point as a *news* medium. Apart from a few news and sport items and the TV listings, how much of Monday's *Mirror* or *Sun* could not equally well be published on the following Thursday or Friday?

Media qualifying as 'mass media' therefore vary, in particular with changes in technology but also with the changing interest of mass audiences and the intricate factor of costs. Some media at any moment might be on the way in; others on the way out. Theatre, in past centuries, might have counted as a mass medium: it was an effective way of spreading ideas, and so it suffered official censorship (not abolished until the 1960s). Beacons, semaphore, morse code were all in their day rapid methods of sending information. The elephantine new medium in the 1945–90 period was obviously TV. Its presence in everyday life became so large and so intense, and in such a short space of time – say 20 years from the Coronation in 1953, acknowledged as the 'take-off' date – that its influence is strictly incalculable, over other media and over most facets of life. The effects – upon violence in society for instance – often seemed self-evident. But they were very difficult to prove, or to use as the basis of generalization, because of the difficulty of isolating TV as a causal factor.

Beside TV, other media that came or went look mouselike. Most were variations of existing media. For example, 78 r.p.m records and wind-up gramophones gave way in the 1950s to LPs and open-reel tape-recorders. These in turn gave way to stereo, cassettes, CDs. Bulky portable radios, larger than the portable TV sets of the 1980s and bulbous with valves and batteries, gave way to the transistor radio in the 1950s. Provincial morning papers continued their slow decline, as TV and the national press ate into their market. The 'general interest' illustrated weekly magazines like *Picture Post* were killed off in the late 1950s by TV, even before the free colour magazines and expanded feature coverage of the Sunday papers, led by *The Sunday Times*, were introduced in the early 1960s.

The new electronic media of the 1980s, such as cable, satellite TV and video recorders, were not variations in the product reaching the audience, as were those changes in the press. They were new *methods* of delivering the product: changes in media technology. Some would qualify as mass media on 'message' and rapidity grounds, but fail on audience size. The telephone 'conference call' for instance, enabled a widely separated group of individuals to share a telephone discussion, but the groups were too small to count as 'mass'. Similarly, telex and faxing were more analogous to mail than to the press.

'Direct mail' (often known as 'junk mail'), on the other hand, even though it came through the letter-box dressed up as a personal letter and not as a newspaper, arguably met the mass medium definition of reaching large numbers of people quickly and simultaneously. The amount of such mail handled by the Post Office increased threefold from 1975 to 1987, reaching 1,626 million items and making up 7.7 per cent of total national expenditure on advertising. Junk mail can be placed clearly on a continuum with the press. At one end is the newspaper or magazine, delivered by the newsagent and paid for by the reader. Next is the publication paid for by subscription and received through the mail. Next, the 'free sheet', unsolicited and arriving by mail or private delivery. Finally there is the 'letter', free, unsolicited and mailed. Only in size and restricted contents (advertising goods, charities, insurance, unit trusts) does junk mail differ much from the newspaper or magazine as a medium.

Might advertising be regarded as a mass medium on similar grounds? The widest commercial usage of the word 'media' in the post-war period did indeed refer to just that. 'Senders' (advertising agencies) existed specifically to produce advertisements. They reached mass audiences, whom their 'messages' frequently interested much more than the news or the programmes that the advertisements indirectly helped pay for. There is no distinct technology of advertising, but this could be thought an arbitrary objection, especially when the boundaries between media technologies that were quite sharp in the 1940s — between print and photography, or film and TV, for example — were dissolving in the 1980s.

Books raise a similar difficulty, for they too have no technology of their own. Unlike advertising, however, they could be excluded from a definition of mass media because by twentieth-century standards they did not spread their messages quickly and simultaneously, nor to audiences that were large in relation to the communities within which they circulated.

These are arguable cases. A few other media met the conditions of technology, but simply failed to catch on with a mass audience. 3-D movies were an early example: cinema audiences in the 1950s donned spectacles that produced a three-dimensional image. Quadraphonic sound sought a comparable multidimensional effect for music-lovers: instead of two speakers and signals from your amplifier, you had four. More fundamental were the videodiscs marketed in competition with videotapes in the early 1980s. These had advantages in handling and in instant access to a desired image without any winding. They were no use for recording programmes, however, and the public opted for video cassette recorders instead.

What may be included in the term 'mass media' is thus not a precisely defined set of products and technologies, but a rather loose and variable collection. Newspapers, magazines, TV and radio feature on most people's lists, with the refinements of the 'new technologies' of the 1980s. Books, discs and posters feature less. Advertising is a key element in the finance and contents of most media but is not always regarded as a medium in itself.

The history of such a loose collection, even for such a short period as 1945–90, could obviously be a large enterprise. Each element in the communication processes of which media are a part has a history of its own: the media organizations, the changing technology, the contents, the audiences. Then there are the changing relations between each. What difference to the contents of TV programmes followed from the setting up of the ITV companies, for example? Did nudes in the tabloid press proliferate in the 1970s in response to readers' demands, or were readers' expectations aroused by the supply, as a marketing device?

Apart from media's own history, there is the wider question of the relation of media to their society. What needs did they satisfy? Beneath such general terms as 'news' and 'entertainment' lay deeper needs. 'I like to hear the sound of voices in my house' and 'It's like having a good chat' were the kinds of response given to audience surveys of radio and TV in the 1970s. These media were clearly better than the press in helping to combat loneliness and isolation, allegedly more common in the 1970s and 1980s than in the post-war decades, especially among an ageing population.

Such responses help to make the important point that just because mass media were good at spreading news and information, those were not the only purposes they served. The

history of media will look different according to whether you
explore their economic and financial character; their links to
politics and government and to other possible centres of power;
their social aspects, providing certain types of occupation and
status and, through their contents, helping to shape their society's
culture from one generation to another; or their psychological
importance, of the kind indicated in the response to the surveys
about TV and radio in the 1970s.

One complicating result of these diverse ways of looking at
media is that they can easily seem to have more in common
with *non*-media organizations and products than with each
other. 'Mass media' can then start to seem an even more
incoherent term than has already been suggested. Going to the
cinema in the 1940s and 1950s, for example, was an important
part of courtship among young people: it had more in common
with other courtship rituals than with other forms of media
use, such as reading the paper. Similarly, the 1947 Royal
Commission on the Press, the first official, across-the-board
inquiry into the modern press and the first of three in the
1945–90 period, judged the press by three standards, one
of which was as an industry. Yet that was not how most
politicians pressing for the inquiry had seen it. They were
concerned with variety of opinion, editorial freedom, partisan
bias – values having nothing directly to do with economics and
industry. Again, the print and production workers who used
union power to force overmanning and inflated salaries upon
Fleet Street managers in the 1960s and 1970s, put priority on
conditions of work and were not dissuaded by arguments that
such tactics risked reducing the range of titles and thus of
voices heard in the national press. To a typesetter, the closure
in 1960 of the last Liberal daily, the *News Chronicle*, might
simply mean he must take his typesetting skills elsewhere, and
not necessarily to a newspaper. To Liberal party activists,
however, it was the extinction of a lamp, the end of an era. In
production terms, the morning paper perhaps had more in
common with the assembly line than with the production of
most TV programmes. In terms of delivery, curiously, it most
resembled milk, and in 1990 these two products, uniquely,

were still delivered fresh — and perishable — each morning to the doorstep.

If there is a general unifying character to mass media, beyond the relativities of speed and audience size, it may lie in their progressive use, during the post-1945 era, as *leisure* commodities. They made employment for a workforce and were used in the work of other occupations; but mainly they were used for recreation. In this there is a parallel, by no means fanciful, with the motor car — surely the only product that might challenge TV's claim to have made the greatest difference to most people's daily lives between 1945 and 1990. We did indeed use our cars rather like a TV set. Most of us drove fairly similar models. We spent a lot of time looking through the window at 'pictures'. These, like the routines of a news bulletin, chat show or soap opera, were a mixture of the familiar and the unexpected: townscapes and landscapes, high streets and roundabouts which, even when we repeatedly travelled the same routes, were never 'identical' journeys, never entirely the same experience. We shared our motoring experiences with friends, as we shared our reactions to TV. The motor car was a private space, like the rooms in which we watched TV, shared with family and friends; yet, like TV, it was a window on the world — but taking us out whereas TV brought the world in. Though we each traced individual patterns in our cars, the range of experiences and purposes (shopping, going for a drive, getting to work) gave the 'content' of our journeys much in common.

The analogy must not be overstretched, but the fact that it can be made at all shows how integrated mass media were into the rhythms and activities of society. The amount of time we spent using media, their virtual inescapability and thus the extent of their potential influence, all make their history important. What is there in the nest that this cuckoo did not touch? But their character as well as their scale makes them important. For not only are the press, radio and TV, in particular, a key part of the organism of a society that endlessly recreates itself: they are also the chief means through which a society observes and evaluates itself. This is obvious in politics. TV became both an arena in which political discussion is carried on, like the House of Commons or a party meeting, and simultaneously a medium in which politicians could be held to account before the people.

This dual character makes mass media almost inevitably contentious. In observing society and providing the means of its evaluation, media tend to change what they observe – to exert influence, unwittingly or by intent. Sport provides clear examples. Cricket in 1990 was a somewhat different game from 1945, due to the 'needs' of TV. The finances and popularity of some sports, such as snooker, darts, tennis and athletics, were transformed by that medium. But not everybody preferred one-day cricket: in sport, as in other social activities, the effects of media were controversial.

When media themselves are put to scrutiny they are therefore judged both on their own performance and also on their relations with the rest of society. For this reason, most questions about the importance of media turn out to be questions about something else: the interest in media will typically be in its possible role as a *cause* of some particular effect. Do media cause violence? Here the wider concern is the increased violence in society at large. Has the press been persistently biased against Labour since 1945? Here the question is prompted by an interest in the competition for political power. Is *Lady Chatterley's Lover* obscene? The concern of the prosecution in 1960 was with the corruption of public morals.

This book does not go into such broader questions. Many are discussed exhaustively in the literature on 'effects' or 'bias', for example (see Bibliography). This is a history of the media, rather than of their times. Firstly, the book is limited to those media which most absorbed people's attention in the post-war era, and which met most fully the criteria of a mass medium – television, radio and newspapers. Other media are mentioned only in relation to these. Chapters 3 to 6 analyse what was available and what people used – the numbers and circulation of the press, the expansion of TV and radio channels, the patterns of ownership and audiences.

Seen in those terms, three main features of the period were media concentration, conglomeration and internationalization.

Concentration of ownership increased both within particular media, from national daily papers to local radio, and between them. Conglomeration meant that media companies diversified or were bought up by larger corporations whose media interests were only a part of their whole activity. These often worked on an international scale, and the results showed in their products. For instance, co-production TV series were scripted and cast to appeal to an international audience. Publishers calculated their advances for best-selling authors like Frederick Forsyth on the basis of sales hyped in international markets. Readers of Rupert Murdoch's papers in different continents might read the same syndicated articles.

Those features were not new. The model British press baron, Lord Northcliffe, 'bestrode Fleet Street like a colossus' before the First World War, fat with national and provincial daily and Sunday papers, magazines and children's comics. Films were cast for an international market in the Hollywood of the 1920s; and international press syndication had a long history. Nor did the post-war trends happen at the same rate in every medium. Far more than before, however, and far more substantially because of the growth of TV and other new media, they stand out as dominant features.

The book's later chapters focus mainly upon aspects of media accountability. In 1945 the public arguments were still largely about the nature of a 'free press'. Broadcasters and politicians largely left each other alone. In 1990 the free press argument had become over-shadowed by debate about TV. For the citizen/viewer/elector, TV could be the sling of David against the Goliath of government. Or it might be the weapon of Goliath himself, used by governments in the exercise of power. The 1980s ended not only with disputes about an unprecedented governmental curb on broadcasts by Irish extremists, but with a reconstruction of the broadcasting system that put in question the very principles of traditional 'public service broadcasting'. The more media permeated life from 1945 to 1990, and the more they became concentrated in international conglomerates, the more important the account-ability of media themselves became.

3 Media 1945–1990: the Press

The general pattern

National daily and Sunday papers dominated British newspaper reading more recently than might be thought. In 1920, the circulation of the provincial morning and evening papers was still one-third greater than the national dailies. But the nationals quickly expanded: they overtook the provincials in 1923 and by 1945 sold almost twice as many copies.

Wars makes us hungry for news. Despite newsprint rationing, fewer pages without any reduction in price, and pegged circulations, sales rose during the war. They continued to do so among all kinds of paper until about the early 1950s (Table 3.1). Newsprint restrictions lasted until 1955, initially because of the post-war dollar crisis and the Korean War — both of which hit imports. Most papers did not mind, however, for the government restrictions kept their paper and printing costs low and enabled them to make good profits from the big demand for advertising space.

1957 was the peak year for total sales, before the competition from ITV for advertising revenue had started to bite. The next 30 years saw a drop of about 30 per cent, very unevenly distributed and with many fluctuations. The traditional London evening paper market virtually disappeared. In 1920 there had been six London evenings. Post-war there were still three, but *The Star* closed in 1960 and by 1989 an amalgamated *Evening*

Table 3.1 Newspaper circulations

Year	National morning[a] (m)	National Sunday[b] (m)	Provincial morning (m)	Provincial evening (m)	Provincial Sunday[c] (m)	London Evening (m)	Weekly & bi-weekly (m)
1939	10.53	15.48	2.16	4.99	.48[d]	1.71	8.5[d]
1945	12.35	19.76	2.38	5.39	?	2.38	7.3[?]
1947	15.63	26.60	2.87	6.41	1.66	3.48	11.3[]
1949	16.45	29.32	3.03	6.79	?	3.80	13.32
1951	16.62	30.59	2.94	6.84	1.00	3.75	13.6[]
1953	16.07	30.20	2.80	7.13	1.07	3.29	13.6[]
1955	16.22	30.22	2.35	7.06	1.14	2.98	16.2[]
1957	16.71	29.08	2.30	6.85	1.16	2.85	16.0[]
1959	16.11	26.84	2.56	6.39	1.05	2.51	16.7[]
1961	15.69	23.33	1.89	6.61	2.09	2.25	14.7[]
1963	15.55	23.51	2.05	6.24	2.80	2.12	13.9[-]
1965	15.59	23.98	2.01	5.72	1.20	1.96	13.5[]
1967	15.41	24.27	2.06	6.65	2.36	1.91	13.2[]
1969	14.80	24.37	1.97	6.89	2.02	1.68	14.4[]
1971	14.24	22.74	1.95	6.68	2.55	1.49	13.1[]
1973	14.55	22.10	2.03	6.60	2.30	1.33	12.7[]
1975	14.11	20.50	2.09	6.51	1.34	1.13	12.28
1977	13.95	18.95	2.00	6.17	1.28	.96	11.78
1979	15.19	19.26	2.11	5.96	2.26	.81	12.2[]
1981	15.39	17.82	2.03	5.64	2.31	.57	11.5[]
1983	14.95	18.13	2.00	5.25	2.24	.48	10.1[]
1985	14.73	17.83	2.03	5.22	2.73	.49	9.0[]
1987	14.92	18.10	1.98	5.07	2.66	.49	7.6[]
1988	14.96	17.74	1.99	4.90	2.64	.46	?

[a] Excluding *Daily Worker/Morning Star*
[b] Including *Empire News*
[c] Figures fluctuate, as some circulations were confidential.
[d] 1937 figure.
Source: Royal Commissions on the Press, Press Council, ABC, Belson (1967)

News and *Evening Standard* survived alone, with a reduced circulation area and no Saturday edition.

The provincial evening papers suffered a steady decline, steepest in the later years. The biggest drop was among the Sundays — a massive 10 million sales — and the weeklies. The provincial mornings managed to stay at their 1957 level, but this was already down by one third from their immediate postwar peak. The national dailies peaked later, in 1957, but fluctuated within a comparatively narrow range. Apart from fairly intangible external factors like changes in the cost of living or unemployment, the fluctuations were caused by the immediate effects of newspaper closures (the *News Chronicle* and *The Star* in 1960, for example), by price increases, and by changes such as 'tabloidization', colour printing and the launch of weekend magazines, and by promotional gimmicks like bingo.

The survival of the nationals may seem remarkable, in view of the much greater choice of alternative media at the end of the period than at the beginning, with TV an obvious competitor for the reader's time and the advertiser's money. Other kinds of attraction altogether — sport, motoring, holidays — consumed time and money too. This survival reflects the extent to which the daily papers' contents and appeal tied in with these various alternatives: they were complementary more than competitive. When regular radio broadcasting began in 1922, the press refused at first to publish free the daily programme schedules. It took the London store magnate Gordon Selfridge, who included them in his own advertising copy in the evening papers, to show that publishing them would increase the value of the paper to its readers, rather than make them desert to a rival medium. Similarly, in the post-war period, the national dailies managed to adapt their appeal so that people continued to find them useful, and advertisers therefore went on providing the essential economic base for most of them.

What made a paper 'national'?

The categories of the previous section need breaking down.

What made a paper 'national'? The term was purely conventional — and vague. A London base and nationwide circulation were generally essential, but there were exceptions. The *Guardian*, for example, had a national reputation without a London base and with a limited circulation (its home was in Manchester up until 1959). Similarly, in 1978, the *Daily Star* was successfully launched as a national tabloid from Manchester.

'Nationwide circulation' was also something of a fiction. The expansion of the London dailies by Northcliffe and his imitators, including Lord Beaverbrook and the Berry brothers (Lords Kemsley and Camrose) was made possible partly by printing separate northern editions. In 1947 all the London dailies except *The Times*, *Daily Mirror* and *Daily Worker* printed large editions in Manchester, and the *Daily Mail* and *Daily Express* also printed in Scotland (until 1966 and 1974 respectively). Much of the domestic news was different in these from the London editions.

The nationals did not cover the country evenly either, and their contents had distinct biases. Northern Ireland was largely excluded, both from circulation and, until the renewed troubles after 1969, from coverage. Scotland had papers like the *The Scotsman* and *Glasgow Herald* that were too Scottish to be 'national' yet were of a quality that depressed the Scottish sales of papers such as *The Times* and *The Daily Telegraph*. The *Daily Mirror* did not even pretend that its Scottish edition was the same paper and sold it as the *Daily Record*. In England, the north-east region was the last to be penetrated fully by the London papers, with Newcastle and Darlington remaining important newspaper cities into the 1980s. As to contents, the Royal Commission on the Press in 1947 judged that the nationals 'tended to reflect the life and interests of three or four regions rather than those of the whole country' (p. 8).

Content contributed to the woolly definition in an extra way. Was the *Financial Times* a national daily? The 1947 Press Commission thought not: its contents were too specialized (no sport, for instance). The 1961 Press Commission thought differently, however, for by then the paper had broadened its range and increased its penetration. Again, the *Morning Star* (*Daily Worker* until 1966) was 'specialist' in the sense that its columns reflected strongly its brand of Marxist ideology and the work of the Communist party and parts of the Labour movement. Its circulation (and perhaps its party's sizeable electoral support) qualified it unquestionably as a national daily in 1947. By 1961 it was fading: lack of resources kept it to four or six pages when other broadsheets were three or four times as big. By 1974, the third Press Commission excluded it from its tables and statistics. The Press Council, on the other hand, continued to count it as a national daily. Finally, two very small, short-lived papers defined themselves as 'nationals' in 1953 and 1960. These, the *Recorder* and the *New Daily*, were idiosyncratic, right wing, anti-trade union papers. They would have had more chance of getting established in the late 1980s.

One factor which by itself had no bearing on the idea of a 'national' paper was circulation size. In 1947 several provincial papers still had circulations rivalling some of Fleet Street's: the Manchester *Daily Despatch* (475,000) and *Evening News* (224,000), the *Newcastle Journal* (146,000), *Yorkshire Evening Post* (204,000) and *Birmingham Mail* (200,000). *The Times*, at this point, sold 195,000 and *The Daily Telegraph* and tabloid *Daily Graphic* were both under 900,000. The best example was a Sunday paper, the Manchester *Empire News*. This had a circulation approaching two million at the end of the war, ranking it ahead of six out of ten national Sundays. It was edited in Manchester and was founded as a sporting paper — the *Umpire* — but the 1947 Press Commission called it 'distinguishable from a national newspaper only in its place of origin' (p. 13). Moreover it printed in London as well as Manchester for most of the post-war years until its closure in 1960.

The London evening papers complicated the picture as well. Their position in the capital meant that insofar as London's affairs were the nation's, they had national contents and a national voice. They were close to Westminster politics, to City interests, and to national and international gossip about the arts, show business and 'society'. People in those worlds probably treated them rather like national papers, too. Each was owned, moreover, by one of the national dailies – the *Evening News* by the *Daily Mail*, the *Evening Standard* by the *Daily Express* and the *Star* by the *News Chronicle*. But of course they did not circulate beyond the commuter belt, so they failed to qualify as nationals on that ground.

The recipe for a national paper was thus a mixture of national reputation, geographical reach and breadth of content. The precise ingredients changed across the years after 1945, as they had before. Before the first World War, a London-based metropolitan press had coexisted with a vigorous provincial press, whose luminaries (*Yorkshire Post, Manchester Guardian, Scotsman*, and so on) were not completely overshadowed by the London papers in either circulation or editorial authority. The *Manchester Guardian* in the late 1950s was the last survivor of that era. The removal of its editorial offices to London and of 'Manchester' from its mast-head symbolized the change to a dominant national press with the provincials dwarfed in circulation and resources.

The national press

Numbers

Changes in the number of national dailies from 1945 to 1989 were very few and took three forms: launch or closure, relaunch, and change of status. The *Guardian* and *Financial Times* joined the list, and arguably the *Morning Star* left it, by change of status. The *Sun*, top seller by 1989, was a tabloid relaunch, twenty years previously, of an ailing broadsheet paper with an entirely different character, some of whose readers nevertheless stayed with it and were a base on which the new ownership could build.

Because of abundant advertising revenue and continued newsprint restrictions (which limited competition) the first closure – the *News Chronicle* – did not come till 1960. The way it was done, with absolutely no warning, was traumatic for the staff and startling for its subscribers, of whom there were well over a million. Moreover it was the last mass circulation Liberal daily and was closed by abrupt merger with the *Daily Mail* — a Conservative paper. On 18 October, *News Chronicle* readers were simply delivered a copy of the *Mail*, with *News Chronicle* in small type on the mast-head. The shock was increased for Londoners by the simultaneous merger of *The Star* with the *Evening News*.

Despite gloomy predictions over the next 20 years, including forecasts that only one 'quality' daily would survive, with one middle-range paper (the *Express*, for example) and one tabloid, only two other established papers died. In 1971 Lord Rothermere merged the tabloid *Daily Sketch* with his *Daily Mail*. The *Sketch*, in comparison with the *Daily Mirror*, was thin in size and content and Conservative in politics. The new *Sun* was clearly going to provide a Conservative voice for the tabloid market and would eat further into its declining sales, so the *Sketch* died a quiet and unsurprising death.

The death of the old *Daily Herald*, the longest surviving Labour daily, founded in 1912 and owned by the Labour party for a period between the wars, was more agony than trauma when compared with the demise of the *News Chronicle*, but equally disturbing for its supporters. The paper had an ageing readership and a bad position in the advertising market, because of its working class skew. Its owners, especially when the *Daily Mirror* took over, were reluctant to make the contents brighter, less political, less class-conscious. That might have attracted more women and young readers — but by taking them partly from the *Mirror*. Instead, Cecil King, who had pledged the TUC he would keep the paper alive till the end of the decade (providing its obvious description as King's cross), tried to take it up market and appeal to the younger voters, better off but 'socially radical', whose support had just helped elect Harold Wilson into office. The paper was relaunched in a new format as the *Sun*, but it failed to win up-market readers, while the old loyalists were put off. It struggled on as an 'underfinanced, deradicalized hybrid', in Curran and Seaton's phrase (1988, p. 99), until King's pledge expired and it was sold to Rupert Murdoch in 1969.

The only other closure in the period (leaving aside the *Recorder* and *New Daily*) was *The Post*. This was a tabloid launched by the founder of *Today*, Eddie Shah, which lasted only 33 issues at the end of 1988.

The enormous risks and start-up costs of launching a new daily from scratch prevented anyone trying, until new technology and a successful challenge to the strength of the trade unions transformed Fleet Street economics in the mid-1980s — making 'Fleet Street' itself an archaic term, since the construction of production plant elsewhere, notably Wapping, was part of the process. The one exception was the *Daily Star*, founded in 1978 by the owner of the *Daily Express*, Trafalgar House. The object was to use spare printing capacity in Manchester to compete with the London-based *Sun*, which the *Star* was therefore designed to resemble extremely closely. Sales varied but were well down by the end of the 1980s, and the paper remained a rather marginal venture.

The 'Wapping revolution' was truly a transformation — of newspaper technology, industrial relations and costs. Forces that had kept the size of Fleet Street under continuous pressure for more than 25 years were broken. Newspaper production was labour-intensive. Although newsprint (the other major cost) had doubled during 1972–5, the Press Commission of the mid-1970s found labour was still the largest cost, at 40–50 per cent. This was partly due to the nature of the business, but partly because management bought off the threat of trouble with high wage settlements in the prosperous 1950s. The industry was 'notorious for the generosity of its manning levels, and its workers have traditionally been very highly paid', commented the Press Commission (1977, p. 42).

The production unions' success had various causes, including an effective closed shop and weak newspaper managements. The strike threat was formidable: there is no way lost production on a newspaper can ever be made up. The new technology available in the 1970s offered the promise of massively reduced manning levels and higher productivity. In effect, through computer-typesetting, journalists could become their own printers, and whole echelons of intermediaries could be eliminated.

For years unions and managements argued over the terms

of change. The Mirror Group, for one, invested heavily in plant that stood idle. *The Times* and *Sunday Times* closed down in dispute, for what turned out to be a whole year.

The unions overplayed their hand in the end. Eddie Shah, who had built up a group of free weeklies based in Stockport, determined to launch a national daily, *Today*. His weeklies were produced by new technology in defiance of union opposition, and he planned the same methods for *Today*. One advantage of computerized typesetting was the speed with which it could be learned. Rupert Murdoch decided to do the same thing with *The Times*. When the unions took industrial action against a no-strike clause in the latest contract proposals, Murdoch moved production of his papers overnight to the plant at Wapping – previously said to be for the *News of the World* alone. This was a classic *fait accompli*. Non-print union labour was bused in; 'Fortress Wapping' was the scene of picketing, boycott, physical attacks, confrontations with (some said by) the police. Crucial to Shah's and Murdoch's success was the Thatcher government's industrial relations legislation that limited the unions' power to respond.

Murdoch's success was the cue for the rest of Fleet Street to forge ahead with new investment (sometimes long planned) in buildings and plant. Workforces were slashed: the Express group, for example, cut one-third of its 6,000 staff. The flurry involved further new launches. *Today* was followed by the *Independent*, *The Post*, and a number of Sunday and London evening papers, of which only the *Sunday Sport* survived. Right at the end of the period a new *Sunday Correspondent* and an *Independent on Sunday* were launched. There had been nothing like it since the heyday of Northcliffe in the early years of the century.

The attempt to launch new London evening papers reflected an enduring belief that the capital ought to be able to support more than one. Since 1980 the *Standard* had been the only survivor of the flourishing trio in 1945. These had peaked in 1950 with combined sales of 3.8 million but had gone steadily downhill thereafter. When it closed in 1960, *The Star* was roughly half its 1950 size. Its closure provided only a breathing-space. In 1974 the *Standard* dropped its Saturday edition and the *Evening News* went tabloid. When the two amalgamated in 1980, they had a joint circulation of little more than 600,000.

The 1974 Press Commission suggested the evenings' decline was due to their rapid increase in price in the early 1970s, the effects of TV, changing family budgets in a time of inflation, and the growth of evening papers in commuter towns. Around 27 per cent of adults in Brighton, for instance, saw a London evening paper in 1963, but only 7 per cent did in 1975.

With the much lower production costs of the late 1980s, small circulation was no longer the same barrier to profitability. Robert Maxwell launched the *London Daily News* as a 'round the clock' paper in February 1987. It lasted five months. Partly it died, no doubt, from its own defects (including distribution difficulties), and partly from the spirited response of the *Standard*. But Lord Rothermere, sole owner of the *Standard*, spoilt the market too by relaunching the old *Evening News* on the very same day. He closed it a few months after Maxwell's paper folded − with a circulation of only about 100,000.

Until Wapping, the number of national Sundays contracted quite severely, compared with the dailies. The economics of Sunday journalism were different, being much affected by what happened to the staff and printing plant during the rest of the week. Thus, two new launches had proved possible at a time when new dailies were generally still unpractical. Both were sister papers of established dailies, the *Telegraph* and *Mail*, which could be expected to provide a core of readers and whose presses had spare capacity. The *Sunday Telegraph* (February 1961) cashed in on the rapidly expanding quality Sunday market, built up most effectively by the *Sunday Times* (whose colour magazine started in the same year). The *Mail on Sunday* (summer 1982) had more difficulty, since it aimed chiefly to take readers from the less buoyant middle market long dominated by the now declining *Sunday Express*.

Unlike the dailies, the number of titles was not swelled by relaunches and changes of status: all other changes were closures. First went the *Sunday Chronicle*, a failing product faced with stronger middle market competitors and pressure on each side from the quality papers and the downmarket tabloids. Its owner, Lord Kemsley, leased the presses instead to the *Sunday Pictorial* (renamed *Sunday Mirror* in 1963). At the end of 1960, in the same period that the *News Chronicle* and London evening *Star* closed, the *Sunday Graphic* and the *Empire News* were closed by new owners, the Thomson organization. Thomson, again, could make more money by leasing the presses to another newspaper — in this case the *News of the World*. It was this subordination of the social and political value of a newspaper to commercial priorities that so exercised politicians and helped get the second and third Royal Commissions on the Press set up in 1961 and 1974.

In June 1961 the *Sunday Dispatch*, another middle-ground paper squeezed into unprofitability by competition for sales and advertising revenue, was sold by Lord Rothermere and amalgamated with the *Sunday Express*. The previous 12 months had therefore seen unprecedented contraction of plague-like proportions. Five important papers had died (three Sundays, one daily and one London evening), with a total circulation of six million. Most of the readers, of course, moved to other papers.

One other Sunday paper died in the 1960s, after struggling on with subsidies from the Cooperative movement. This was the *Sunday Citizen*, relict of one of the popular Victorian papers, *Reynolds' News*, relaunched with a new name in a tabloid format in 1962.

The Sunday innovations of the late 1980s have already been mentioned. *Sunday Today* started alongside *Today* but made no mark. *Sunday Sport* thrived on its advertising but was a cheaply produced magazine more than a newspaper. *News on Sunday* was an earnest attempt in 1987 to establish a popular radical paper, backed by trade unions and Labour controlled local authorities. Its planning and management were reportedly rent with the schisms for which the left is sometimes ridiculed. Its circulation never approached the 800,000 target and was about 112,000 when, after little more than six months, the estate agent and local radio entrepreneur, Owen Oyston, who sought to rescue it, closed it down.

'Qualities' and 'populars'

Trends in each paper's circulation are clear in Tables 3.2 and 3.3. Changes were the result of many factors. Some were general, like the good economic conditions (for the press) in the late 1940s and 1950s and the bad ones in the 1960s. Others concerned specific papers – their comparative attractiveness to advertisers; the age, wealth and education of their readers; their special style and contents. Many of the last were intangible. Discovering how to reverse a declining circulation was famously difficult and, as the figures show, was not often achieved. Great success, such as that of the *Daily Express* at its peak (around 1960), might contain the seeds of decline. Both the *Express* and the *Mail* went into the 1970s with an ageing readership, for they failed to replace their old readers with young new ones in the same numbers. Yet if they changed their style, they risked making things worse by alienating the old readers and still failing to attract new ones.

The great circulation successes were the *Daily Mirror* and *Daily Express* into the 1960s; the *Sun* from 1970 onwards, when it bit hard into the *Mirror's* market; *The Daily Telegraph* until the 1980s and the *Guardian*, in a quiet way, after it had settled in London. The *Express* and *Mirror* successes were repeated by their Sunday companions. Nearly all the Sundays fell back more or less steeply later in the period, however. Of all Sunday papers the most distinctive success was *The Sunday Times*, which soared ahead from the late 1950s on a formula of serialized war memoirs and increasingly diversified and segmented review and magazine sections.

Rather than trace individual papers in detail, it is more useful to look at the development of particular classes of paper. One of Northcliffe's many effects upon the press was to sharpen the division, comparatively minor in the late nineteenth century, between the mass circulation 'popular' papers and the low circulation 'qualities'. Northcliffe founded the *Daily Mail* in 1896 and pushed its circulation to one million in 1900. This was unprecedented for a daily paper: most were selling in the range 90–250,000. In the 1930s, circulation wars pushed the

Table 3.2 National daily newspapers: circulation (thousands)

Newspaper (launch date)	1945	1950	1955	1960	1965	1970	1975	1980	1985	1988
'Qualities'										
Daily Telegraph (1855)	822	976	1,055	1,200[a]	1,337	1,409	1,331	1,433	1,202	1,128
The Times (1785)	195	254	222	260	254	388	319	316	478	436
Financial Times (1888)	(35)	(57)	(80)	122	146	170	181	196	234	279[b]
(Manchester) Guardian (1821)	(80)	(140)	(156)	212	270	304	319	379	487	438
The Independent (1986)	–	–	–	–	–	–	–	–	–	387
Total	1,017	1,230	1,277	1,794	2,007	2,271	2,150	2,324	2,401	2,668
(%)	(8)	(7)	(8)	(11)	(13)	(15)	(15)	(16)	(16)	(18)
(including *Financial Times* and *Manchester Guardian*)	(1,132)	(1,427)	(1,513)							
'Middle market'										
Daily Express (1900)	3,239	4,116	4,036	4,270	3,987	3,563	2,822	2,194[c]	1,902	1,637
Daily Mail (1896)	1,752	2,225	2,068	2,825	2,464	1,890	1,726[d]	1,948	1,815	1,759
Daily Herald/Sun (1912)	2,000	2,017	1,759	1,418	1,273	–	–	–	–	–
News Chronicle (1930)	1,454	1,534	1,253	–	–	–	–	–	–	–
Today (1986)	–	–	–	–	–	–	–	–	–	548
Total	8,445	9,046	9,116	8,513	7,724	5,453	4,548	4,142	3,717	3,944
(%)	(68)	(60)	(57)	(53)	(49)	(37)	(32)	(28)	(25)	(26)

'Mass market' tabloids										
Daily Mirror (1903)	2,000	4,567	4,725	4,649	5,019	4,570	3,968	3,625	3,033	3,157
Daily Sketch/Graphic (1908)	883	717	950	1,075	844	785	–	–	–	–
Sun (1970)	–	–	–	–	–	1,615	3,446	3,741	4,125	4,219
Daily Star (1978)	–	–	–	–	–	–	–	1,034	1,455	967
(The Post [1988])e	–	–	–	–	–	–	–	–	–	?f
Total	2,883	5,344	5,675	5,724	5,863	6,970	7,414	8,400	8,613	8,343
(%)	(23)	(32)	(35)	(37)	(38)	(47)	(53)	(56)	(58)	(56)
Daily Worker/Morning Star (1930)g	115	115	?f	60	?f	?f	?f	33	?f	?f
Total (including Daily Worker)	12,345 (12,460)	16,520 (16,717)	16,068 (16,304)	16,031	15,594	14,694	14,112	14,886	14,731	14,955

a Estimate. b By 1988, 81,571 of this number were overseas sales. c Tabloid since 1977. d Tabloid since 1971. e The Post lasted or e month. f figure not certain. g Circulations only available intermittently. Guardian and Financial Times not counted as national dailies until 1960.

Sources: Audit Bureau of Circulations, Press Council Annual Reports; individual newspapers. Some figures are part-year averages.

Table 3.3 National Sunday newspapers: circulation (thousands)

Newspaper (launch date)	1945	1950	1955	1960	1965	1970	1975	1980	1985	1988
'Qualities'										
Observer (1791)	299	422	564	738	824	830	730	929	736	722
Sunday Times (1822)	460	535	606	1,001	1,290	1,439	1,380	1,419	1,251	1,314
Sunday Telegraph (1961)	–	–	–	–	650	764	752	1,003	686	693
Total	759	957	1,170	1,739	2,764	3,033	2,862	3,351	2,673	2,729
(%)	(4)	(3)	(4)	(6)	(12)	(13)	(14)	(18)	(15)	(15)
'Middle market'										
Reynolds' News/Sunday Citizen (1850)	580	705	579	329	233	–	–	–	–	–
Sunday Chronicle (1885)	1,150	1,118	830	–	–	–	–	–	–	–
Sunday Dispatch (1801)	1,372	2,378	2,549	1,520	–	–	–	–	–	–
Sunday Express (1918)	2,114	2,967	3,235	3,706	4,190	4,263	3,715	2,989	2,449	2,033
Mail on Sunday (1982)	–	–	–	–	–	–	–	–	1,631	1,919
(News on Sunday [1987])	–	–	–	–	–	–	–	–	–	–
(Sunday Today [1986–7])	–	–	–	–	–	–	–	–	–	–
Total	5,216	7,168	7,193	5,555	4,423	4,263	3,715	2,989	4,080	3,952
(%)	(26)	(24)	(24)	(20)	(18)	(18)	(18)	(16)	(23)	(22)

'Mass market'										
Empire News (1884)	1,812	2,085	2,049	2,100	–	–	–	–	–	–
News of the World (1843)	5,000	8,444	7,971	6,664	6,176	6,229	5,479	4,198	5,103	5,360
People/Sunday People (1881)	3,447	5,089	5,075	5,468	5,538	5,140	4,188	3,846	2,962	2,743
Sunday Graphic (1915)	1,026	1,169	1,220	893	–	–	–	–	–	–
Sunday Pictorial/Mirror (1915)	2,500	5,094	5,539	5,461	5,082	4,826	4,251	3,831	3,009	2,953
Total	13,785	21,881	21,854	20,586	16,796	16,195	13,918	11,875	11,074	11,056
(%)	(70)	(73)	(72)	(74)	(70)	(69)	(68)	(65)	(62)	(62)
Total	19,760	30,006	30,217	27,880	23,983	23,491	20,495	18,215	17,827	17,737

The Sunday Correspondent (1989) and Independent on Sunday (1990) were launched too late for inclusion. News on Sunday and Sunday Today lasted only for a short time, with circulations of 100–200,000.

Sources: Audit Bureau of Circulations; Press Council Annual Reports.

figures far higher, aided by a big increase in daily paper purchases among the working class.

The popular press needed the sales revenue from large circulations to cover their costs. Advertising revenue would certainly help, or would boost profits, but much of it went simply on the paper and production costs of printing the advertisements. The quality papers ran on different lines. The sales revenue from their smaller circulations covered a much lower proportion of costs; but the greater purchasing power of their readers, some of whom spent 'corporate' money, not just their own personal incomes, enabled the qualities to charge far higher advertising rates and break even at circulation levels completely unrealistic for the populars.

The quality–popular distinction was sharply drawn by 1945. Thereafter it was complicated by the immense success of the *Daily Mirror*, which had been turned into Britain's first mass market tabloid in 1935. Both dailies and Sundays can thus be sorted into 'quality', 'middle market' or 'popular broadsheet', and 'mass market', or 'popular tabloid' groups. The differences roughly corresponded both to the nature of the contents and design (including length of articles and size of headlines) and to the social class distribution of their readers.

Table 3.2 shows how the groups changed. The advance of the qualities was dramatic – sales in 1988 were two and a half times those of 1945, with five quality dailies instead of two. The number of populars (excluding the *Daily Worker/Morning Star*, which fitted easily into neither category) was six in each year, but total circulation was down by nearly 10 per cent. The absolute figures are less impressive. Despite the great increases in formal education since 1945, fewer than one person in five was interested in the kind of reading matter offered by the qualities.

For the mass of the population, indeed, the shift of interest arguably went in the other direction. In 1945 most people read a broadsheet paper – four populars and the two qualities, compared with two tabloids. The broadsheet populars comprised a middle market – middle class and middle brow – which became steadily less distinguishable over the following decade.

In 1945 the *Mail*, *Express*, *News Chronicle* and *Herald* dominated the number of titles and the sales of the qualities and tabloids either side of them. Forty years on, the *Mail* and *Express* remained, with the new *Today*, but found themselves squeezed between sectors that had doubled in size.

In the Sunday market the quality–popular division became even sharper than among the dailies when the qualities turned themselves into large scale Sunday magazines. The popular broadsheet category eventually almost disappeared, however, as one by one the popular broadsheets changed their format to tabloid (see Table 3.4). Only the *Sunday Express*, among all the middle market populars, was still a broadsheet in 1990.

Table 3.4   Date of adopting tabloid format by national newspapers

Before 1945	*Daily Mirror* (1935)
	Daily Sketch (1908)
	Sunday Pictorial/Sunday Mirror (1915)
1962	*Sunday Citizen*
1969	*Sun*
1971	*Daily Mail*
1974	*Sunday People* (*The People* from 1986)
1977	*Daily Express*
1978	*Daily Star* (at launch)
1982	*Mail on Sunday* (at launch)
1984	*News of the World*
1986	*Today* (at launch)
	Sunday Today (at launch; closed 1987)
	Sunday Sport (at launch)
1987	*News on Sunday* (at launch; closed 1987)
1988	*The Post* (at launch; closed 1988)

Ownership

What kind of people owned the national press? Many seemed larger than life. The image of the 'press baron' partly reflects literal reality: politicians continually courted publishers with peerages to secure or reward their support, in case the intangible 'power of the press' turned out to be real. But the image also suggests character. The 'barons' were often supreme egotists: flamboyant, assertive, idiosyncratic, ostentatious, ruthless — yet inspiring great loyalty and affection. A newspaper suits such behaviour. It involves the daily expression of opinion and its smallest details can be changed by the direct intervention of the proprietor. By comparison, other mass production barons of the mid-twentieth century — motor manufacturers such as Lord Nuffield, for instance — could not so quickly, easily and frequently shape their products. The newspaper is a natural tool for the autocrat.

Barons could most readily huff and stomp when they did indeed own their papers, rather than being chairmen, liable to be sacked by their directors. Cecil King behaved liked a baron at the *Daily Mirror* in the 1960s, scolding the Wilson government and toying with the idea of political office. Readers may have thought his front page squibs came from the pen of a dominant shareholder. Not at all: King went too far and was out on his ear in an overnight boardroom coup in 1968. Northcliffe, Beaverbrook, Kemsley or Thomson, on the other hand, could not easily be jettisoned: their press empires were more substantially *theirs*. All, in fact, were self-made men — which no doubt is a clue to their style and motives. There is more than a touch of rags to riches in the story of the outsize barons. Despite great wealth, too, the barons were not generally profit-maximizers. If they had just wanted to make money, there were far better ways. By the late 1960s, indeed, half of Fleet Street was running at a loss (Economist Intelligence Unit, 1966), and the situation (though cyclical) got no better in the 1970s. Titles were often kept going on the profits of provincial partners or other businesses.

With his own property, it was perhaps easier too for a baron to take risks or sail close to the wind. Tiny Rowland (latterly owning the *Observer*) was dubbed the unacceptable face of capitalism by Prime Minister Heath in the early 1970s. Robert Maxwell was once declared unfit to be in charge of a major public company by an official inquiry. It needed considerable force of character, whatever the merits of the issue, for the

Thomson family to shut down *The Times* and *The Sunday Times* for a year and for Murdoch to move the papers to 'fortress Wapping' later, in his struggles with the unions.

Some owners, of course, inherited papers — and their fathers' flair or good fortune. Rupert Murdoch's father built an empire in Australia: his son did so on a world scale. Lord Hartwell inherited *The Daily Telegraph*, saw it flourish and launched its Sunday partner. Vere Harmsworth proved a shrewd strategist at Associated Newspapers in the 1980s. Other heirs had less flair, luck or stomach. Beaverbrook's Express group did not prosper under his son Max Aitken, who sold out some ten years after Beaverbrook's death. Nor did Colonel John Astor's *Times* under his son Gavin.

Inheritors needed a motive for getting out. The motives of those getting in could be as varied as the role of a newpaper. Some saw the press as an industry and had no other object than to sell a product, provide employment and make a fair profit. Lord Thomson was the best example in the post-war period. He was all the more striking because the boast that he ran his papers just to make money contrasted strongly with the more complex motives, combining profit with politics, that were still typical of the proprietors of the early 1960s. The boast went bluntly against the claim by Thomson's fellow Canadian, Beaverbrook, that his own objective was purely propaganda. Forerunners to the Thomson view included nineteenth-century printers, such as the early owners of *The Daily Telegraph*, who took over papers in settlement of unpaid printing bills. Lord Southwood of Odhams Press acquired his 51 per cent shareholding in the *Daily Herald* between the wars on much the same basis. Southwood was not much interested in the tactics of the Labour movement. He happily entered an agreement, which lasted until 1961, 15 years after his death, to leave political policy to the 49 per cent shareholders, the TUC.

The Thomsons and Southwoods were exceptions. Another, in the 1980s, was Eddie Shah, founder of *Today*. Most barons saw their papers as means to an end. This was usually the advance of a political cause or party, and, less often than before 1945, the pursuit of their own public or political career.

The Beaverbrook and Astor empires were both founded, before and after 1900, by rich men from overseas (Canada and the USA) who wished to buy their way into British public life.

With international multimedia empires and conglomerates, motives were more complicated. To ask Rupert Murdoch what were his 'goals' would have been to pose probably rather a difficult question (if the answer were serious). On the other hand, for Tiny Rowland of the conglomerate Lonrho, and for the Atlantic Richfield Oil Company of California, his predecessor as owners of *The Observer*, the control of a national paper might be no more than a useful form of corporate public relations and personal prestige.

Who, then, owned the national press in 1945? Typically, papers were controlled by a dominant family, relatives of a pre-war, first generation empire-builder, politically partisan but demure. No company had more than one daily, although there was a family connection between Lord Kemsley's *Daily Sketch* and his brother Lord Camrose's *Daily Telegraph*. Similarly, four of the eleven Sundays (including the *Empire News*) belonged to Lord Kemsley. The others were separately owned, but several were in partnership with a daily. The only fully independents were *The Observer*, belonging to a different branch of the Astor family from *The Times*, the Co-operative movement's *Reynolds' News*, and the huge *News of the World*, to become larger still, run by the Carr family.

Kemsley was less flamboyant than other barons of the earlier generation, like Northcliffe and Beaverbrook. Quietly Conservative, he did not seek major political office, as they had. Nor did his brother Lord Camrose. The second Lord Rothermere, now in control of the *Daily Mail*, was similarly reticent. Beaverbrook, though a wartime minister and intimate of Churchill, lived until 1965 but was a spent political force.

The dominant families of the other papers had what now would be called a low profile too. Colonel Astor had bought *The Times* in 1922 specifically to keep it out of the clutches of Lloyd George, who was seeking a personal political base and had money to spend from his earlier sale of honours when Prime Minister. Astor was a classic non-interventionist proprietor, rumoured to own *The Times* but not actually to read it. The Cadbury family, newspaper publishers since the Victorian heyday of the Liberal 'chocolate press', still ran the *News Chronicle* in a party interest. The *Guardian* was controlled by a family trust, dominated by relations of the formidable owner-editor (and sometime MP) C P Scott, one of the great Liberal voices of British journalism for half a century into the 1920s. *The Financial Times*, still fairly small and specialized, was controlled by the Crosthwaite-Eyres.

Very few papers indeed, therefore, had a wide spread of shareholders. The unusual structure of the *Daily Herald* certainly prevented it being dominated by a small group, apart from the elected brothers of the TUC council. The *Daily Worker* was run as a co-operative. The *Daily Mirror* and *Sunday Pictorial* were in interlocking ownership; but the first Lord Rothermere, one of the founders (in 1903, when the *Mirror* was to be *for* women, edited *by* women — the women failed, and sacking them, the Harmsworths' henchman said, was like drowning kittens) had dispersed his shares on the Stock Exchange in 1931. The 1961 Press Commission was told that there were 40,000 shareholders.

Taking a strict definition of a national paper (that is to say, excluding the *Guardian* and *Financial Times*), twelve companies in 1945 controlled between them nine dailies and eleven Sundays. This pattern continued relatively undisturbed until 1959, when a short period of major upheaval began. More changes came in 1969–71 and again in the 1980s, which was a decade dominated by battles over new technology and the establishment of new titles. All these phases involved closures or the threat of closures. When proprietors sold, at any stage, whether anticipating amalgamation (like the *News Chronicle* and *Daily Mail*) or a continuing future, they did so because of flagging interest or energy, or because they had not the resources to turn round a weak paper in an increasingly competitive market.

Not counting sales associated with closure, there were some 16 major changes of ownership of national dailies and 17 of Sundays between 1945 and 1988. Most involved both dailies and Sundays. Nearly half took place in the 1980s. Table 3.5

Table 3.5 National newspapers: changes of ownership, 1945–89

Newspaper	Controlling owner in 1945	Purchaser			
		1945–59	1960–69	1970–79	1980–89
Daily Express	Lord Beaverbrook			Trafalgar House 1977	United Newspapers 1985
Daily Herald/Sun	TUC/Odhams		Mirror Group 1961/1964 Murdoch 1969		
Daily Mail	Lord Rothermere (Associated Newspapers)				
Daily Mirror	Various			Reed 1970	Maxwell 1984
Daily Sketch/Graphic	Lord Kemsley	Lord Rothermere 1952 (closed 1971)			
Daily Star	(1978: Trafalgar House)				United Newspapers 1985
Daily Telegraph	Lord Camrose/Berry family				Conrad Black 1985
Daily Worker/Morning Star	Communist Party co-operative				
Financial Times	Eyre Trust	Pearson 1957			
(Manchester) Guardian	Scott Trust				
Independent	(1986: various)				
News Chronicle	Cadbury family		Lord Rothermere 1960 (closed)		
The Post	(1988: Eddie Shah. Closed after 33 issues)				
The Times	Col. J. Astor		Roy Thomson 1966		Murdoch 1981
Today	(1986: Eddie Shah)				Lonrho 1986 Murdoch 1987

Newspaper					
Empire News	Lord Kemsley	Roy Thomson 1959	Carr family 1960 (closed)		
Mail on Sunday	(1982: Lord Rothermere)				
News of the World / News on Sunday	Carr family (1987: various)		Murdoch 1969		Owen Oyston 1987 (closed)
Observer	D. Astor			ARCO 1976	Lonrho 1981
People/Sunday People	Odhams		Mirror Group 1961	Reed 1970	Maxwell 1984
Reynolds' News/Sunday Citizen	Co-op Press: closed 1967				
Sunday Chronicle	Lord Kemsley: closed 1955				
Sunday Dispatch	Lord Rothermere		Lord Beaverbrook 1961 (closed)		
Sunday Express	Lord Beaverbrook			Trafalgar House 1977	United Newspapers 1985
Sunday Graphic	Lord Kemsley	Roy Thomson 1959 (closed)			
Sunday Pictorial/Sunday Mirror	Various			Reed 1970	Maxwell 1984
Sunday Telegraph	(1961: Berry family)				Conrad Black 1985
Sunday Times	Lord Kemsley	Roy Thomson 1959			Murdoch 1981
Sunday Today	(1986: Eddie Shah)				Lonrho 1986. Closed 1987

In general, individuals and families have been named as owners: this does not mean they owned all the stock.

shows the distribution of papers and dates. The *Guardian* and *Daily Mail* alone stayed in the same ownership throughout the period. Most papers changed once or twice.

The first changes were minor — Kemsley's sale of the *Daily Sketch* to Lord Rothermere in 1952 and the Pearson/Westminster Press purchase of *The Financial Times* in 1957. Then in 1959 Lord Kemsley, apparently worried by falling income and the prospect of heavy death duties, decided to sell up completely. This was a major destabilizing move, at the provincial level too (see below). The main purchaser was Mr (not yet Lord) Roy Thomson, who got a national foothold through *The Sunday Times*. In March 1961 the Mirror Group bought Odhams, which gave them the *People* and 51 per cent of the *Daily Herald*. Also in 1961 the *Guardian* became London based and fully 'national' and *The Sunday Telegraph* was launched. Taking account too of the closure of the *News Chronicle*, the *Sunday Dispatch* and several other Sundays following the Kemsley sale, five out of twelve dailies and six out of eleven Sundays — half the entire national press — saw their ownership, existence or status (as a 'national') affected during less than two years between August 1959 and June 1961.

In 1964 the TUC sold its 40 per cent of the *Herald* to the Mirror Group, which relaunched it as the *Sun*. Then Thomson bought *The Times* late in 1966 and poured resources into it in an attempt to make it profitable. More significant were the changes at the end of the 1960s, with the irruption of Rupert Murdoch. After a tough battle with Robert Maxwell he bought the *News of the World* early in January 1969, and at the end of the year he bought the still failing *Sun*. The Mirror Group's decision to sell it to him was perhaps the greatest miscalculation in post-war press history. Murdoch immediately relaunched it as a tabloid and turned it against the flagship of its previous owners. Linked to the disposal of the *Sun* was a takeover of the Mirror Group by the papermaking conglomerate Reed International, which already had a large shareholding in the *Mirror*. In 1971 the *Sketch* and *Mail* merged. In the three-year period 1969–71, then, three out of ten dailies and three out of seven Sundays changed ownership or status.

Failing energy and resources accounted for two sales in the mid-1970s. *The Observer*, lagging behind *The Sunday Times* and without a daily partner as a cushion, was sold in 1976 by David Astor to Atlantic Richfield — a quite unexpected knight galloping out of the mists. The following year the Beaverbrook papers were sold to the Trafalgar House conglomerate. Unlike, say, Rothermere's Associated Newspapers, Beaverbrook had never seriously diversified, not even into the provincial press, and although the *Sunday Express* remained profitable, the *Daily Express* and London *Evening Standard* were in trouble. Victor Matthews, Trafalgar's vice-chairman, was in the familiar self-made baron mould and duly acquired his barony from Mrs Thatcher.

Changes in the 1980s came more frequently. Half the dailies existing in 1981 changed hands by 1988. Two new dailies started and survived, one of which changed hands twice. A third new daily quickly failed. Three Sundays started, of which one survived. The *Independent* and the *Sunday Correspondent* both emphasized the fact that they were not dominated by a 'baron'. Much of their money came from City institutions and insurance companies. All the existing Sundays except the *News of the World* (six out of seven) changed hands between 1981 and 1985.

Some of these sales were to existing publishers. When Roy Thomson's son decided to pull out of national papers, having spent millions on *The Times* in pursuit of production economies, Murdoch was the purchaser. When ARCO tired of losses at *The Observer*, Tiny Rowland's Lonrho, already owner of a Glasgow daily, bought it. In 1986 Rowland rescued *Today*, when its founder Eddie Shah ran out of cash after the paper's shaky launch. Rowland sold it on to Murdoch.

There were three notable newcomers, however. First was Robert Maxwell, who in 1984 achieved his long ambition to play the press baron role and won the *Mirror* papers from Reed at an acceptable price. Next came the latest Canadian, Conrad Black, a businessman of conservative views, who bought the *Telegraph* papers from the last of the Berry family in the newspaper business, Camrose's younger son Michael, Lord Hartwell.

The *Telegraph*, too, had never diversified, and it lacked the resources to modernize. Finally the expanding provincial group, United Newspapers, bought the *Express* group in 1985 from Trafalgar House.

Such a sketch oversimplifies the pattern of ownership and the complexities of the underlying economics. It conceals elements of cross-ownership, for instance, such as Murdoch's 15 per cent ownership of shares in *The Financial Times*' parent company. For many years too, various papers printed each other under contract (for example, *The Times* printed *The Observer*, and the *Guardian* printed *The Sunday Times*). To concentrate on the barons is to stare at the public face.

These other connections give point to the issue of concentration. Table 3.6 shows each major ownership group's share of titles and circulation at 10 year intervals. The pattern was not a simple and consistent move towards concentration, either of titles or of circulation. The enormous Sunday circulations of the post-war years meant that even without owning more than one paper, the *News of the World* had the equal largest market share in 1947. In contrast, Kemsley had five papers but ranked only fifth.

The circulation share of the three largest groups grew greatly between 1947 and 1967. But they were not all the same groups within the different daily and Sunday categories each year: for instance, Beaverbrook was a top daily but not a top Sunday group in 1947. Nor were they the same top three from one decade to the next: groups such as Kemsley disappeared, and the market share of a survivor such as Associated Newspapers fluctuated quite widely. Nor were the largest shares by an *individual* group to be found at the end of the period: they were the Mirror Group's (more than 40 per cent in each category) in 1967. If the figures were shown year on year, other variations would appear too.

The large concentration of circulation in the late 1960s was due to the Mirror Group's purchase of the *Daily Herald* and the *People* at a time when Murdoch had not yet arrived to challenge the dominance of the *Daily Mirror* over the tabloid market. Once he had, the pattern changed. His own success, with its accumulation of titles, meant that by 1987 the circulation share of the top three groups had slipped back — but the number of titles within them was greater than ever. Overall, it is important to note that while Fleet Street was dominated by large groups, only one, Associated, survived the whole period from 1945 to 1990. It was the *combination* of large circulation share and a large number of titles that gave concentration its distinctive character in 1990.

The provincial press

The main features of the provincial press were set well before 1939. The period 1945—90 saw the number of morning papers decline, with total sales fluctuating; gains and losses among the evening titles, with a long term decline in sales; and more losses than gains among the weeklies, whose market changed sharply towards the end with the arrival of free sheets. Chain ownership, built up between the wars by the manoeuvres of the press barons (mainly seeking economies of scale), remained a crucial factor.

The number of provincial mornings dropped by one-third from 29 to 18 (Table 3.7). They fell one by one, like apples off a tree, but with the largest loss between 1955 and 1964. Circulations differed greatly, and there was no consistent trend. Some great names of the past survived at a much reduced level (*Yorkshire Post, Newcastle Journal*). Some had much the same sales after forty years as before. Others had more than doubled. Circulation size was no clue to survival. Provincial newspaper economics were a complex matter, including the size of the market, proximity to competing markets, the range of other media and membership or otherwise of a chain. The particular towns on the list thus had no obvious logic. Glasgow, Edinburgh and Cardiff were to be expected. But why on earth Leamington? If Nottingham, why not Leicester? If Plymouth, why not Exeter or Southampton? The historical explanations lie mainly in the middle and late nineteenth century, when newspapers were founded often in a political cause, or in

Table 3.6 National daily and Sunday newspapers: major group ownerships

Group	1947		1957		1967		1977		1987	
National dailies										
Associated Newspapers (*Mail*, etc.)	1	13	2	21	2	19	1	13	1	12
Beaverbrook (*Express*)	1	24	1	25	1	25	—	—	—	—
Mirror Group (*Mirror*, etc.)	1	23	1	28	2	41	—	—	—	—
Kemsley (*Sketch*)	1	5	—	—	—	—	—	—	—	—
Odhams (*Herald*)	1	14	1	10	—	—	—	—	—	—
Thomson (*Times*)	—	—	—	—	1	2	1	2	—	—
News International (*Sun*, etc.)							1	27	3	32
Reed (*Mirror*)							1	28		
Trafalgar House (*Express*)							1	17		
Maxwell (*Mirror*)							—	—	1	21
United (*Express*, etc.)							—	—	2	19
Total, 3 largest	3	61	4	74	5	85	3	72	6	72
National Sundays										
Associated Newspapers (*Dispatch*)	1	8	1	8	—	—	—	—	1	10
Beaverbrook (*Express*)	1	9	1	12	1	17	—	—	—	—
Mirror Group (*Mirror*, etc.)	1	15	1	20	2	45	—	—	—	—
Kemsley (Various)	4	18	3	15	—	—	—	—	—	—
News of the World	1	29	1	25	1	25	—	—	—	—
Odhams (*People*)	1	17	1	17	—	—	—	—	—	—

Number of titles and percentage of circulation

Thomson (*Times*)	—	—	—	—	1	6	1	7	—	—
News International (*N.O.W.*, etc.)	—	—	—	—	—	—	1	26	2	36
Reed (*Mirror*, etc.)	—	—	—	—	—	—	2	42	—	—
Trafalgar House (*Express*)	—	—	—	—	—	—	1	17	—	—
Maxwell (*Mirror*, etc.)	—	—	—	—	—	—	—	—	2	33
United (*Express*)	—	—	—	—	—	—	—	—	1	13
Total, 3 largest	6	64	3	62	4	87	4	85	5	82
National dailies and Sundays										
Associated Newspapers	2	10	3	13	2	8	1	6	2	11
Beaverbrook	2	15	2	17	2	20	—	—	—	—
Mirror Group	2	18	2	23	2	43	—	—	—	—
News of the World	1	18	1	16	1	16	—	—	—	—
Kemsley	5	13	3	10	—	—	—	—	—	—
Odhams	2	16	2	14	—	—	—	—	—	—
Thomson	—	—	—	—	2	5	2	5	2	—
News International	—	—	—	—	—	—	2	26	5	34
Reed	—	—	—	—	—	—	3	36	—	—
Trafalgar House	—	—	—	—	—	—	2	17	—	—
Maxwell	—	—	—	—	—	—	—	—	3	27
United	—	—	—	—	—	—	—	—	3	16
Total, 3 largest	5	52	5	56	5	79	7	79	11	77

Table omits small circulation papers or groups.

Sources: Royal Commission on the Press, 1947; Press Council Annual Reports.

Table 3.7 Provincial morning newspapers

Town	Newspaper	1945 owner	Circulation (thousands)	Purchaser/closure (date)	1988 circulation (thousands)
Birmingham	B. Post	Iliffe family	40	Ingersoll (USA) (1987)	25
	Gazette and Express	Westminster Press	98	merged (1956)	–
Bradford	Yorks. Observer	Westminster Press	27	merged (1956)	–
Brighton	Sussex Daily News	Infield family	6	merged (1956)	–
Bristol	Western Daily Press	Allen family	25	Bristol Evening Post (1960)	74
Darlington	Northern Echo.	Westminster Press	114		88
Ipswich	E. Anglian D. Times	Colman family	30		51
Leamington	Morning News	3 local families	4	EMAP[a]	10
Leeds	Yorks. Post	Various	139	United (1969)	92
Liverpool	Daily Post	Various	62	Trinity International Holdings[a]	70
Manchester	M. Guardian	Scott Trust	80	Goes national (1959)	–
	Daily Dispatch	Lord Kemsley	475	merged (1955)	–
Newcastle	Journal	Lord Kemsley	146	Thomson (1959)	58
Norwich	Eastern D. Press	Colman family	35		90
Nottingham	N. Journal	Westminster Press	30	merged (1953)	–
	N. Guardian	T Bailey Forman	na	closed (1973)	–
Plymouth	W. Morning News	Sir H Harmsworth	36	Thomson (1959); United (1967); closed (1986)	56
Sheffield	Morning Telegraph	Lord Kemsley	116	Thomson (1959)	–
Cardiff	Western Mail	Lord Kemsley	74	Thomson (1959)	77
Aberdeen	Press & Journal	Lord Kemsley	53	Thomson (1959)	108

	Title	Owner	Circ.	Subsequent ownership	Circ.
Glasgow	G. Herald	Outram (various)	78	Lonrho (1964)	123
	Daily Record	Lord Kemsley	300	Mirror Group (1955); Maxwell (1984)	773
	Bulletin	Outram (various)	155	closed (1960)	
Dundee	Courier & Advertiser	D C Thomson	80		122
Edinburgh	Scotsman	Findlay family	60	Thomson (1953)	86
Belfast	News-Letter	Henderson family	30	Century Newspapers[a]	41
	Northern Whig	Cunningham family	48	closed (1963)	
	Irish D. Telegraph	Baird family	6	merged (1952)	
	I. News & B. Morning News	Irish News Ltd.	32		43
Total Circulation			2,379		1,987
Number of titles		29		21 (1960); 19 (1975)	18
Number of separate owners		19		17 15	15

[a] Dates not known.

connection with news about trade and commerce. All of the other towns just mentioned, moreover, also had evening papers. The eighteen morning survivors in 1989 were the remnants of an army that had numbered over fifty in 1900.

Birmingham, Manchester and Nottingham had competing morning papers in 1945, but only Glasgow and Belfast did in 1989 (the *Glasgow Herald* really competed more with the Edinburgh *Scotsman* than with the *Daily Record*, and the two Belfast papers reflected different sectarian viewpoints). Manchester lost its morning papers altogether when the *Guardian* left. Bradford, Brighton and Nottingham also lost their papers. No town got a new morning paper. Staff of the Scottish *Daily Express* tried to fill the gap when local publication of their paper was ended in 1974. With Labour government backing they founded the *Scottish Daily News* but failed to capture a market. Copies of the *Express* continued to be available, shipped up from England.

Few large towns lacked an evening paper. The 1947 Press Commission listed nine with a population of over 100,000 but no paper, and 41 from 50,000–100,000. Only 10 of these were far distant from an existing paper. The precise number of evening papers has not always been easy to fix, since some of those with distinct names (such as the *Evening Mail* of Sandwell and Dudley in the late 1970s) were in fact local versions of a 'series' title (in this case, the Birmingham *Mail*). The number varied between 70 and 80. Unlike the mornings, the number of titles remained much the same, but total circulation fell. Evening papers still reached 90 per cent of their local households in the early 1960s: by 1980, they were down to 60 per cent. (Clark, 1981, p. 6).

The first wave of closures did not come until between 15 and 20 years after the Second World War. These were all in towns that still had evening paper competition: Birmingham, Bristol, Leeds, Leicester, Liverpool, Manchester, Nottingham, Edinburgh. In each case the lower circulation title went under. The fate of the Manchester *Evening Chronicle* (1963) was typical. In the two years before its death, advertising volume dropped by a quarter and circulation by about 10 per cent (Clark, 1981,

p. 12). Its competitor, the Manchester *Evening News*, outsold it by a ratio of 2:1. Where a paper closed in these circumstances, the survivor picked up on average rather more than half its circulation.

This shake-out left only Glasgow with two evening papers. Glasgow, uniquely, had had three at the end of the war. The weakest, the *Evening News*, closed in 1955. The two others continued till 1973, when the closure of the *Evening Citizen* meant that no town outside London was supporting more than one evening paper — and London went the same way in 1980.

In contrast to the morning papers, which suffered most heavily from the competition of the nationals, the evenings also had scope for growth in towns where an evening was not already established. At exactly the same time that the 'shake-out' was happening — the early 1960s — the largest expansion of evening titles since the 1890s was under way . Twelve new papers were launched between 1959 and 1970, either in locations on the edge of the circulation area of a 'parent' paper (such as in Hereford, Peterborough, Bromley, Doncaster and Telford) or in outer-London towns like Reading, Luton, Slough and Watford. A few of these papers became firmly established (and the latter helped kill the London evenings), but more, including some founded later in the 1970s (such as the Chelmsford *Evening Herald* and the Guildford *Daily Advertiser*), did not survive long into the 1980s. Altogether (including 'series' papers) about 20 evening papers were launched in the 30 years before 1985.

The post-war trend in evening papers, then, was a clear-cut elimination of towns with more than one locally based paper; the establishment of papers in perhaps 20 towns that did not have them in 1945; and the survival of all the existing papers that faced no home town competition as early as 1945.

As with the morning papers, circulation size was no clue to profitability. In 1945, papers in Bath, Carlisle, Darlington, Scarborough and North Shields all published not more than 15,000 copies a day (the Scarborough *Evening News* published 8,000). Papers in Glasgow, Manchester and Liverpool published over a quarter of a million. By 1985 the average had dropped but the spread was narrower, with a few exceptions at the extremes (the Manchester *Evening News* with 300,000 and the Darlington *Evening Echo* with 12,000). A full list of titles is given in the appendix while Table 3.8 consolidates some of the information.

Trends in the number and location of morning and evening titles can also be set side by side. At the end of the war, Glasgow had three morning and three evening papers; Belfast four and one. Birmingham, Manchester and Nottingham had two mornings and two evenings each. Bristol, Edinburgh, Leeds and Liverpool had one morning and two evenings; eleven towns had one of each, and Leicester had no morning but two evenings. By 1985, Glasgow and Belfast had two mornings and an evening each, and 17 towns had one morning and one evening.

Put another way, 21 towns outside London had a morning or evening choice in 1945; 16 did by 1989 (but a more limited choice in nearly half of them). The reality of such choice depended on whether a reader cared who owned the papers. In 14 of the 21, morning and evening papers were in the same ownership, and some of these were themselves in national or regional chains. This situation continued.

At the end of the war, provincial newspaper ownership took three forms. Some papers were still in local companies, with or without a morning/evening partner, and controlled by one or two families or a scatter of shareholders. This was, so to speak, the 'historic form'. Others were part of a provincial newspaper group. The remainder were in chains, some of which belonged to the national press undertakings.

Table 3.9 shows the size of these categories and, with Table 3.8 and the appendix, the decline of independence over the years. In 1947 over half the mornings and one-third of the evenings were owned by companies with few or no other newspaper interests elsewhere. Eight of these companies owned both a morning and an evening paper (the *Scotsman* and the Edinburgh *Evening Dispatch*, for example, and the Nottingham *Guardian* and *Evening Post*). Eight owned only a morning paper (such as the *Liverpool Daily Post*) and a ninth, Outram's, owned

Table 3.8 Provincial evening newspapers

	1945	1961	1975	1987
Total number of titles	76	74	79	73
New since previous date	–	1	17	4
Closed	–	3	12	10
Titles with circulation[a]				
35,000 or less	29	19	21	21
36–70,000	20	16	29	24
71–105,000	10	11	8	12
106–140,000	6	6	8	5
141,000 or more	10	16	13	9
Total circulation (thousands)	5,389	6,613	6,515	5,074
Smallest	8	10	8	12
Largest	293	412	386	291
Mean average	71	97	82	70
Total number of owners	39	31	31	25
Owners with	27	18	19	13
1 title	5	6	5	5
2	3	1	3	3
3	1	3	–	–
4	3	2	1	3
5–9	–	–	2	–
10–12	–	1	1	1
13				

Includes England, Scotland, Wales, Northern Ireland. Some titles are in 'series' (i.e. similar content but different name) and numbers vary in different sources.
[a] Some circulations are confidential. Number of titles does not always add up to 'Total number' above.

Sources: Royal Commissions on the Press; Press Council Annual Reports; ABC.

two in the same town (Glasgow). Nineteen owned only evening papers. Some of the family firms went back generations. Tillotsons, who controlled the Bolton *Evening News* until 1970, when it joined a chain, had done so for 104 years. Graham of Wolverhampton, Grimes of Blackpool, Hawkins of Bristol and Jeans of Liverpool, were all in the saddle in the 1940s. Most were unhorsed in the 1970s.

The provincial groups with papers in two or three towns were little different from the other independents. The Iliffe

Table 3.9 The provincial press: concentration

Type of paper	1947 Number of titles	1947 Percentage of circulation	1961 Number of titles	1961 Percentage of circulation	1974 Number of titles	1974 Percentage of circulation	1987 Number of titles	1987 Percentage of circulation
Morning								
5 major chains	11	63	8	36	9	38	8	30
Other main groups	18	37	4	40	4	46	4	37
Other			9	24	6	16	6	33
Total	29	100	21	100	19	100	18	100
Evening								
5 major chains	33	44	37	50	43	58	37	55
Other main groups	42	56	8	23	7	16	5	14
Other			30	27	27	26	31	31
Total	75	100	75	100	77	100	73	100
Weekly (paid for)								
5 major chains	82	8	135	13	211	24	133	16
Other main groups	1,080	92	19	2	84	9	122	8
Other			1,069	85	844	67	547	76
Total	1,162	100	1,223	100	1,139	100	802	100
Weekly (free)								
5 major chains	—	—	—	—	—	—	144	20
Other main groups	—	—	—	—	—	—	177	22
Other	—	—	—	—	—	—	499	58
Total							820	100

The five major chains are the same for each category each year but vary between years. Pearson/Westminster Press and Associated Newspapers are the only two represented in each year.

Sources: Royal Commissions on the Press; Press Council Annual Report.

family had papers in Birmingham and Coventry, the Colmans in Ipswich and Norwich, the Storeys in Portsmouth, Sunderland and Hartlepool. The fourth group, Southern Newspapers, was represented in Southampton and Bournemouth.

The growth of chains between the wars had been dramatic. In 1923 they controlled only 10 per cent of evening titles. By 1947 they controlled 11 of the 29 mornings and 33 of the 76 evenings (with minority interest in six more). Lord Kemsley's group was largest, with six mornings, nine evenings and three Sundays (including the *Empire News*). The Westminster Press, controlled by the Pearson family (Lord Cowdray), had four mornings, nine evenings and the Birmingham *Sunday Mercury*. The Harmsworth family interests, chiefly derived from the brothers Alfred and Harold, Lords Northcliffe and Rothermere, and trading as Associated Newspapers, had seven evenings and a major interest in four others (as well as managing, but not owning, a twelfth). A separate Harmsworth chain owned a morning and three evenings, and United Newspapers controlled or had a major interest in six.

The trend of ownership across the post-war years had four interlinked parts: independent ownerships declined; the provincial groups carried on; there were manoeuvrings among the major chains; and – the greatest upheaval – Kemsley left the market altogether and was replaced by a new player, the international Thomson organization.

The decline of the independent mornings was produced as much by amalgamations and closures as by sales. Only a few papers, notably the *Scotsman* and the *Yorkshire Post*, were sold to chains (Thomson and United). Provincial groups like Iliffe (*Birmingham Post*) and the Colmans (Norwich and Ipswich mornings) generally stayed with their papers. The activities of the chains, however, meant that only a third of the mornings still published in 1988 were in the same ownership as in 1945.

The independent evenings survived less well. Fewer than 10 of the 27 'single town' companies of 1947 remained in control by 1988, and most of these ran smallish papers in towns like Halifax, Oldham and Scarborough. The others sold out in the late 1960s and 1970s, often to the chains.

Kemsley's disposal of his provincial papers in 1959, of course, was part of the larger sale of his national newspaper interests. Thomson had bought *The Scotsman* in 1953, as an entry to the British market. The purchase of 11 provincial dailies and one Sunday was followed by various manoeuvres. In 1963 the Manchester *Evening Chronicle* was closed, and the two Sheffield papers were swapped with United's Edinburgh *Evening News*. Thomson then closed the weaker Edinburgh *Evening Dispatch*, which he had bought with *The Scotsman*. The following year he tried to buy Outram's Glasgow papers but was beaten off by nationalist feeling (Thomson being Canadian) and the resources of the Scottish financier Lord Fraser. The papers eventually passed with the rest of Lord Fraser's holdings to the multi-national conglomerate Lonrho. Meanwhile, Westminster Press and Associated slightly enlarged their chains, partly, as with Thomson, by new launches. Thomson, in particular, brought to the industry a dynamic concern with techniques of selling and marketing.

The Iliffe interests expanded too, through launches and the purchase of the Birmingham *Sunday Mercury* from the Westminster Press. They became, like United, relatively much more important than in 1947. By 1977, when the third Press Commission reported, five organisations stood out because of their provincial interests: Thomson, Westminster, Associated, United and Iliffe. United and Iliffe alone had no national press interests. But by 1988 Thomson had sold theirs and United had acquired some.

It is difficult to build details about the weekly press into this account, not least because of problems of definition. The 1974 Press Commission found that nearly a third of weekly papers shared editorial content with other weeklies, and half shared advertising. Many, in other words, were in series of associated titles.

This development had certainly been increasing steadily since the war. The 1947 Press Commission had already pointed it out – but the proportion sharing at that time was only one-fifth. Moreover, the total number of titles was very much larger. The decline shown in Table 3.9 was continuous, although the net figure conceals a considerable number of births. About 200 new titles were launched between 1961 and 1974, for example, but 300 probably died. In the same period, 40 per cent of the new titles were actually new editions of existing papers. Most people launching weeklies were already weekly publishers, many of whom were also contract printers.

As weekly ownership declined, it also became more concentrated. The number of towns with a choice of weekly papers was down from 226 in 1961 to about 150 in 1974. As Table 3.9 shows, while the largest category of owners was still the independents, the number of weeklies taken into the provincial and national chains increased enormously.

The later pattern of weeklies was further complicated by the growth of free sheets. These began to flourish in the early 1970s, and by 1975 there were 185. They increased steadily and in the late 1980s outnumbered the paid-for weeklies. Because they were delivered door-to-door, their 'guaranteed' circulation far exceeded the others' – 37 million compared with 7.6. The response of the existing publishers was traditional: they founded their own free weeklies or bought up the newcomers. By 1987, two-thirds of the titles and circulation were concentrated among two-dozen established publishers, with Pearson, Thomson, Associated and other familiar names controlling 20–40 each. Half a dozen groups of some size produced free weeklies only. Largest was the Yellow Advertiser Group, second only in circulation (two million) to Thomson. In Birmingham, uniquely, a free daily paper was launched in 1984, to compete with the old morning and evening papers.

The implications of concentration of provincial press ownership are greater when its geographical variation is taken into account. The chains generally concentrated in particular regions, although not to the extent of local monopoly. (In 1961, for instance, the 'leading publisher' had more than 50 per cent of evening sales in seven regions. By 1974 this number had dropped to four.) Associated Newspapers, for example, was strongest in the south-west, with five evenings and two mornings in Cornwall, Devon, Somerset and Gloucestershire, and 60 per cent of Cornwall's circulation of weeklies in 1974. Iliffe, similarly, concentrated in the west midlands, especially Birmingham and Coventry. With nine weeklies acquired from 1961–74, their morning and evening interests accounted for most of the sales in the major part of the Birmingham conurbation. United Newspapers expanded strongly into Lancashire. Westminster Press had three dailies and nineteen weeklies in the north and a spread of publications across the south. In turn, 'a striking development', as the 1974 Press Commission researchers called it, was 'the concentration of the ownership of newspapers in contiguous towns into a few hands' (Hartley et al., 1977, p. 73).

Three economic factors explain much of that concentration. First, firms economized through the *joint production of evenings and weeklies*: one sign of this was the closure of 79 printing centres by dailies and chains between 1961 and 1975, leaving 126 in production. Second, 'series publications' gave scope for *editorial economies of scale*. Third, a compact market made for *more efficient advertising sales*.

Similar considerations helped to explain the survival of the provincial dailies in the face of competition from the nationals. Provincial mornings could keep down their overheads and editorial costs if they had an evening partner. Even so, the 1974 Press Commission estimated that perhaps eight out of fifteen mornings they examined were being subsidized by an evening paper. Provincials also benefited from local display advertising (linked directly to retail sales activity) and from classified ads (dependent on households and population size).

In principle, the effect of concentration upon competition was, of course, to reduce it. For the provincial press, any calculation is complicated by questions of market boundaries and different types of publication. Thus provincial mornings, we have seen, competed chiefly with national mornings. Monopoly evening papers often competed with a morning paper from elsewhere (such as the Bradford *Telegraph and Argus* with the *Yorkshire Post* from Leeds), for morning papers circulated far more widely than the evenings. Evening and weekly papers faced the stiffest competition at the fringes of their circulation areas. In the mid-1970s, evening papers in about 30 towns faced competition from a rural-owned weekly. The effect of all such variations was to make it in the interests of publishers not to specialize in one type of paper but, as they did increasingly over the post-war decades, to spread their interests across morning, evening and weekly papers – and, in a few cases, Sundays. In addition, there was obviously competition from non-print media for advertising revenue and from other goods and services for the money in the newspaper reader's pocket.

Finally, the links between the provincial and the national press are summarized in Table 3.10. The baron with a finger in every pie was in fact less common than might be supposed. Most groups had most kinds of paper; only a few had all. The most 'complete' baron, in this sense, was Kemsley in 1947, with a large share both of titles and circulation. No group was directly comparable in 1961; but by 1976 the Thomson group was strong in all sectors. So was United, in 1987, having acquired national papers by purchasing the Beaverbrook/Trafalgar titles.

In general the pattern reflects the changes previously discussed in the national press. Owners such as Kemsley, Beaverbrook and Odhams dropped out. Newcomers such as Reed and Thomson entered but then partially withdrew. Other newcomers such as Murdoch and Maxwell stayed. Many of the Kemsley provincial papers were still in the same group in 1987 as in 1947, but now under a different owner. The greatest continuity of ownership was in the Rothermere Associated Newspapers combine and the smaller and narrower Pearson/Westminster group. But for a 'weakness' in the Sunday sector during most of the period, Associated would have been a consistently comprehensive group.

The addition of the provincial press, therefore, does not much affect the earlier conclusion about concentration among the nationals. Neither of the two major national groups in 1990, Murdoch and Maxwell, was strong in the provincial sector. Nor were the strongest provincials, United and Associated, dominant in either the quality or the popular national market. The large issues about press concentration concerned the national sector and the incorporation of the press with other media and financial interests.

Table 3.10 The national and provincial press: concentration (number of titles and percentage of circulation)

Group	1947 National mornings (no.)	(%)	1947 National & provincial Sundays (no.)	(%)	1947 Provincial dailies (no.)	(%)	1961 National mornings (no.)	(%)	1961 National & provincial Sundays (no.)	(%)	1961 Provincial dailies (no.)	(%)
Associated Newspapers	1	13	1	7	8	8	2	23	–	–	14	11
Beaverbrook	1	25	1	9	1	*	1	27	1	17	1	3
Mirror Group	1	24	1	14	1	*	2	39	3	42	1	6
Kemsley	1	5	6	20	15	23	–	–	–	–	–	–
News of the World	–	–	1	27	–	–	–	–	1	25	–	–
Odhams	1	14	1	16	–	–	–	–	–	–	–	–
Pearson/Westminster	–	–	1	*	13	7	1	1	–	–	9	5
United	–	–	–	–	4	3	–	–	–	–	4	5
Iliffe	–	–	–	–	3	?	–	–	1	1	5	8
Thomson	–	–	–	–	–	–	–	–	2	4	13	17
Murdoch/News Int'l	–	–	–	–	–	–	–	–	–	–	–	–
Reed	–	–	–	–	–	–	–	–	–	–	–	–
Lonrho	–	–	–	–	–	–	–	–	–	–	–	–
Maxwell/Pergamon	–	–	–	–	–	–	–	–	–	–	–	–

Group	1976 National mornings (no.)	(%)	1976 National & provincial Sundays (no.)	(%)	1976 Provincial dailies (no.)	(%)	1987 National mornings (no.)	(%)	1987 National & provincial Sundays (no.)	(%)	1987 Provincial dailies (no.)	(%)
Associated Newspapers	1	12	–	–	14	10	1	12	1	9	14	12
Beaverbrook	1	18	1	16	–	–	–	–	–	–	–	–
Mirror Group	–	–	–	–	–	–	–	–	–	–	–	–
Kemsley	–	–	–	–	–	–	–	–	–	–	–	–
News of the World	–	–	–	–	–	–	–	–	–	–	–	–
Odhams	–	–	–	–	–	–	–	–	–	–	–	–
Pearson/Westminster	1	1	–	–	12	7	1	2	–	–	8	7
United	–	–	–	–	8	8	2	19	1	11	8	8
Iliffe	–	–	1	1	5	6	–	–	–	–	–	–
Thomson	1	2	2	7	14	15	–	–	1	*	12	15
Murdoch/News Int'l	1	26	1	23	–	–	2	32	2	31	–	–
Reed	1	27	4	41	1	7	–	–	–	–	3	2
Lonrho	–	–	–	–	–	–	–	–	1	4	3	4
Maxwell/Pergamon	–	–	–	–	–	–	1	21	3	32	1	11

* Less than one percent.

Source: Royal Commissions on the Press; Press Council.

4 Media 1945–1990: Radio and Television

Public service broadcasting

Regular radio broadcasting started in 1922 and the BBC was founded in 1926. From its early days, broadcasting was therefore seen to be a legitimate field of public policy and its development was shaped by periodic government inquiries. In contrast with the press, whose three Royal Commissions stemmed from the fear or fact of concentration and contraction, these concerned the management of expansion. Pre-war were the Sykes (1923) and Crawford (1926) Committees, which set the pattern of 'public service broadcasting' run by the BBC, and the Ullswater Committee (1936), which confirmed it. Post-war came Beveridge (1951), Pilkington (1962), Annan (1977) and Peacock (1986). The Beveridge report ensured that TV would expand on the same lines as radio. Pilkington determined the allocation of the third TV channel to the BBC not ITV. Annan set the scene for the introduction of Channel 4. Peacock, strictly about finance, cut open the large can of worms about the organization of broadcasting in the era of satellites, cable and new information technology. In addition there were occasional narrower, often technical, reports.

These inquiries necessarily formulated explicit principles of broadcasting organization and practice. Too expedient and unsystematic to be called a philosophy, they comprise even so a kind of official doctrine, rather as though a series of government inquiries on the press had set down an official theory of 'the Fourth Estate'. They have been continuously unpicked or embroidered in the process of open criticism and riposte which the idea of public accountability imposes, part legally part morally, upon the broadcasters. Memoirs, prestige lectures and academic treatises have all added to the argument. Thus the BBC's proposals for *Broadcasting in the Seventies*, for example, published in July 1969 as a kind of White Paper, provoked what the BBC called 'vehement debate' and the Annan Committee 'a public row of splendid proportions' (Annan, 1977, p. 12), including debates in both houses of Parliament.

Throughout the period 1945–90, then, the system governed by these principles can be characterized as 'public service broadcasting'. The phrase itself was not perhaps in common currency until it came under challenge in the 1980s. Previously people were as likely to talk of a 'public broadcasting system'; but this became confusing when the distinctive US TV network with that name was established, often using British programmes.

The principles referred both to the *goals* of broadcasting and to a particular *form of organization* through which (alone?) they could be achieved. As with other principles, there could be arguments about whether they were in fact implemented in particular practices (finance by advertising, for example, or the quality of news coverage). They had to be flexible, too, adjusting to the new post-war broadcast medium of television; then to a new scale and range of programmes, increasingly controversial, and to changes in the society they served; and above all to the introduction of what at first was known as 'commercial television' in 1955.

The first principle was that radio should be run as a monopoly. Since the airwaves were limited, they were 'a valuable form of public property', as the Sykes Committee put it. Secondly, the monopoly was controlled by the government. Partly this was because the division of the radio spectrum was fixed internationally, and the government was guarantor of British conformity to the agreement. There were other users in addition to broadcasters, too, (wireless telegraphy, for example) whose interests needed protection. As radio caught on, politicians became increasingly aware also of the latent, intangible influence of the medium and its possible danger if unchecked. This danger might be greatest in the government's hands. A third principle, firmly established by the Crawford Committee, was that the public monopoly should be run at arm's length from the government. The private monopoly of radio set manufacturers, set up in 1922 from the applicants for government broadcasting licences, was turned into a public monopoly: the British Broadcasting Corporation.

The point about a public corporation was its midway status between the politicians and their civil servants on the one hand and the people running the broadcast services day to day on the other. It was a quintessential institution of British government: its success depended upon informal, tacit habits and understandings, rooted in the shared values and experiences of an educated class, more than on legal forms and niceties. In this it resembled the British constitution itself, which, as apologists delight in explaining to foreigners, is nowhere embodied in a single document having the force of law.

For the BBC, the government, in the person of the responsible Minister, (the Postmaster-General in 1945, as in 1926) appointed the seven Governors, set the licence fee and retained certain general powers. In theory its powers went no further. In practice, however, the BBC's position was epitomized in the government's power to require or ban the broadcast of any specific matter. This was used in 1955 to enforce the 'Fourteen-Days rule', which the BBC wanted to abandon, about broadcasting matters due for debate in Parliament; and it was the authority for the general ban on BBC 'editorializing' and on party political broadcasts outside the annual series agreed with the BBC. If it had been used more often, politicians and broadcasters alike would have regarded that as evidence not of the system's success but of its failure. Programmes likely to produce such action ought, rather, to be spotted within the BBC in advance and either adjusted suitably or else supported by the Governors in such a way that the politicians would be quietly told, in effect, that if they wished to object they risked on this occasion a larger row than they might want.

As intermediaries, the members of the public corporation — the Governors, who legally *were* the BBC — thus faced both ways. They shielded the broadcasters from outside pressure — from all directions, not just from the politicians — and they reviewed the broadcasters' work, explaining, justifying and sometimes excusing it to government and the public. This did not mean sitting on the fence but, in theory, jumping to and fro. In practice, it meant protecting the broadcasters from politicians and pressure groups more than the other way round. Pressure generally came at moments of crisis, such as Suez in 1956 or the Irish conflict in the 1970s and 1980s, and tended to focus on particular programmes. This meant that details of the Governors' procedures, which might seem unimportant to outsiders — such as whether they watched a contested programme in advance of its first transmission — sometimes had great symbolic importance for the broadcasters.

The BBC was not the first public corporation and by no means the last. As a device for separating 'general matters of policy' from 'day to day administration' it seemed a comfortable way of combining public accountability with business efficiency in a parliamentary system of government: Ministers dealt with the former and the corporation's employees with the latter. Public utilities such as electricity supply and London Transport were put under public corporations between the wars, and they were the standard form of nationalization in the Attlee government for railways, air and freight transport, coal and steel. Few of these, from the vantage point of 1990, flourished as corporations so successfully as the BBC, which gained a reputation as one of the great creations of social and cultural policy in the twentieth century.

A public corporation managing a monopoly might do so in a sectional interest. A fourth 'public service' principle was that the BBC should be, in the Crawford Committee's words, 'trustee for the national interest'. Radio must serve the interests of everyone, not of particular religions, regions or social and economic groups, and it could best do this if not subject to the direct control of a ministry. The Governors were to represent a broad cross-section of the public.

Consistent with the 'national interest' idea was a fifth principle, about the key matter of finance. Rather than concentrate the raising of revenue at the production end of the broadcasting process, by selling airtime to advertisers, the Sykes Committee recommended raising it by charging a flat rate annual licence fee to the consumer. This was considered fairer because the amount of advertising time would be small and expensive, which could favour the wealthiest clients. The size of the fee was set and reviewed periodically by the government, for whom it was a useful source of leverage in the informal manoeuvrings typical of government–broadcaster relations. For the broadcasters, the licence fee had the advantage too of being an assured and predictable form of income.

A sixth principle, more easily taken for granted by audiences, perhaps, than the others, was geographical 'universality of service'. Wherever people lived, they had an equal right to receive programmes, just as the BBC's parent department, the Post Office, delivered the mail to the remotest communities. This would have meant little if the charge to the receiver reflected the true cost of delivery, so the flat rate licence fee was an important element in 'universality'.

These principles chiefly concerned broadcasting organization, and the organization, of course, was designed to achieve complementary public service goals. In these, one is dealing with programme content and specifically with a certain kind of programme quality. The word 'service' here needs emphasizing, too, for while it is simple to establish that the law requires the appointment of twelve Governors and that twelve have been appointed, a broadcasting service is organic, extensive, continuous – and difficult to evaluate.

Applied to broadcast programmes, then, the public service principles were in the nature of flexible guidelines. Their practice felt the stamp of personalities, starting with the formidable John Reith. Reith's domination of the BBC as first Director-General (i.e. chief executive) until 1937 is well described as 'massive, totalitarian and idiosyncratic, and for many decades the traditions of the BBC seemed to flow directly from his personality' (Curran and Seaton, 1988, p. 118). Reith's notion of public service was rooted in a strict sense of selfless moral rectitude, derived from Scottish presbyterian values. Sir William Haley, Director-General from 1944 to 1952, was a self-made man whose career started as a telephonist on *The Times*, and he had much of Reith's commitment to the enlightening and educative value of broadcasting. But he failed to appreciate the potential of television. Another Director-General whose vision of broadcasting had a major influence in a period of important change in social attitudes was Hugh Greene, who oversaw a more liberal interpretation of 'public service' in the 1960s.

Obviously the stamp of personality was felt at all levels of the BBC. Official committees of enquiry tended to duck the task of too detailed an account of the stuff of public service, falling back on the Pilkington Committee's observation that 'good broadcasting is a practice not a prescription' (Pilkington, 1962, p. 12). The principles were encapsulated in the requirement that public service broadcasting should 'inform, educate and entertain'. Those words, and in that order of priority, were included in the BBC charter (and were passed on to ITV in much the same form in 1955).

The particular order of priority avoided, firstly, the risk of simply 'giving the audience what it wants' and settling at a lowest common denominator of taste. The stress on 'information' justified, in due course, strong news services, documentaries and international coverage. Education meant infinitely more than good schools programmes; a whole approach, rather, to broadcasting as a means of widening horizons, opening doors, increasing awareness – all the well meant speech–day cliches of the educationist, working with the privilege of experience and knowledge and with a sense of responsibility for the improvement of those they serve.

Information does not properly inform unless it is accurate. Principle, as well as expediency, therefore ensured that public service broadcasting was to be impartial. This meant both that the BBC itself was not to 'editorialize' about the news (or 'matters of public policy', as the Postmaster-General put it in

1927) and that it kept strict control over access to the airwaves. As the Annan Committee pointed out, the public service principles, and the BBC's position as 'trustee for the national interest', did not mean 'that anyone with a claim to broadcast had a right to broadcast. They do not give the press or the universities or the churches the right to broadcast respectively the programmes on the news, education or religion, or to determine how they should be broadcast' (Annan, 1977, p. 9). The same principle meant that in theory, too, there was no subject about which the broadcasters might not make a programme, if they judged it right.

These kinds of argument could be almost infinitely refined. In practice, they were inevitably contestable. How did you recognize and measure impartiality? Who should be excluded from the air? Was it 'against the national interest' to have very many foreign programmes? What was the right balance between creativity and innovation on the one hand and familiarity and repetition on the other? The refinements also had to cover the new forms of broadcasting. Once ITV started, rules about advertisements were needed, concerning length, frequency, position in schedules, content and so on. What about the question of foreign ownership of ITV companies, too? (Not permitted, was the answer.)

Later chapters indicate how some such questions were answered. The answers naturally varied. But the essence of 'public service' practice was the broadcasters' day to day independence. However much encumbered by advisory councils, complaints commissions and the shifting apparatus of consultation and audience research, the broadcasters' own judgement about programme standards and quality − what it meant to inform, educate and entertain − prevailed.

The greatest challenge to the continuing applicability of public service principles to broadcasting structure and content was not the arrival of TV itself, which slid comfortably into the BBC system in 1946, where it had started 10 years earlier, but the Churchill government's decision to introduce a second TV network in 1955. It was to be financed by advertising revenue, but was it best described as 'commercial' or as 'independent', as complementary to the BBC or as competitor? The direct competition with the BBC was for the audience. This did indeed run counter to the original principle of a benign public monopoly. If the BBC really was being run in the 'national interest', what benefit could competition bring? The idea that competition for audience share would be *virtuous* was thus an innovation. On the other hand, it did not necessarily contradict the public service principles, especially as the new Act of Parliament obliged ITV to 'inform, educate and entertain' according to the same standards. Along with them went the baggage of impartiality, high quality, good taste and decency. In news programmes, quality and range were sought by setting up a distinct company, ITN, which was jointly owned by the other companies and supplied news for the whole channel, and later for Channel 4.

Competition for finance did not in theory exist, since the BBC's licence fee was untouched by the new system. In practice, however, the BBC knew that as its audience share fell, the case for a compulsory fee would become weaker and that getting the fee raised at the regular three-yearly review would be trickier (no government was going to win votes by raising the licence fee, even during the years of monopoly). The popularity of programmes therefore did become a factor in BBC calculations in a qualitatively different way from previously.

But what of the very idea of advertising in a public service system? The Beveridge Committee, which reported shortly before the Churchill government took office in 1951, saw no conflict. It drew a parallel between broadcast advertising and the advertising columns of the press, which did not (or need not) affect editorial independence. 'Slots' – spot advertisements – were the form chosen for ITV. Although the ITV companies sold them and collected the revenue, their frequency, duration and content were regulated by the supervising body, the Independent Television Authority. In this way the influence of revenue source over programme content was minimized.

At the top, ITV organization followed public service principles closely. The ITA was a public corporation like the BBC, with a small group of Governors and comparable (though not identical) intermediary functions of oversight and control. But where the BBC Governors appointed a Director-General to run the service, the ITA selected companies from competing applicants and awarded franchises to run the service in different geographical regions, subject to meeting the ITA's programme standards. The franchises initially lasted seven years. The ITA also owned the transmitters, for which the companies paid a rent.

The other supposedly distinctive feature of ITV, along with advertising revenue, was the principle of regionalism. This fitted perfectly well into the public service world, but in practice it was considerably diluted for viewers by the networking arrangements of the four (later five) larger companies. These were guaranteed a national, not just a regional, showing for their programmes for a number of peak hours each week.

The case against ITV had initially to be made against something that did not yet exist. Much was therefore made of the horrors of American TV — again, by hearsay, since the BBC did not show the worst American TV programmes and none of the ads. The pernicious influence of sponsorship on content may have been a fact in the States but was irrelevant to the proposed British system. Arguments about the more intangible effects on 'quality' of the need to generate large audiences to provide enough advertising revenue, and of the intrusion of the profit motive in general, appealed to people's broader social and political prejudices. But obviously they cut no ice with a Conservative government that was busy dismantling wartime controls and reviving the notion of 'choice' in people's everyday lives.

So ITV was 'commercial'; but was it 'independent'? Hardly, except from the BBC; and perhaps the word might fairly be used to describe the divorce of advertisers from programme makers. Was it complementary or competitive with the BBC? ITV in fact was both. Initially it seemed more competitive. The BBC was the public service broadcaster: ITV was the commercial broadcaster. The BBC Director-General Hugh Greene was scathing in 1960 about an ITA claim to the public service label. Only with the passage of time did the two channels come to be seen widely as part of a *single* public service system. In particular the idea of competition for audiences but not for revenue seemed increasingly an expression of the British genius for making practical contraptions which then turn into beautiful machines. Competition, feared at first for its degenerative effects on programme quality, was rationalized as consistent with public service principles, because it was not driven by competition for a single source of revenue, as in the USA, but ensured a proper sensitivity to audience needs. Each system enjoyed what Reith in the beginning regarded as one of the public service essentials – assured finance.

The introduction of BBC2, Channel 4 and local radio posed no such challenges to the public service ideas. But breakfast time TV provides a footnote. The BBC started its own cut-price breakfast time service because of, and just before, ITV's TV-AM. This was, in part at least, in pursuit of the idea that 'if it's broadcasting, then the BBC does it' (even if someone else does too). Similarly, the BBC felt that it should have a stake in the (abortive) satellite plans of the early 1980s. These were echoes of the old days – of the BBC as a public service broadcasting system in itself. By the time of the changes introduced for the 1990s, they had died away.

A careful distillation of the principles of public service broadcasting submitted by the Broadcasting Research Unit to the Peacock Committee in 1985 showed that the old values that were in place in 1945 could still be made to fit the diverse and vastly changed system forty years on. In structure, the main difference was that advertising, once grudged, was now embraced. In programming, the shifts were of emphasis – towards the needs of minorities, for example – that reflected the different society and culture of 1980s Britain and that took a pluralist not a paternalist view of the meaning of 'service'. The benign monopoly had become a benign duopoly.

The BRU summed up the principles in eight points. They claimed broadcast programmes should be available to everybody ('geographic universality'), should cater for all interests and tastes, and should make particular provision for minorities (especially the disadvantaged). Broadcasters should 'recognise their special relationship to the sense of national identity and community', should be distanced from all vested interests, particularly the government, and should be 'liberated rather than restricted' by the public guidelines for broadcasting. One main broadcasting organization should continue to be funded by 'the corpus of users' (that is to say, the licence fee, or something like it), and broadcasting should be structured so as to encourage competition in good programming rather than for audience numbers (BRU, 1985).

Would these principles survive into the next period of change in the 1990s, or had they outlived their time? The Thatcher government's policy, effected in the Broadcasting Act of 1990, provoked intense debate. For the first time, there would in the future be direct competition for income, since a new, fifth TV channel would compete with the existing ITV channel for advertising revenue. Franchises were to be allocated on both channels by auction, giving them to whoever would pay the government the highest fee, subject to an abstract 'quality threshold'. The IBA's successor, moreover, was to have fewer powers over programme content.

The fear of opponents was that the new system would push down production budgets; drive out minority programmes and 'serious' projects; subject ITV to the needs of advertisers more than before; force the BBC down market to maintain its audience share. In short, it was feared the system would restrict, not liberate – viewers, as well as broadcasters – and put ratings and rubbish above quality (in every kind of programme) and range. The government, of course, argued otherwise. But those were controversies for a new decade.

Radio

Of all the major media, radio had the most varying fortunes between 1945 and 1990. The BBC emerged from the war with immense prestige and popularity. For the next 10 years it basked in its monopoly, with radio still supreme, as TV came slowly out of the shadows. The rude intrusion of ITV in 1955 changed all that. Radio now was becalmed, for another 10 years. Then it was noisily invaded by the pirates of Radio Caroline, illegally broadcasting pop music offshore in the North Sea. The BBC reorganized its channels, took the pirate disk jockeys on board the new Radio 1 and entered the 1970s with little of the direct Reith influence remaining.

In the 1970s, local radio was greatly expanded, and a pattern was set. Technical developments made possible both a greater variety and quality of signals and also more convenient ways of listening. The transistor transformed the portable radio, culminating in the spectacle – bizarre if it had been witnessed 20 years earlier – of people going around with earphones and Walkmans. Car radios also proliferated. Obviously radio would never recover the prominence of the post-war years, but it successfully re-established itself as meeting a need complementary to TV, whether judged by audience figures or by advertising revenue. A word such as 'moribund', used by Annan to describe its position in the late 1950s, was no longer remotely appropriate.

Before the war the BBC ran two stations, one of which included regional programmes. One of these became the General Forces Programme, which soon provided the light entertainment and relaxation which the Forces clearly wanted and which were easily justified by their importance to morale. The 'home front' had similar needs, met by shows like *Workers' Playtime*. This was geared to communal audiences, such as factory workers, who wanted background listening, and it was broadcast from the factory floor. The second station, the Home Service, was more 'serious': for example it carried the main news bulletins that naturally attracted huge wartime audiences. The war also saw the BBC staff more than double in size, from about 5,000 in 1938 to 11,000 in 1946. The increase no doubt contributed to the Beveridge Committee's attitude five years later that the organization was bureaucratic, top heavy and over-centralized in London.

The BBC's pre-war conception of the audience had been

more like that of someone reading a book — a deliberate and solitary or individual habit, though it may be done in company — than of a collective social entity. This fitted in with the idea of mixed programming, whereby music, talks, variety and drama appeared on each station, exposing the listener to a varied choice, rather than the stations being specialized. This policy was broadly retained after the war, but with the populist elements intact. *Workers' Playtime* continued for many years. The Forces Programme was renamed the Light Programme in 1945, 'designed to appeal not so much to a certain class of listener — but to all listeners when they are in certain moods' (BBC, 1946, p. 53). The Home Service remained, with regional variations, and a new station was launched in 1946. This was the Third Programme, brainchild of the Director-General, William Haley, though really pure Reith in character. Haley cheerfully explained, as no successor could have dared after, say, 1965, that he saw society as a cultural pyramid, slowly aspiring upwards. He himself had aspired with eminent success: the conception was a self-educator's dream. The Third was a highbrow station, with a tiny proportion of the audience.

In these final years of radio prominence in the late 1940s and early 1950s, then, listeners had a choice of three BBC stations, including some regional variation. A part-time chairman of governors was assisted by other part-timers (Table 4.1 lists the chairmen, the directors-general and the number of governors, and their counterparts at the IBA, for the years 1945–89). Inflation was comparatively low and the licence fee, swelled by the increasing income from the separate TV licence, did not need to be raised often in order to provide an adequate income. Revenue would be more of a problem in the future. Table 4.2 shows the changes in the licence fee for the whole post-war period. In the later decades it was raised more often. The gradual eclipse of radio is shown by the growth in the number of TV licence holders, until the separate radio licence was abolished in February 1971. Other ways in which the eclipse can be measured are the changing numbers of radio and TV staff (Table 4.3) and the changing ratio of expenditure (Table 4.4).

The Third Programme's elitist appeal (as it would now be called) to a minority 'whose tastes, education and mental habits enable them to take pleasure in close and responsive listening to broadcasts of artistic and intellectual distinction' (Annan, 1977, p. 12) was so limited that in 1957 it was confined to weekday evenings and weekends from 2.30 onwards. The rest of the time it was called Network 3, broadcasting specialist but less arcane programmes — on gardening, religion, music and so on. In 1964 'serious' music took over altogether and daytime Network 3 was renamed the Music Programme.

In 1964 too the first pirate, Radio Caroline, hove to in a ship just outside UK territorial waters off the Thames Estuary. It was soon followed by others. The pirate image was entirely fair. They broadcast on wavelengths allocated by international agreement and national laws to other services (in other countries, not just Britain), including maritime communications. They 'stole' the pop music that they broadcast by ignoring the law about royalties. The audience was their treasure, and they delivered it to their backers, the advertisers. There was even a buccaneering Robin Hood element, in that their programmes had a genuine popular appeal.

The Labour government was bound to take action: indeed there was a coordinated response through the Council of Europe. In 1967 the appropriately schoolmarm-sounding Marine & Broadcasting (Offences) Act banned the placing of advertising with the pirates. Equally, though, a Labour government could not ignore the public demand, and the BBC was authorized to provide a 'continuous popular music programme' on a medium wave frequency used by the Light Programme. So in September 1967 came 'wonderful' Radio One, with its patter and jingles that sounded like ads but were not ads. The other services were named Radios 2, 3 and 4.

Radio 1 was the most complete form of specialization on a radio station and the last before the BBC accepted that the Reith/Haley commitment to 'mixed' programming on each station simply did not correspond to listening preferences. In 1970, after the famous public row, Radio 1 stayed as an all-pop network, Radio 2 became exclusively 'light' music, Radio 3

Table 4.1 BBC/ITV Governors and Directors-General

Date of appointment	BBC chairman	Main/previous occupation	Total governors	Director-General
1939	Sir A Powell	Administrator	7[a]	
1944				W Haley
1947	Lord Inman	Businessman		
1947	Lord Simon of Wythenshawe	Engineer/politician		
1952	Sir A Cadogan	Diplomat	9	Sir I Jacob
1957	Sir A fforde	Lawyer/headmaster		
1959				HC Greene
1964	Lord Normanbrook	Civil servant		
1967	Lord Hill of Luton	Conservative politician	12	
1968				C Curran
1973	Sir M Swann	Academic		
1977				I Trethowan
1980	G Howard	Landowner/businessman		
1982				A Milne
1983	S Young	Accountant		
1986	M Hussey	Businessman		
1987				S Checkland

ITA/IBA Chairman[b]

1954	Sir K Clark	Art historian/administrator		Sir R Fraser
1957	Sir I Kirkpatrick	Diplomat		
1963	Lord Hill of Luton	Conservative politician		
1965			10	
1967	Lord Aylestone	Labour politician	12	
1970				B Young
1975	Lady Plowden	Educationist		
1981	Lord Thomson of Monifieth	Labour politician		
1982		Industrialist		J Whitney
1989	G Russell			

[a] The number of governors was raised from 5 to 7 in 1937.
[b] The ITA was renamed the Independent Broadcasting Authority in 1972, when it took responsibility for Independent Local Radio.

Sources: Various.

Table 4.2 Radio and TV licences: numbers and fees at selected dates[a]

Date	Total licences (thousands)	Radio Licences (thousands)	Radio Fee (£)	Black & white (thousands)	Combined radio and TV Fee (£)	Colour (thousands)	Fee (£)
1945	9,710	9,633	0.50				
1946	10,396	10,348	1.00		2.00		
1947	10,778	10,713		15			
1948	11,180	11,082		45			
1950	12,219	11,819		344			
1952	12,754	11,244		1,449			
1954	13,437	10,126		3,249	3.00		
1955	13,980	9,414		4,504			
1957	14,525	7,496		6,966	4.00		
1959	14,736	5,423		9,255			
1961	15,177	3,858		11,268			
1963	15,699	3,213		12,443			
1965	16,047	2,759	1.25	13,253	5.00		
1966	16,178	2,580		13,567			
1968	17,646	2,530		15,068	6.00		10.00
1969	17,960	2,439		15,397			11.00

1971	15,943	—[b]	15,333	7.00	610	12.00
1973	17,125	—	13,793		3,332	18.00
1975	17,701	—	10,120	8.00	7,580	21.00
1977	18,056	—	8,098	9.00	9,958	25.00
1978	18,149	—	7,100	10.00	11,049	34.00
1979	18,381	—	6,250	12.00	12,131	46.00
1981	18,667	—	4,888	15.00	13,780	
1983	18,494	—	3,796		14,699	58.00
1985	18,716	—	2,896	18.00	15,820	
1987	18,953	—	2,414		16,539	
1988	19,354	—	2,220	21.00	17,134	62.50

[a] Includes alternate years and dates when the licence fee was changed. Total includes free licences for blind persons up to 1971, excluded from righthand columns.

[b] Radio licences were abolished on 1 February 1971.

Source: BBC.

Table 4.3   BBC staff: radio and television

	1962 (no.)	(%)	1967 (no.)	(%)	1988 (no.)	(%)
Radio	5,650	39	5,600	29	6,618	28
Television	8,700	61	13,675	71	17,272	72

Source: BBC Handbooks.

Table 4.4   BBC expenditure on radio and television

Year	Radio (m)	Television (m)	Ratio (%)
1955–56	10.9	7.0	61:39
1960–61	12.6	18.0	41:59
1965–66	17.1	38.5	31:69
1970–71	24.6	68.4	26:74
1975–76	52.4	131.8	28:72
1980–81	116.2	300.1	28:72
1985–86	225.2	582.1	28:72

Source: A. Briggs, *The BBC: The First Fifty Years* (OUP, 1985); BBC Handbooks.

(limited to VHF) provided 'serious' music by day and high culture by night. Radio 4 was for talk — news, current affairs, drama and general entertainment. This system was described by the ungainly name 'generic broadcasting', and it survived, with changes of wavelength and broadcast hours, throughout the 1970s and 1980s. It was also accompanied by a large expansion of programme output, which nearly doubled between 1962 and 1975.

While putting these changes in place, the BBC had also been developing local radio. The Pilkington Committee recommended a BBC monopoly, and in 1966 the government authorized an experiment on VHF with eight stations. Starting with Leicester, these were all on air by mid-1968 and 12 more were added before 1970. These reached a potential 70 per cent of the English population and were dotted in such obvious places as Birmingham, Bristol, Leeds, Manchester, Liverpool, Nottingham – and London. Another 20 stations would have increased the range to 90 per cent. Scottish, Welsh and Northern Irish radio already had a considerable local element.

The new Conservative government in 1970 had different ideas and not surprisingly favoured a competing set of commercial stations. To make room on the dial, various BBC medium frequencies were released. This meant the end, in 1972, of the old system of regional variations on the national radio network. The BBC's local stations were kept at 20, and the IBA was authorized to licence up to 60, reaching much the same total percentage audience. Capital Radio and LBC opened in London in October 1873 and 17 others quickly followed, chosen from more than 60 applicants.

A change of government produced a temporary halt, when Labour, who returned in February 1974, stopped further expansion until after the Annan inquiry. But under the Thatcher Government new franchises were again allocated and by 1988 46 ILR stations were covering about 85 per cent of the UK population. The BBC's stations increased to 30 (Table 4.5).

BBC local radio was a shoestring operation. As with any extra BBC service, it had to be financed out of existing revenue, for there was no separate licence fee or earmarked increase. ILR, of course, depended on the sale of 'spot' advertising, controlled by the IBA (renamed from ITA when its role was extended to radio). There was certainly a distinct local advertising market available to support it. But the revenue was not just there for the taking, and a station had to get its programming right to win the necessary audience. Even then, income was liable to fluctuate. Several stations had financial problems in their early days. Both Capital Radio and LBC in London, the former geared to pop music and the latter to talk, made near-disastrous starts and recovered under new Canadian ownership (a reflection of the north American style most appealing in local radio). At least two stations went bust, and others, such as Invicta Radio in Kent, had to relaunch before getting firmly established.

With ILR the question of ownership arises once more.

Table 4.5 BBC and Independent Local Radio stations: launch dates

Year	BBC	ILR
1967	Leicester (Nov.); Sheffield (Nov.); Merseyside (Nov.)	
1968	Nottingham (Jan.); Sussex (Jan.); Stoke-on-Trent (Mar.); Leeds (Jun.)	
1970	Bristol (Sep.); Manchester (Sep.); London (Oct.); Oxford (Oct.); Radio WM (Birmingham) (Oct.); Kent (Dec.); Solent (Dec.); Cleveland (Dec.)	
1971	Newcastle (Jan.); Lancashire (Jan.); Humberside (Jan.); Derby (Apr.)	
1973		LBC (Oct.); Capital (Oct.); Clyde (Dec.)
1974		Birmingham (Feb.); Piccadilly (Manchester) (Apr.); Metro (Tyne & Wear) (Jul.); Swansea (Sep.); Sheffield (Oct.); City (Liverpool) (Oct.)
1975	Cumbria (Nov.)	Forth (Edinburgh) (Jan.); Plymouth (May); Tees (Jun.); Trent (Jul.); Bradford (Sep.); Portsmouth (Sep.); Orwell (Ipswich) (Oct.)
1976		Reading (Mar.); Belfast (Mar.); Wolverhampton (Apr.)
1980	Norfolk (Sep.); Lincolnshire (Nov.)	Cardiff (Apr.); Mercia (Coventry) (May); Hereward (Peterborough) (Jul.); Bournemouth (Sep.); Severn (Oct.); Tay (Oct); Devon (Nov.)
1981		Aberdeen (Jul.); Aire (Leeds) (Sep.); Essex (Sep.); Chiltern (Luton) (Oct.); Ayr (Oct.); GWR (Bristol) (Oct.)
1982	Jersey (Mar.); Guernsey (Mar.); Cambridgeshire (May); Northampton (Jun.)	Inverness (Feb.); Wyvern (Hereford etc.) (Oct.); Red Rose (Preston & Blackpool) (Oct.); Saxon (Bury St. Edmunds) (Nov.)
1983	Devon (Jan.); Cornwall (Jan.); York (Jul.)	Guildford (Apr.); Marcher (Wrexham) (Sep.); Signal (Stoke) (Sep.); Brighton (Sep.)

Table 4.5 (cont.)

Year	BBC	ILR
1984		Viking (Humberside) (Apr.), Leicester (Sep.); Invicta (East Kent) (Oct.); Norwich (Oct.); Mercury (Reigate) (Oct.)
1985	Shropshire (Apr.); Bedfordshire (Jun.)	
1986	Essex (Nov.)	Northampton (Nov.)

ILR Subsidiary stations are excluded. Stations are listed by location, if their names do not indicate this.

The idea of local radio fitted snugly with local ownership, like the provincial press. But comparison with the press cannot go very far. An individual might build a local paper from nothing and retain the ownership intact. The costs of ILR were different. They did not expand with the audience to the same extent as with a newspaper. Nor were newspapers controlled by a public authority and subject to competitive franchising. From the start, local radio companies had a fair spread of local investors. As they became established, shares in many of them became quoted on the Stock Exchange. This in principle dispersed ownership, though working against a local character.

ILR thus did not develop ownership chains like the local press. Broadcasting law influenced the pattern, too. No ITV company was allowed a controlling interest in an ILR station in the same area, and vice versa (though there could be joint directors). The IBA could regulate the extent of foreign ownership, and foreign control was completely forbidden. For the rescue operations of Capital and LBC, for example, Canadian interests were preferred over US alternatives, which were reckoned incompatible with public service values.

The law gave local newspapers a privileged position, virtually prescribing an element of radio/press concentration. Papers with substantial circulation in ILR areas were guaranteed a shareholding if they wanted it and if the IBA felt their advertising revenue might be hit. The Annan Committee disliked this arrangement, for even the local newspaper publishers' association itself did not think the amount of advertising likely to go to ILR was great enough to be a threat. Annan wanted press interests limited to 25 per cent in any station, with 10 per cent for any one paper. But this was ignored, and by 1988 several of the 46 stations were 20–30 per cent owned by the press. Table 4.6 gives the details. Only one out of nineteen in 1976 had no press involvement at all, and four out of forty-five in 1987. The same names and groups that have already featured in the discussion of the provincial press therefore appear again as owners of local radio. This is true both of the small and narrower groups, such as the Eastern Counties group in East Anglia, or Portsmouth and Sunderland newspapers, and the national groups with major provincial holdings, such as the Westminster Press and Associated Newspapers. (Radio holdings by the main press groups are indicated alongside their TV holdings in Table 4.11.)

Ownership links between ITV and radio were often indirect and came through a third party, including newspaper groups. Table 4.7 shows direct links in 1988. One striking development was the two clusters of ILR stations accumulated by Crown Communications and Capital Radio (themselves part owned by other organizations). These two companies each had holdings in 1988–9 in 18 stations (Table 4.8). While these links involved the provision of some common services, they did not constitute chains in exactly the traditional newspaper sense, since the holdings were not in every case large enough to be a controlling interest. Obvious exceptions were Crown's 100 per cent ownership of LBC and Capital's of Devon Air.

Crown's other interests were in TV production, computer graphics and business communications. In 1989 it was the first British company to take a significant stake in the French commercial radio network. Capital, a longer established business, was part owned by the BET conglomerate.

The full picture of ILR ownership over a period of nearly twenty years is difficult to trace. But clearly from the beginning the stations were included within media conglomerates, partly by government and IBA design and partly by the natural interest of media investors.

Table 4.6 Press shareholdings in Independent Local Radio, 1976–87

Voting shares held by press (%)	1976	1981	1987
Nil	Bradford	–	Ayr; Red Rose; Tees; Wyvern
5	–	Bradford; Cardiff	Brighton; Chiltern; Marcher; Wolverhampton
5–10	–	Ayr; Bournemouth; Bristol	Bournemouth; Clyde; Guildford; Invicta; Liverpool Mercury; Ocean; Trent
10–15	–	Aire; Gloucester; Aberdeen	Aberdeen; Belfast; Cardiff; Edinburgh; Essex; Gloucester Inverness; Leicester
15–20	Belfast; Metro; Orwell; Trent	Belfast; Devon; Edinburgh; Hereward; LBC; Metro; Orwell; Swansea; Trent	Bristol; LBC; Norwich; Plymouth; Severn; Sheffield; Swansea; Viking
20–25	Birmingham; Capital; Edinburgh; LBC; Liverpool; Plymouth; Portsmouth; Sheffield; Swansea; Tees; Wolverhampton	Birmingham; Capital; Essex; Mercia; Plymouth; Portsmouth; Reading; Sheffield; Tees; Wolverhampton	Birmingham; Capital; Devon; Metro; Reading; Stoke
25–30	–	Liverpool	Aire; Orwell; Saxon
30–35	Clyde	Clyde	Hereward; Mercia; Piccadilly
35–40	Piccadilly	Piccadilly	–
40–45	–	Tay	–
45–50	Reading	–	–
Total	19	31	44

Names are mostly of locations, not stations. (See table 4.5).

Sources: Annan Committee; Press Council Annual Reports.

Table 4.7 ITV companies' holdings in ILR companies, 1988

ITV company	Radio stations (location)
Anglia	Bury St Edmunds; Chiltern; Norwich
Central	Birmingham; Coventry; Leicester; Trent
Grampian	Edinburgh
Scottish	Edinburgh; Glasgow
Thames	Bournemouth; Reading
TSW	Capital Radio group
Tyne Tees	Newcastle; Teesside

Source: The Journalist. Holdings are mostly small.

Table 4.8 Capital Radio and Crown Communications: ILR holdings, 1988–9

	Crown		Capital	
Station	Holding (%)	Station	Holding (%)
---	---	---	---
Brighton	24	Birmingham	?
Chiltern	10	Chiltern	10
Edinburgh	30	Coventry	?
Guildford	5	Devon	100
Inverness	9	Essex	28
Invicta	30	Gloucester	8
LBC	100	Inverness	22
Leicester	19	Leicester	7
Marcher	39	Liverpool	6
Mercury	30	Metro (Newcastle)	28
Ocean	23	Norwich	3
Orwell	15	Ocean	<1
Piccadilly	12	Pennine	3
Saxon	15	Sheffield	3
Stoke-on-Trent	1	Tees	28
Tay	30	Trent	7
Trent	19	Viking	3
Wolverhampton	31	Wyvern	13

Sources: Daily Telegraph, The Journalist (NUJ)

Television

The BBC had run a TV service from 1936 until 1 September 1939, two days before war broke out. By then, 23,000 people within range of Alexandra Palace in London had been able to watch Shakespeare, variety, the Derby and the return of the King and Queen from a visit to Canada.

There was never much doubt that TV would be regarded as an extension of radio. 'One thing cannot be stated too often,' wrote Sir William Haley, Director-General of the BBC in 1951, '... Television is an integral part of Broadcasting. The essence of Broadcasting is that it is a means of communication capable of conveying intelligence into every home simultaneously' (BBC, 1952, p. 9). A government committee under Lord Selsdon in 1935 had already affirmed this, when investigating the form TV development should take. An analogy with the film industry, or treatment as an entirely distinct medium requiring its own organization, was inappropriate. TV began, therefore, as part of the public service radio monopoly. 'The responsibilities are identical,' wrote Haley. 'The purpose should be the same.'

The broadcasters recognized, even so, that there were important differences, particularly in the costs of TV and in the way people might use it. In 1939 the estimated cost of producing an hour of TV was twelve times that of the most expensive radio programme. On the production scale of 1962 it was still seven times as much, and in 1980, perhaps ten times (Tunstall, 1983, p. 34). This meant that within the BBC itself sources of finance beyond the licence fee were not ruled out altogether; nor by the Beveridge Committee in 1951.

As for audiences, 'viewing television is a very different activity from listening to sound broadcasts,' explained Maurice Gorham, the new head of BBC TV, in 1946 (BBC, 1946, p. 26). 'The radio set can remain on for hours at a time; you can enjoy it as background to reading, writing, homework, housework. ... The television set demands your attention; you cannot enjoy television from the next room. You must sit facing the set, with the lights down or shaded, and if you are a normal viewer you will find yourself very reluctant to be disturbed during a programme that you enjoy.'

At first some 15,000 households seized the opportunity to sit in darkened rooms when the post-war service started in 1946. The government had started to take expert advice on how TV might be extended as early as 1943; so the BBC had the signal to go ahead almost as soon as the war ended. The Alexandra Palace transmitter gave a range of about forty miles, or 12 million people. New transmitters in Sutton Coldfield (1949), Holme Moss, near Huddersfield (1951), Kirk O'Shotts (1952) and Wenvoe soon extended the service to a potential 36 million, and by 1956 almost the whole population was included.

The actual audience, as Table 4.2 showed, grew rapidly from its tiny base, partly in line with the new transmitters and partly with the sort of fillip provided by the Coronation. Initially, as Gorham's account suggests (with no exaggeration: the weak signal and eight-inch screen required the darkened room), watching TV was a fairly unsociable activity. Alternatively something of a ritual might be made of inviting friends round to watch a particular programme. The Coronation helped to make TV respectable, in addition to simply showing people its potential.

For nearly 10 years, then, BBC TV gradually established itself, with more programmes, more viewers and (rather slowly) more resources. In 1957–8 licence revenue from TV exceeded sound for the first time, and the following year TV expenditure overtook radio. In the early days, of course, radio listeners had heavily subsidized the generally more affluent TV watchers; while the richer parts of the country, following public service values, paid for the provision of the service to the remote and poorer parts.

Considering the engineering effort and investment, the necessary large-scale manufacture of TV sets, the lack of priority for TV inside the BBC, and the shift in social habits involved, the growth of TV in a decade still pinched by post-war austerity was remarkably quick.

The origin of ITV can be explained in many ways: as a

classic case (perhaps the first, post-war) of high pressure political lobbying; as Churchill's revenge on the BBC for its disdainful treatment of him during the 1926 General Strike and in his wilderness years in the 1930s, when he was largely kept off the air; or as part of the Conservative move to 'set the people free' from the bureaucracy and greyness allegedly intrinsic to Labour planning and the construction of the welfare state (sweets, be it remembered, did not finally come off ration until 1953).

The growth of TV at the BBC was stately compared with the hasty start of ITV. The ITA was simultaneously having to work out the details of its own role; formulate rules that met the legislation's requirements for quality, balance and so on, some of which — about imported American programmes, say — would affect the companies' finances; and ensure both that there was proper competition for the franchises, yet that the operation did not collapse through mismanagement or financial miscalculation.

The Television Act was passed in 1954 after great controversy, including a powerful attack by Lord Reith in the House of Lords. The first four contracts were awarded on 26 October. The London service went on air on 22 September 1955, with the Midlands in the following February and the Northern Region in May.

This haste carried risks. For example, Lord Kemsley, who had taken a 30 per cent interest in one of the successful bidders (and been a major factor in its success) decided subsequently to withdraw. The company collapsed, the ITA had to re-advertise the contract in July 1955, and the ABPC film company, one-third owned by the American Warner Brothers, was persuaded firmly to accept it the very day before ITV started in London.

Such episodes were a portent. In principle, the London Region included an estimated 13 million viewers, with 7.5 million in the Midlands and 12 million in the Northern. In practice, viewers preferred to wait and see — or rather wait for other people to see — before converting their TV sets to receive the new signal. ITV began with only some 3 per cent of households equipped to receive it. Yet to win the big audiences that would attract advertising, the companies had to spend large sums on attractive programmes. The result was a near disastrous first year.

The smaller, regional companies, that filled the gaps in the system between 1957 and 1962, escaped this traumatic experience and were able to enjoy what Roy Thomson, owner of Scottish Television, unwisely described as a 'licence to print money'.

The Television Act intended competition between ITV companies, not just between ITV and the BBC – which was what effectively developed. Fraser assumed, indeed, that the government would by degrees allocate frequencies such that more than one ITV station would be able to broadcast in a given area. Not until the 1990s would this in fact happen. What Fraser and his colleagues decided to do, therefore, was try and introduce an element of competition first by dividing the three available stations – London, Midlands, Northern – 'vertically', and secondly to move programmes from station to station 'horizontally'. 'Vertical' competition meant giving weekday contracts to one company and weekend contracts to another. 'Horizontal' competition, the network system, might in an ideal world have meant companies vying to buy and sell the best programmes from each other. In practice it led to the 'carve-up' (described in more detail in chapter 6), whereby the four big companies (five, from 1968) were guaranteed national access for agreed amounts of their programmes, with the ITA/IBA controlling certain 'quality' aspects of content and the proportions of programme types (news, drama, and so on). By 1968 the franchise terms *obliged* the big five to produce network programmes.

The successful applicants accepted these offers of split contracts, though without massive enthusiasm. The financial interests thus gelled into four organizations that soon became instantly recognized household names and logos: Associated-Rediffusion, Associated Television (ATV), ABC Television and Granada. To provide a national and worldwide news service, the ITA set up Independent Television News, under the companies' joint ownership. Table 4.9 lists the original franchise

Table 4.9 ITV franchises: regions, companies and years awarded

Region	Estimated population[a] (millions; 1982 in brackets)	1955 (or later start)	1964	1968	1982
Network companies					
London	12.9 (12.7)	Associated-Rediffusion (weekdays); Associated-Television (weekends); ABC Television (weekends)	All companies were reappointed in 1964	Thames (ABC/AR merger); London Weekend TV	same; same
Midlands	7.4 (9.6)	Associated-Television (weekdays)		Associated-TV (whole week)	Central TV
North	12.5 (7.7) (6.8)	Granada TV (weekdays); ABC Television (weekends)		Lancs: Granada (whole week); Yorks: Yorkshire TV (whole week)	same; same
'Regional companies'					
Central Scotland	4.0 (3.9)	Scottish Television (1957)		same	same
S. Wales and West	3.3 (4.6)	Television Wales and West (1958)		Harlech Television	same
Southern	4.3 (6.2)	Southern Television (1958)		same	Television South
North East	2.7 (2.6)	Tyne Tees Television (1959)		same	same
East Anglia	2.6 (4.3)	Anglia Television (1959)		same	same
Northern Ireland	1.4 (1.4)	Ulster Television (1959)		same	same
South West	1.6 (1.7)	Westward (1961)		same	Television South West
Borders	0.5 (0.6)	Border Television (1961)		same	same
N. E. Scotland	0.9 (1.2)	Grampian Television (1961)		same	same
Channel Islands	0.1 (0.1)	Channel Television (1962)		same	same
West & N. Wales	1.0 (–)	Wales (West & North) TV (1962)	merged with TWW	–	–
Breakfast channel		–	–	–	TV-AM
Number of applications		25	22 (including 8 new)	36 (from 30 groups, including 17 new)	42

[a] 1982 population figures are for people aged 4 and over: IBA Guide, 1982.

Sources: B. Sendall, *Independent Television in Britain*, vol. I (Macmillan, 1982); various.

holders and their successors, from 1955 to 1988, including the smaller companies that started slightly later.

Who provided the money and driving force? The combination of competition, regionalism, previous relevant experience and piety about public service values determined the pattern. It meant also that ITV companies were from the start a kind of conglomerate – by definition. The money had to come from somewhere, and while old newspapers might spawn new newspapers there was not, of course, any 'old' ITV.

One natural source of finance and experience was the world of show business – live theatre and cinema. This included 'talent' organizations like those of Lew Grade (ATV) and Jack Hylton (TWW), and theatre and cinema chains (the latter much larger enterprises in the 1950s, obviously, than later, when so many became bingo halls instead). These included Howard and Wyndham (Scottish TV), Moss Empires and J Arthur Rank (Southern TV). Rank were also involved in film production: and a few other, much smaller film makers, such as Launder and Gilliat, took an interest too (TWW). Another obvious source was firms that had become wealthy through the hire of radio and TV sets – chief among them Rediffusion (Associated-Rediffusion).

Regional finance was strongly encouraged by the ITA, especially in the smaller companies. In the early days it was not always easily secured. TWW, for instance, with a base in Bristol, was part owned by the local Imperial Tobacco Company. TWW, in fact, was a good example of a consortium put together from interests reflecting the shape of the franchise area, which was partly dictated by the fact that the signal for Wales would also be picked up in the West Country.

'Regionalism' also meant the presence of local notables on the companies' boards, sometimes bringing finance with them, as in the case of Lord Derby, chairman of TWW, and sometimes prestige, contacts and local influence. Regionalism also overlapped with the very important question of newspaper finance. From the start this was bound to be contentious, for it tied in so obviously with concern about newspaper chains, the power of large circulations and the alleged dangers of a too one-sided party press. With Labour in opposition, and perhaps ready to dismantle ITV when back in office, the issue featured prominently during the passage of the Television Act in 1954.

Moreover it was a complex issue, rather than simply splitting opinion on party lines. The provincial press was a strong expression of regionalism. It competed with Fleet Street (with difficulty, as has been seen). To exclude it from ITV, its competitor for advertising revenue, might weaken it further. Yet the links between the provincial and the national press meant that it would be complicated, if not illogical, to allow investment by the former but not by the latter.

Involvement by the national press was thus the trickier issue for the ITA. They handled it initially by seeking political balance, hoping, for instance, that the *Manchester Guardian* would join a consortium to balance the Kemsley bid and the 50 per cent holding of the Conservative Associated Newspapers (*Daily Mail*) group in Associated-Rediffusion. When Kemsley dropped out, the prospect of *News of the World* or Beaverbrook investment, also Conservative, was most unwelcome, and the Authority looked unsuccessfully for Odhams (*Daily Herald*), *News Chronicle* or *Daily Mirror* interest.

Cecil King, *Daily Mirror* chairman, preferred 'to wait until after the second bankruptcy'. The bankcruptcies did not happen, but he bought the *Daily Mirror* into ATV when bankruptcy looked possible, after the traumatic first year. ATV had run out of cash, as a result of large start-up costs, a delayed opening of its Midlands service and general under-capitalization. At about the same time (July 1956) Lord Rothermere decided to sell most of his 50 per cent *Daily Mail* stake in Associated-Rediffusion; and he sold the remainder when he took a third of the shares in the new South/South-East franchise holder, Southern TV, in 1958.

The Amalgamated Press, controlled by Lord Camrose, also had a third share in Southern. But almost immediately, Amalgamated was sold to the Mirror Group, which now had holdings in two companies – to which the ITA objected. King, therefore, sold the Southern shares to D C Thomson of Dundee – about as far removed from a 'regional' interest as could be imagined. Meanwhile the Central Scotland franchise (and 80 per cent of its voting shares, and all the non-voting) had gone to Roy Thomson, Canadian owner of *The Scotsman*. The press element in ITV finance was thus significant in several ways. It was 'natural' and defensible, on the ground that one medium might reasonably seek to protect itself by investing in a competitor. It was contentious, because of the political implications and the potential for concentration. It fluctuated, through the manoeuvres of the press groups, and it tended to attract publicity. It was the subject of legislation in 1963 and of particular scrutiny whenever official inquiries into the press or broadcasting were set up.

As time went on, the ITA/IBA tried to reduce press holdings. The 1990 Broadcasting Act limited newspapers to a 20 per cent stake in TV companies. Table 4.10 summarizes the holdings at various dates across the period. Table 4.11 identifies them by newspaper group, and includes ILR. The position is slightly complicated by the question what constitutes a 'press' company. British Electric Traction (BET), for example, was regarded as such by the Press Council and the 1974 Press Commission, but not initially by the ITA. BET had a major holding in Associated-Rediffusion. Apart from that, Table 4.10 shows clearly how the number of network companies part-owned by the press increased, while the size of holding diminished. All the regional companies had press holdings – most of them large – from the beginning. They amounted to 28 per cent of the whole, when the Annan Committee investigated. By 1987 most had been reduced or sold.

The holdings of particular newspaper groups fell into no tidy pattern. Certainly Fleet Street as a whole never plumped for ITV. Nor was there great continuity. The Pearson, *Guardian*, D C Thomson and BET interests were the most sustained, but only the *Guardian* and Pearson's *Financial Times* represented Fleet Street. Ignoring its own changes of proprietorship, the Mirror Group's papers were the largest group continuously associated with ITV. In 1990, the Murdoch papers' association with Sky TV was the subject of most controversy, but that story does not belong in this post-war period.

Table 4.10 Press holdings in ITV: summary of the percentage of voting shares held by press companies, from starting date

ITV company (starting date)	At start	1961	1968	1976	1982	1987
Network companies						
ABC (1955)	–	–	b			
Associated-Rediffusion (1955)	75[a]	50[a]	b			
ATV (1955)	–	40	40(?)[c]	43	–[d]	
Granada (1956)	–	–	–	–	–	–
LWT (1968)			22	32	32	*
Thames (1968)			50[a]	50[a]	50	29
Yorkshire (1968)			18	18	35	21
Central (1982)					40	40
Regional Companies						
Scottish (1957)	80	80	25[e]	25	–	–
Southern (1958)	62	62	62	62		
TWW (1958)	39	39				
Anglia (1959)	34	34	34	34	34	9
Tyne-Tees (1959)	21	21	?[f]	?[f]	7	–
Ulster (1959)	9	9	9(?)[c]	7	1	*
Border (1961)		39	39(?)[c]	43	40	21
Grampian (1961)		3	3(?)[c]	2	2	2
Westward (1961)		2	2	1		
Channel (1962)			?[f]	29	15	–
Harlech (1968)			?[f]	5	7	*
TSW (1982)					15	–
TVS (1982)					*	*
TV-AM (1983)					33[g]	–

* Less than one per cent.
[a] Holdings by BET, which the ITA did not define as a press company, but the Press Council did.
[b] Formed Thames jointly.
[c] figure uncertain.
[d] Partly formed Central.
[e] Press holding reduced in 1964 to 55 per cent.
[f] figure unknown.
[g] 1983 figure.

Note: the size of the companies differs greatly, so the percentages cannot be made into a meaningful average.

Sources: Pilkington Committee, Annan Committee, Press Council.

Table 4.11 Main newspaper groups' holdings in ITV and ILR

Newspaper group	ITV Company (% voting shares)			Number of radio stations	
	1961	1976	1987	1976	1987
Associated Newspapers	Southern 38	Southern 38 / Harlech 2	–	4	12
BET	Associated Rediffusion 50	Thames 50	Thames 29	1	2
Guardian	Anglia 21	Anglia 20	Anglia 5	1	2
Mirror/Reed	ATV 28	ATV 30	–	2	–
News of the World	TWW 25	–	–	–	–
Westminster Press/Pearson	ATV 7	ATV 5 / LWT 4	Yorkshire 21	3	2
SUITS	Border 12	Border 14	–	1	–
D C Thomson	Southern 25	Southern 25	Central 20	1	2
Thomson International	Scottish 80	Scottish 25	–	5	4
Beaverbrook	–	ATV 8	–	2	–
News International	–	LWT 10	*	2	–
Observer	–	LWT 9	–	1	–
Maxwell/Pergamon	–	–	Central 20	–	6

* Less than one per cent.
BET was not defined as a press group by the Royal Commission on the Press in 1961, nor by the ITA, but it was by the 1974 Commission.

Sources: Royal Commission on the Press, 1974–77, Pilkington Committee, Press Council.

Apart from the press and the other sources mentioned, ITV finance came from institutions such as banks and pension funds and, in due course, investors on the stock market (usually limited to shares without voting rights). Table 4.12 lists them by rather general categories, partly adopted from the Pilkington Committee. Categories such as 'theatre and entertainment' or 'cinema and film' did not include quite the same things in 1987 as in 1961, or not in the same proportions. It is difficult to discern a strong trend or pattern in the types of finance.

One other noteworthy source of support to franchise bidders, bringing resources less of money than talent (though they often acquired shareholdings later) were the experienced broadcasters, many of whom came from the BBC (inevitably, in 1955). They added an essential element of credibility to the high-sounding rhetoric required of franchise bids by the 'public service' conditions set by the ITA. Even though there was contact between the ITA and bidders before the formal application date, the grand interview between Governors and applicants in 1954 was by no means ritualistic. Nor was it in 1967, when decisions to disenfranchise as well as to enfranchise were a possibility. Considering the scale of the consequences, it is remarkable that the interviews carried so much weight. The 'creative' people were not necessarily most important in the interviews: but with their reputations as programme controllers, producers, editors, lay an applicant's chief prospects of attracting further talent and, ultimately, the best ratings.

The initial allocation of franchises in 1954, then, was absolutely not a matter of the ITA folding its arms and waiting for consortia to spring fully formed before it. Franchises were re-allocated by competition in 1964, 1967 and 1981, and although there was each time a public invitation and a grand interview, the procedure involved a good deal of preliminary contact and discussion, not least about such important but apparently secondary factors as studio locations and offices.

Those re-allocation dates should not be underemphasized. For TWW (1967), Southern (1981) and Westward (1981) they were execution dates; and major surgery dates for ABC and A-R (1967) and ATV (1981). They were the moments, too,

Table 4.12 ITV network companies: categories of shareholder and percentage of voting shares

Network company	1955 (%)	1961 (%)	1968 (%)	1976 (%)	1982 (%)	1987 (%)
Associated-Rediffusion						
Press	75	50				
Radio/electronics	25	37	See Thames			
Individuals		12				
ABC						
Cinema/films	100	100	See Thames			
Granada						
Cinema/films	100	100	100	100	100	100
ATV						
Press	26	40				
Radio/electronics	11	16	?	?	See Central	
Theatre/entertainment	27	27				
Thames						
Press	–	–	50	50	50	29
Cinema/films			50	50		
Yorkshire						
Press			?	18	35	21
Banks, insurance, etc.	–	–				6
Business (WH Smith)						20
LWT						
Press			22(?)	32	32	1
Radio/electronics ⎫						
Banks, insurance, etc. ⎬	–	–	50	40(?)		27(?)
Other corporate ⎭						
Staff			30	?		5(?)
Central						
Press					40(?)	40
Radio/electronic						20
Banks, insurance, etc.	–	–	–	–		18
Other corporate					50(?)	?

Ownership figures are not easy to trace, and these may be unreliable.

Sources: Pilkington Committee; Royal Commissions on the Press; Press Council.

when new franchise areas were set up, such as Yorkshire in 1967, and new services such as Breakfast TV (1981) and Channel 4 (1981). But changes in the ownership and control of companies also took place between these dates, sometimes on virtually the same scale and certainly with the same consequences for programme contents. Too much focus on the re-allocation competition risks understating the extent to which ownership and control changed by an irregular but continuing process of adjustment and negotiation with the ITA/IBA about the buying and selling of interests, either on the Authority's or a franchise-holder's initiative.

The award of a franchise to an entirely new company, from scratch, was thus the extreme case. It was done for Harlech and LWT (1967) and for TVS and TSW (1981) in pre-existing regions, and for Yorkshire TV (1967) and TV-AM (1981) with new franchises. Even then there were elements of adjustment. For instance, TWW, supplanted by Harlech, was given the opportunity by the ITA of buying 40 per cent of the shares in the new company. Lord Derby, furious at losing his franchise, declined. New but unsuccessful bidders were sometimes invited by the Authority to join a winner. For instance the *Yorkshire Post* and three other local press groups joined their former competitor as junior partners in Yorkshire TV in 1967. *The Daily Telegraph, Observer* and *Economist,* unsuccessful in groups bidding variously for the Yorkshire and Central Scotland franchises, were given holdings in LWT.

Another variation was the forced marriage. Thames, awarded the London weekday contract in 1967, was formed by an ITA-initiated merger between A-R, the previous holder, and ABC, the previous holder of Midlands and Northern weekday and weekend contracts. To rub salt into A-R's wounds, ABC was given a majority of voting shares and on the board. In 1981, Central TV was formed rather similarly out of the previous contractor (ATV) and some new shareholders. In the latter case, as in 1967, one factor in the Authority's calculations was a decision to alter the shape of the franchise region.

Changes not brought about directly by the Authority happened in two ways. The more dramatic was the salvage operation. ATV provided the first example in 1955–6, as we have seen, with Mirror Group capital injected at a key psychological moment. In 1964 the tiny Wales (West and North) company effectively went bust, and merged, with its region, into TWW. Then LWT, whose galaxy of creative talent in 1967 just 'had to have its chance, whatever the repercussions,' as the ITA chairman, Lord Hill, put it (Sendall, 1983, p. 364), failed disastrously at company management. In 1971 it was rescued by Rupert Murdoch, who alone was prepared to risk the capital to keep it afloat. LWT was bulging with production talent, headed by Michael Peacock, one of the BBC's golden boys; performance talent, with David Frost a star (and an important shareholder); and a string of business tycoons on the board. But the former knew little of business and the latter little of TV. Against a BBC policy of scheduling popular entertainment opposite LWT's 'serious' programmes, the company made little headway. Peacock was sacked after a year, and other staff followed.

While other network companies mooted various ideas with the ITA for absorbing LWT or making London a single franchise – ideas that were anathema – Murdoch won reluctant ITA approval to buy the General Electric Company's 7.5 per cent of the voting shares (and a larger block of non-voting shares, which did not require approval). With this foothold, and after further controversial sackings, he took control, eventually bringing in John Freeman, the eminently respectable journalist and ex-Ambassador to the USA, as chairman. So far was the company now from its original shape that the ITA, in a face-saving operation, submitted the new team to a full-scale franchise-style interview, after which it declared itself satisfied.

TV-AM, equally star-studded, failed equally flamboyantly in 1982. Again, Australian money and management (from Kerry Packer) turned it round. In each case, grand programme ideals were abandoned, with the Authority's connivance, to keep the franchise going.

Less dramatic were changes in company ownership following changes in a parent company. Sometimes these resulted in contravention of an Authority rule about foreign ownership or conflict of interest, and further sales followed.

The formation of the original four network companies has already been described. The remainder of those first franchises divided into second and third tiers according to the economic base provided by the populations they served. The third tier was chiefly at the physical and cultural extremities of the nation – the Channel Islands, Ulster, North-East Scotland, South-West England and (the exception) the Anglo-Scottish borders. All started later than the network companies and missed the dreadful first year. Scottish TV came first, launched on the enthusiasm of Roy Thomson, who had difficulty convincing Scottish backers that ITV had a bright future. He thus began with 80 per cent of the voting shares and all the non-voting shares. Lord Derby's consortium for TWW has been mentioned. The Southern region, so close to London, attracted nine applicants, among whom the Rank/Associated Newspapers/Amalgamated Press group, which became Southern TV, was clearly the strongest. The ITA decided that in this region it did not matter if the finance was not 'local'.

Not long after the last regional ITV company went on air, the focus of interest shifted back to the BBC. For the BBC, the Pilkington inquiry had been a vindication and a triumph, confirming the superiority of its own service over the commercial values of ITV, which was moving rapidly into surplus. It was therefore no surprise when the Macmillan government allocated the third TV channel to the BBC in 1963, with a 1964 opening date.

It was becoming the rule not the exception that launches did not go right first time, but BBC2 settled down quite quickly as a recognized minority channel. It could be little else. The government wanted it broadcast on the new UHF/625 lines frequency (the rest of TV was on VHF/405 lines). This meant it was available for the first two years only in London and the South-East and to people who bothered to fit a new aerial. Moreover, it broadcast only for about four hours each evening; and ten years later it was still on air only 60 per cent as much as BBC1. There was no increase in the licence fee to pay for a 50 per cent jump in programme hours. Expenditure on TV in the year after BBC2 started increased from £27.6 million to £35.8 million (BBC, 1966, p. 194).

The BBC and ITA joined in a major construction programme

in the late 1960s to build 50 high powered UHF stations and more than 400 low powered, so that UHF was available to 95 per cent of the population by 1974. Even so, BBC2 remained, as the BBC told the Annan Committee (p. 90), 'the channel for initiation, for large scale departures as well as for tryouts and experiments'. Colour, for example, was introduced in 1967 on BBC2 (not until 1969 was it available on BBC1). BBC2 settled down with about 10 per cent of the total TV audience and heavily subsidized by BBC1, which had four times the viewers at only twice the cost. Until the coming of Channel 4 in 1982, a very rough and varying 40 and 10 per cent audience share for BBC and 50 per cent for ITV was an implicit part of the equilibrium of the duopoly.

While BBC2 was gearing up, the ITA was concerned in 1963–4 with its first round of re-franchising, very low-key compared with what was to come. Contracts were to be awarded for only three years, as the ITA hoped that by 1967 a fourth channel would be available and require more radical reorganization. All the companies had their contracts renewed. Three of the smaller regionals (Border, Grampian and Ulster) were not even opposed. The London weekday franchise attracted five applicants. There were 22 altogether, contrasted with 36 in 1967–8 and 42 in 1981–2.

The ITA took the 1964 competition very seriously, nonetheless. It came in the aftermath of the Pilkington Report, which had roundly condemned ITV, and at a time when profits were fat, as a result of which the government was introducing a tax, in the form of a levy on advertising revenue. The Authority set out new principles governing ownership. Existing companies infringed some of them and Rediffusion, for example, had to adjust its shareholdings.

By 1966 it was clear that a fourth channel was some way off. The ITA decided to split the Northern region into separate Lancashire and Yorkshire franchises, each of which would be large enough to support a network company, increasing the number of these to five. The 'vertical' division of London was adjusted so that the weekend franchise would run from 7.00 pm on Friday, not from Saturday morning. This proved a miscalculation, which added to the financial crisis of the new contractor, LWT, a few years later.

Seventeen new groups entered the competition in 1967 (out of 'two to three hundred' who requested particulars) (Sendall, 1983, p. 337). This time six of the smaller regions were unopposed. On the other hand, there were ten bidders alone for the new Yorkshire contract. Several groups bid in more than one region. Much of the trumpeted 'new talent' came from the BBC.

How were the ITA to proceed? They were not in an easy position. Allocating the new Yorkshire franchise was straightforward: the ITA played matchmaker between two strong, locally based groups. But how should the existing franchise holders be treated? If all were re-appointed, in a replay of 1964, the claim that franchises were 'competitive' would begin to look hollow, and would simply confirm the Pilkington Committee's judgement that to all intents 'the appointment of a programme contractor is virtually irrevocable' (Pilkington, 1962, p. 165). As Lord Hill replied to an outraged Lord Derby, whose TWW had 'stood on its record' and been brusquely dismissed, newcomers such as Harlech could offer only promises, 'but if promise is never to be preferred to performance, then every television company will go on for ever' (Sendall, 1983, p. 359).

On the other hand, the realities of the situation made disenfranchisement both drastic and risky. The ITA could not regard itself as starting with a blank sheet. Disenfranchisement would mean upheavals for staff, start-up costs and teething troubles for the new contractor, and a danger that the service would indeed turn out to be demonstrably less popular than the old contractor's or different from what was promised. Lord Derby complained that he had been given no warnings. ITA powers over programming would make it more difficult, even, to argue that poor performance was wholly a contractor's fault.

The sacrifice of TWW and the merger of ABC and Rediffusion into Thames were acts of some courage and panache, in which the ebullient personality of ITA chairman, Lord Hill, a former broadcasting star as the Radio Doctor in the 1940s and a cabinet minister under Harold Macmillan, were an important factor. Beyond that, the ITA was influenced by the existing configuration of franchise holders, by new applicants' promises and broadcasting talent, by their performance at interview and the extent to which they met the conditions of regionalism and financial soundness. Thus TWW had to compete not only with the mundane but necessary business skills of the Harlech consortium but with the presence of famous Welsh names from the arts — Richard Burton, Stanley Baker, Geraint Evans — and the authority of Lord Harlech himself, a former minister and Ambassador to the Kennedy White House. Lord Harlech's concluding statement at interview, the official ITV history oddly comments, almost as though the process were a debating competition, 'was the finest piece of spoken prose heard at any of the thirty-six ITA interviews' (Sendall, 1983, p. 358).

Where performance (at interview and in prospect) was decisive for Harlech, the forced marriage of ABC and Rediffusion showed the influence of the existing pattern of weekday/weekend franchises split between the four network companies. With the creation of a new Yorkshire region came a decision to end this split except in London. The Midlands, Lancashire and Yorkshire would now be seven-day contracts. With a new applicant taking Yorkshire, with Granada strongly entrenched in Lancashire, and with ATV well placed to concentrate on the Midlands and give up its London weekend franchise, Rediffusion could reasonably assume that it would keep the London weekday contract and that ABC would move into the weekend slot vacated by ATV.

The dazzling LWT application put an end to that idea. If LWT 'had to have their chance' then ABC was out in the cold. A merger with Rediffusion for the weekday contract was a consolation prize for them both. Rediffusion in particular was bitter about this decision. The company had stuck with the infant system at a time when it could easily have collapsed, and the ITA's credibility with it. It had pioneered children's programming for ITV and the use of videotape. In line with ITA recommendations, its board contained a high proportion of professional TV executives. Why should it suffer simply because the ITA wanted to restructure the North and Midlands parts of the system?

The 1967/68 procedure was essentially repeated in 1980/81, with the addition of regional public meetings by the Authority. These were held in belated recognition that the entirely private exercise last time had given the public not even a token opportunity to comment on the various applicants. The competition was postponed from 1976, to allow for the Annan Committee, set up on 1974, to make its report on the future of broadcasting.

The results were fairly similar to 1967: two summary executions and one piece of major surgery. After 20 years or more, Southern TV and Westward had both become vulnerable, but for different reasons. Southern's absentee landlordism (the 25 per cent holding of D C Thomson of Dundee) was a continuing embarrassment to the regional principle, and the company's programme policy lacked freshness and a clear regional emphasis. Seven or eight serious and strong competitors came forward, and the group headed by former broadcaster and Labour MP, Lord Boston, was successful. Westward had recently been the scene of a public boardroom row that could have come out of a TV series. Again, it was not well placed to withstand the competition.

The major surgery was done to ATV in the Midlands. The IBA decided to make this a 'dual region', with a new centre in Nottingham to balance Birmingham. This involved closing ATV's London base. The IBA hoped to raise half the capital for a new company from Midlands money, with ATV providing the rest. This plan failed on two counts. First, Lord Grade sold ATV to the Australian financier Robert Holmes à Court; second, the 49 per cent of 'Midlands' shares were bought by D C Thomson (who thus made up for losing Southern), the betting company Ladbrokes and the printing and publishing interests of Robert Maxwell. Holmes à Court was obliged by the law against foreign control of ITV to sell his shares, which passed to Sears, a conglomerate including footwear and the William Hill betting shops.

An extra novelty in the 1980–1 franchise competition was the new breakfast time contract. Again events followed a familiar path. Eight groups applied. The IBA was deeply impressed by the star-studded consortium with highfalutin public service plans. Peter Jay, former Treasury civil servant, *Times* economics editor, broadcaster and Ambassador to the USA, provided intellectual thrust; Robert Kee, current affairs experience in depth; David Frost, showbiz contacts; and former ITN news reader Anna Ford, glamour. The company made a disastrous start in February 1983 and found profitability only when it went down market under new management and ownership (partly Australian).

Much more exciting was the launch of Channel 4 in November 1982. Its origins were a combination of expediency and of arguments derived from the public service rhetorical tradition. ITV had assumed ever since the third channel was given to the BBC after Pilkington (as BBC2), that the fourth channel would come to ITV, on the principle of 'fair-dos' and to preserve the balance of the duopoly. Conservative governments were predisposed in that direction. Labour governments leant more sympathetically towards ideas (of which there could be endless variations) for some kind of 'Open Broadcasting Authority' to use the Annan Committee's phrase. The point of this would be to escape the duopoly and some of the rigidity of the franchise system. In practical terms, programme makers increasingly fretted that, in a system now producing many hours of television, it was virtually impossible to work independently of the BBC or an ITV company. On the public service plane, there was a persuasive case that the duopoly was structurally and financially biased towards the common denominators of society and culture, even if not the lowest denominators. Where ITV met the needs of regions viewed as 'minorities' within the nation, the fourth channel should be a national service, but serving social and cultural minorities: blacks, feminists, philosophers, gays, American football fanatics, and so on.

The outcome was determined eventually by the accident of which party was in power. It happened to be the Conservatives, with an accomplished fixer, William Whitelaw, as responsible Minister. Channel 4 emerged as a company wholly owned by the IBA, with directors serving a limited term. Its function was to commission and buy programmes from independents and the franchise companies, not to make them itself. News was supplied by ITN. Finance was provided by the ITV companies as a 'subscription', and the companies raised it by selling the advertising time on Channel 4 in their own regions. The channel thus had financial security without either public subsidy or the need to bow to the ratings. In Wales, a separate fourth channel authority operated on similar lines, producing the channel S4C.

A deliberately experimental service, designed to seek small, specialized and neglected audiences, was a recipe guaranteed to make mistakes. Channel 4 did so, with early programmes attracting audiences too low to register on the ratings. With the help of a few sure-fire successes brought over from ITV, it gradually established itself, though still subsidized by the subscriptions. By 1990 it had gone through the familiar process: what started as a compromising fudge had been rationalized as yet another creative act of policy, fitting in with its unique character to a harmonious pattern of public service broadcasting.

The changes in ownership by salvage operation between franchise rounds have already been mentioned. There might have been more of these. ITV was unavoidably vulnerable to the impact of economic recessions upon advertising revenue (for instance, revenue fell by 12 per cent in real terms in 1969–70). Its ability to respond was limited by the IBA's programme requirements. One of the sharpest recessions came a few years after the Conservative government, sensitive to the enormous profits made in earlier years, had imposed (in 1963) a variable levy rising to 45 per cent on the companies' advertising revenue (as distinct from their profits). The position of one second tier company, Tyne-Tees, was so weak that to save costs it 'affiliated' with the network company Yorkshire TV within a joint holding company, Trident. The ITA gave consent, only reluctantly, in view of the statutory rule forbidding ownership of more than one franchise company. A major factor in the decision was that one of the new UHF transmitters introduced in the switch from VHF overlapped both companies' areas. Tyne-Tees, as the smaller enterprise, feared it would lose out. Both companies transferred their capital to Trident and received interest in proportion to their original holdings. The IBA insisted that each company continue with their separate programme responsibilities. In 1980 the Authority brought the arrangement to an end.

In a rather different example from the same period, Scottish TV was so short of cash by February 1970 that it could not pay its ITA rental, nor the levy, nor its bills, nor get further credit from the bank. The ITA saved it by postponement of sums due. HTV, too, blamed the levy for its problems, though expenditure also played a part. The Labour government eased the position by reducing the levy. Governments could vary the levy at will, and it remained a permanent part of the system of ITV finance. In 1974, it was changed to a levy on profits (later net of Channel 4 costs).

The history of TV until 1990, then, was one of growth and diversification, if not always in the ways intended either by regulators or companies and channels. It took place entirely within the strict limits of 'terrestrial' transmission. One of the ways – perhaps the chief one – in which 1945–90 did indeed make a distinct period was that in 1990 those limits were about to be stretched by the provision of satellite services. Rupert Murdoch's Sky channel started first. The BSB consortium followed some months later, in April 1990. Even though their losses forced them to merge before the end of the year, the assumptions on which TV had been organized could never be quite the same again.

5 Concentration, Conglomeration, Internationalization

Concentration, conglomeration and internationalization — cumbersome words for complex processes — attracted increasing attention in the 1980s. Media of all kinds seemed more and more to be under the control of a few large international corporations, headed by brusque individualists and outsize personalities such as Robert Maxwell and Rupert Murdoch, who were natural heirs, perhaps, to the Beaverbrooks and Kemsleys. This development was undoubtedly happening; but it is important to be clear exactly which features were different from the immediate post-war years and which continued as before. These distinctions are especially important since the development is easier to illustrate in broad terms than to measure precisely.

Media concentration, conglomeration, and internationalization long preceded 1945. Concentration is normally measured by number of newspaper titles (or radio stations, and so on) or market share. Northcliffe had a bigger share of Fleet Street morning circulation in 1910 (39 per cent) than Murdoch in 1989 (35 per cent) and the same number of titles (three) (Negrine, 1989, p. 72). Foreign ownership goes back just as far, in the sense that individuals such as Waldorf Astor and Max Aitken (Lord Beaverbrook) used foreign capital to buy into the English press. Some inter-war newspaper firms were already conglomerates, too, through diversification into allied businesses such as newsprint production. Associated News-papers (*Daily Mail*) controlled the Anglo-Newfoundland Development Company, which owned land, railways, shipping and mines, as well as paper mills. Odhams (*Daily Herald* and magazines) was primarily a printing business. The Cadbury (*News Chronicle*) fortunes were based in cocoa. Like so many other newspaper owners, the Cadburys had been businessmen first and press magnates later — through involvement with party politics. In the cinema, another growth medium inter-war, Hollywood money so dominated British film production that the government introduced protectionist policies.

The distinctive features of concentration, conglomeration and internationalization as they developed into the 1980s can perhaps be described as their *scope, scale, management, balance* and *volatility*. The expansion of new media (and new forms of old media) was obviously a major cause. The growth of ITV, transistor radios and Walkmans, LPs, CDs, audio tapes and VCRs, even free sheets, tended to follow familiar economic patterns. Unless, like ITV, they were regulated, competition and economies of scale gradually reduced the number of sup-pliers and increased market share. More media, equally, meant more scope for conglomeration — horizontally, at local, regional or national level, and vertically between all three. A 'media conglomerate' in 1945 was largely print-based, perhaps with unrealized property assets and some 'trade investments' in subsidiary businesses, such as paper. The arrival of ITV in 1955 transformed the situation, acting as a focal point for previously unconnected interests. By 1990 the conglomerates thus had a much wider range.

The post-war economic recovery and continued growth, added to the new media, meant that the scale of media enter-prises grew both absolutely and as a proportion of the whole economy. By the late 1980s, the largest organizations were likely to operate most efficiently if they did so at an international level, raising capital internationally and supplying international markets. Overseas tycoons, too, such as the Australians Robert Holmes à Court and Alan Bond, saw British firms as a good base in which to expand outside their own domestic market.

Those trends saw the eclipse of the old style media baron. The typical baron in 1945 still owned the majority of shares in his company, perhaps in common with his family. But bigger enterprises and conglomerates increasingly overstretched them. Murdoch and, especially, Maxwell looked and sounded like Northcliffe and Beaverbrook, but the looks deceived.

Two events in the 1960s symbolize the shift. One was the peremptory sacking of Cecil King in 1968 by the Mirror Group board, of which he was chairman. He had behaved like his authoritarian uncle Northcliffe but, as we have seen, without actually owning the paper he managed. Northcliffe could not be sacked; King could. The second was a modest change of name by the Fleet Street trade association, the NPA, at about the same time. Formerly the Newspaper *Proprietors* Association, it now became the Newspaper *Publishers* Association, marking a shift from member groups dominated by a single proprietor to corporations managed on more orthodox commercial lines and with a wide range of finance. Maxwell and Murdoch were no doubt entrenched in their organizations by the complexities of cross-holdings and foreign-registered companies, but their personal holdings were proportionately small, particularly in comparison with their predecessors. The funds they manipulated were substantially other people's. As we saw, Murdoch was able to control LWT in 1971 with initially just 7.5 per cent of the voting shares.

One other change of balance should be noted. This is the rough distinction between non-media conglomerates with a media side-interest and, in contrast, media conglomerates that diversified outwards. This distinction reflects the mixture of accident and design by which they grew. The old newspaper conglomerates of national and provincial daily, Sunday, weekly and periodical publications had an obvious logic, which extended to the acquisition of printing plant and paper mills. Cinema chains and film production made an equally obvious pair. So, in one way or another, did the various combinations participating in the original ITV finances.

Even after they had ceased to be largely print-based, most conglomerates up until the 1970s remained primarily media organizations. ITV companies were bound to diversify because they were banned from holding more than one franchise. Newspapers had to bear in mind restrictions the Monopolies Commission could impose (though this proved a feeble weapon, as Murdoch's accumulation of titles showed). Their ITV holdings were progressively restricted by IBA policy. So they diversified abroad, or into specialized publishing and books, recorded music, radio and leisure activities.

From the 1970s, the balance shifted. Media conglomerates diversified further away, and non-media conglomerates moved into media. Either way, the non-media element of organizations controlling media increased. As the Press Commission put it in 1977 (p. 149), 'Rather than saying that the press has other business interests, it would be truer to argue that the press has become a subsidiary of other interests'.

The Thomson organization was an early example of movement outwards. Indeed, it illustrates very clearly all three features of concentration, conglomeration and internationalization. Roy Thomson assembled from nothing a chain of small-town papers and radio stations in Canada. *The Scotsman*, when he bought it in 1954, was the first significant British daily (Fleet Street included) to go into international ownership. His purchase of the Kemsley newspaper chain was a step in the overall process of press concentration and gave him a Fleet Street prize, *The Sunday Times*. His business methods, including the boosting of small ads and telephone sales, reflected North American management styles. His successful enthusiasm for Scottish TV made the business a media conglomerate, as did the acquisition of book publishers, magazines and the contract for Yellow Pages (another American invention). Purchase of *The Times* itself in 1966 was a culmination, and a further move towards concentration. The success of the TV and press interests (including papers now far from the North American base, in West Africa for instance) led him to diversify, taking an important stake in North Sea oil. (Associated Newspapers did the same, and both groups thereby had a useful cushion when the oil price rises and economic crises of the early 1970s saw newsprint prices quadruple.) He diversified too into the booming package holiday and travel business and by 1989 was the UK's biggest tour operator. Increasingly, his business became a non-media conglomerate.

The later Thomson story illustrates also the volatility of the conglomerate in the 1980s. Companies chopped and changed their holdings, for reasons that might have little to do with the specific nature of the businesses involved. Thomson's son poured so much money into *The Times* in the vain effort to modernize it in the late 1970s that no one could blame him for wanting to sell it. But when he did so (with *The Sunday Times*) to Murdoch in 1981, the reason in fact was the wider international strategy of the organization. The North American interests were paramount (with headquarters in Toronto), concentrating on newspapers, books, data and information systems, travel and oil. The regional UK press interests, and the travel and oil, still made sense, but *The Times* did not. The Scottish TV holdings, too, were a thing of the past.

A similar if less conspicuous story might be told of the Reed conglomerate. Until the 1960s, this was a paper-making company in which the Mirror Group (IPC) held 44 per cent of the shares as a somnolent investment. Under the expansionist management of Don Ryder (a former financial journalist whose later success took him, inevitably it might seem, to the House of Lords) the company diversified – into wallpaper products for example, By 1971, Reed had outgrown its parent company, which it proceeded to take over. The *Mirror* thus passed from owning to being owned by a non-newspaper interest.

In the 1970s and 1980s Reed changed a lot. Early on, it sold its 21 per cent holding in ATV. In 1984, it sold the *Mirror* titles themselves, giving Robert Maxwell his long sought Fleet Street base; and it entered the 1990s essentially as an international paper, packaging and publishing conglomerate – the fifth or sixth largest publishing empire in the world. It was especially strong in business and consumer magazines, with well known titles such as *Woman's Own*, *Country Life* and *New Scientist*, book-publishing mini-conglomerates such as Octopus, and business publications in Europe and North America.

The movement of non-media conglomerates into media has

a more random appearance — a different kind of logic — than the diversification by Thomson and Reed (and Reed's movement back again). Earliest into the national newspaper market after 1945 was the Pearson group, previously interested only in a regional newspaper chain (Westminster Press). This had developed from a side-interest of the original Weetman Pearson (Lord Cowdray), a civil engineer and Liberal activist before and after the First World War. The main Pearson interests remained in international banking, property and business.

When they bought *The Financial Times* in 1957, the Pearsons started to expand further into media. They bought a half-share of *The Economist*, Penguin Books, the Longman publishing group and other familiar book imprints (including Michael Joseph, Hamish Hamilton, Sphere, Ladybird and Pitman). They expanded their financial and business magazines. They took a stake in the BSB satellite company. Their non-media businesses included startling acquisitions such as the prestige Chateau Latour vineyard and the Royal Doulton china business. Behind all this lay the American, British and continental European bank interests, such as Lazard's.

A good later example of a non-media conglomerate moving into the press for non-media reasons is the Trafalgar House purchase of Beaverbrook Newspapers in 1978. Trafalgar was chiefly a property group, with hotel and travel interests and civil engineers such as Trollope and Colls. Its first links with Beaverbrook came through refurbishing the *Express* building in Fleet Street. The Beaverbrook papers were in financial trouble, and Trafalgar beat the competition to buy them, with its main interest being the asset value of the group's properties. The vice-chairman, a self-made businessman, Victor Matthews, gave every appearance of enjoying the role of press tycoon and duly entered the House of Lords after the return of a Conservative government.

Trafalgar moved out of the press again when they sold their titles to United Newspapers in 1985. This was unusual but not unique. *The Observer*, for instance, spent six years in the ownership of the Atlantic Richfield oil company of California. This was the result of a chance encounter in 1975, when the

Astor ownership was frantically trying to fight control passing to Murdoch or the *Daily Mail*. Similarly Sir James Goldsmith, whose fortunes were in the food industry, started a weekly news magazine, *Now*, in 1979, after failing to purchase a suitable established title. The magazine folded two years later and Goldsmith's attention turned elsewhere.

Another important non-media group with media interests at the end of the 1980s was 'Tiny' Rowland's conglomerate Lonrho. Its name (from 'London' and 'Rhodesia') reflected its origins as a Central African trading company. Rowland, as has previously been indicated, was the kind of entrepreneur to attract adjectives like 'maverick'. His interest in media started as a by-product of buying the House of Fraser, initially a large department stores group built up by a nationalistic Scot, Lord Fraser of Annandale. Fraser had bought control of Scottish press and publishing interests, such as the Glasgow *Herald* and *Evening Times* publishers George Outram, specifically in order to prevent them being bought by the Canadian Roy Thomson.

Lonrho's media interests grew, most prominently with its purchase of *The Observer* from ARCO in 1981 and its rescue operation for Eddie Shah's *Today*, which it quickly sold on. Rowland used *The Observer* to fight non-media battles, notably over control of the Harrods store, which at one time had been part of the House of Fraser group. With the Scottish interests had come a stake in Border TV, which Lonrho kept. Overall, its media business was a small part of the whole enterprise.

British Electric Traction was another conglomerate which, as its name implies, moved into media from outside. Its regional press and magazine holdings went back some time but were not large enough to qualify it as a media company. By the late 1980s, however, its 28 per cent share of Thames TV and 13 per cent share of the Capital Radio ILR combine certainly qualified it.

In the late 1980s, too, the Australians Alan Bond and Robert Holmes à Court (neither Australian-born) started to expand into British media. So did the Canadian financier Conrad Black. In 1982 Holmes à Court captured Lew Grade's ACC organization, which owned half of ATV and a variety of film, cinema, theatre and music interests. Grade had overstretched himself and lost money heavily on box office flops such as *Raise the Titanic* and biblical epics. Bond came later, from a base initially in real estate and classic Australian beer and mining companies. But as the 1980s ended, his empire was disintegrating – partly as a result of the 1987 stock market crash – and the future of his 15 per cent holding in the BSB satellite channel looked doubtful. Black, in contrast, had a solid base in Toronto, both in media and other enterprises, and seemed likely to expand his UK interests beyond the *Telegraph* titles.

Neither Maxwell nor Murdoch, so prominent in the last twenty years of the period, fits the simple pattern of a non-media organization moving in or a media one moving out. Instead they illustrate better the shifting balance within conglomerates between one media interest and another and secondly, the trend toward internationalization.

At first Murdoch followed the Thomson path: no-nonsense colonial boy muscles into sleepy British business and starts raising the dust. After a tough takeover battle for the *News of the World* in 1968, financed by the profits of his Australian papers, Murdoch invigorated and streamlined the management, sold off various marginal activities (including Walton Heath Golf Course, allegedly purchased by the paper's one-time proprietor so that he could get to play golf there with Lloyd George, a member) and quickly bought the *Sun*. The move into LWT followed; then *The Times* Newspapers saga and late refinements like the boosting of *Today*.

Murdoch's international side was symbolized by his vanishing sense of nationality. In person and style, he remained the down-to-earth Australian, caustic about the class-ridden antique snobberies of the 'poms'. Periodically he returned to his Australian roots, but for long periods he worked in the UK. Suddenly, however, he turned into an American citizen, a necessary formality if his expanding US empire was to remain legally his. From the 1970s on, he expanded first into US newspapers (the *New York Post*, for example) and then into film and TV, buying control of Metromedia and Twentieth Century Fox (whose massive film archive could feed his TV channels). He entered the 1990s gambling on the long term success of his satellite TV channel, Sky, and his plans to build a fourth US national TV network. In 1989, too, he took control of the publishing conglomerate Collins in a bitter takeover battle, thereby acquiring a string of familiar imprints such as Fontana and Granada Books. He was also an important shareholder in the international news agency turned information business, Reuters.

Murdoch retained some non-media interests, such as a share of the TNT trucking business. This was a key element in the reorganization of newspaper distribution, associated with the transfer to Wapping and the battle against the 'old technology'. But his was largely a media conglomerate: the prime example of those distinctive features listed earlier: large in scope and scale, with modern management and a shifting and volatile balance of interests. The volatility was exemplified in 1989 by his 20 per cent holding in the Pearson Group, which might have been the basis of a takeover bid. It was shown in a different way by sales forced on Murdoch by US and Australian cross-ownership laws. In 1987 new Australian laws forced him to sell his Australian TV stations. In the USA, the Fox purchase, which included seven TV stations, obliged him to sell his New York and Chicago papers that circulated in those franchise areas.

The balance of Maxwell's group was rather different, with origins in printing and in magazine and trade publishing. Maxwell came quite late to newspapers, though not for want of trying: in 1968, for instance, he was a loser in the battle for the *News of the World*. The *Mirror* titles made him a Fleet Street figure to match his other interests. These included 20 per cent of Central TV and 15 per cent of Border; a cable station; and 25 per cent of a satellite music station, MTV. Overseas, he controlled the US publishing firm Macmillan, 10 per cent of a French TV channel; and non-media interests world wide. Maxwell's own nationality symbolized, again, the international quality of his outlook. Despite an English-sounding name, he was born in central Europe and fought with distinction for the British in the Second World War.

In the media jungle, Murdoch and Maxwell grew to be elephants. Over the period since 1945 as a whole, other beasts proved mammoths – of elephantine size but doomed to extinction. The Kemsley press empire was sold up. So, in turn, were groups such as Beaverbrook, with the *Telegraph* being the last. Companies at the core of TV groups, such as Rediffusion, lost their franchises. Film and cinema groups declined or were broken up.

Newcomers picked over the bones. In addition to the conglomerates already discussed, several press groups grew substantially. United Newspapers developed from a modest regional grouping to Fleet Street prominence, latterly under the leadership of Lord Stevens. United bought the *Express* papers when Trafalgar tired of them. By 1990 they controlled eight regional daily papers, nearly one hundred weeklies, and two large magazine and directory publishers – Benn Brothers and Morgan Grampian. They also owned *Punch* and the financial information agency Exchange Telegraph (Extel), formerly a traditional news agency. EMAP (East Midlands and Allied Press) grew in a similar manner but without any national titles. So did Iliffe, from its *Birmingham Post* base.

Outside the press, groups developed in the 1970s and 1980s from several directions. W.H. Smith, originally a nineteenth-century distributor, wholesaler and retailer, moved into TV (25 per cent of Yorkshire TV) and satellite TV services. Its book publishing activities expanded too. Thorn, formerly a manufacturer of electrical equipment, radio and TV sets, acquired the much larger EMI, long established as a major international recorded music, film and TV industry. Equally, names that no one had heard of emerged as important groupings. Richard Branson's Virgin Records, for instance, grew and diversified, including a successful foray into cheap transatlantic flights. Crown Communications, owner of LBC, became one of the two large ILR conglomerates. It had interests also in computer graphics, TV and business film production and services. In 1989 it was the first British company to take a significant stake in French commercial radio.

Carlton Communications came from a broadly similar direction but with even more spectacular growth. Pre-tax profits more than quadrupled from £5 million to over £20 million from 1984–5 to 1987–8. Michael Green, its creator, built it up from a small photo-processing company. After 15 years, this took off when, in 1982, Green moved into video production and copying, hire of TV studios and facilities, and technical electronic services such as digital effects. He was a major beneficiary of the video boom and used his profits to diversify and expand abroad. His attempt to buy into ITV by taking over their share of Thames TV from BET and Thorn EMI was vetoed in 1985 by the IBA, which wanted a broader rather than narrower range of owners. Green had to settle, temporarily perhaps, for 20 per cent of Central TV, which he bought from the betting group Ladbroke in 1987.

An account of the growth of international media conglomeration risks piling example on extravagant example, while the question, 'so what?' gets ignored. That question goes straight to the issues of media accountability raised in the introduction. At this stage, the point to emphasize is the relevance of conglomeration to the very notion itself of 'media'. The conglomerates were commercial organizations. A few had a technical coherence: they were entirely press, or entirely electronic. Most did not. Where was their economic and functional coherence, beyond the simple claim that they served a market? Mostly, they were a product of the energy and inclination of their individual barons and of the sequence of expansionist opportunities those men had made or seized. With concentration, conglomeration and internationalization the issues of power and accountability became substantially more difficult, in both principle and practice.

6 Content and Audiences

Continuities

ITV researchers asked people in 1978 which of nine topics they thought should get more coverage, or less, in TV news and documentaries. Industrial news, Northern Ireland, immigrants' affairs? Yes, those were very important. So would they personally like to watch more about them? Well, as a matter of fact, no. The poll found a clear difference between what people thought should be available and what they personally wanted to watch.

That example shows as well as any the complicated relation between what is available in media, which bits people use, how much, what for, and with what satisfaction. The complexity is natural, given the prominence of media in daily life. Analysts, particularly in the advertising world, ceaselessly try to unravel it, to help clients sell their products in the best markets.

The issues are even more complicated if, as in this book, one is exploring developments through time and comparing different media. There is also the great puzzle, which is central to arguments over media power and accountability, about the direction of influence. How far have media contents followed audience taste and how far created it? The larger a programme's audience or a paper's readership, the more likely it seems that the content must in general be enjoyed, else why the large audience? Equally, though, taste in many subjects, such as fashion (clothes, design, music) also follows media.

This chapter can be no more than a combination of large generalizations and small examples, maybe unrepresentative. To start with, we may note certain obvious and important *continuities of content and audience* between 1945 and 1990. Advertising, first, was crucial in various ways. For instance, it kept down the direct cost of media to the consumer. National daily papers got nearly half their revenue from advertising in 1970 and two-fifths in 1990. Provincial dailies got 60 per cent or more, and weekly papers 80 per cent, at both dates. For free sheets, of course, the direct cost to the reader was nil; and for ITV programmes, the viewer paid directly for the cost only of a TV set and electricity. Advertising made media cheap. On the other hand, one of the consequences of advertising finance was its strong impact on media contents. From the start, ITV programme scheduling was almost entirely determined, apart from the IBA's requirements, by the need to get advertising revenue (in its early years, one-quarter of ITV's money came simply from the great washing-powder war). The time, length, casting and sequence of programmes were all liable to be affected. The shape of programme, audience and advertiser all had to coincide. One simple factor played a major part in the calculations: time of day. Audience size (on radio too) was primarily determined by when a programme was broadcast. Peak-time, between roughly 6.00 pm and 10.00 pm, was the key to scheduling.

The BBC never had to fit audiences to advertisers, but from 1955 it was in competition for its audiences with ITV. So a twice-weekly soap opera such as *EastEnders*, which started in February 1985, was as carefully researched as any commercial programme. It was the first BBC soap since *Z Cars* and *Compact* in the 1960s. Soaps, audience research had long shown, were not the kind of programme the public associated with the BBC. The idea for this one was proposed in 1981, specifically to boost the early evening weekday audience and help to build it for the rest of the evening. From telephone surveys and detailed representative group discussions, the planners developed the programme's shape – the neighbourhood, story line, characters – and launched it successfully four years later.

After its first year it had the widest appeal of any soap opera. Many viewers were 'structuring their lives round it' and spoke of the characters as if they knew them well (BBC, 1986). The early evening audience gap between BBC1 and ITV fell from 20 per cent to less than 10 per cent.

In the launch of *EastEnders*, did content follow audience taste, or audience follow content? Clearly, there was a bit of both. The example gives a glimpse too of the intricacies of scheduling and of the competition for audiences even when revenue was not directly a factor.

For the press, the importance of advertising can hardly be overstated, though it was often indirect. It helped to start whole categories of publication, such as free sheets, Sunday paper colour magazines, and successive speciality magazines (yachting, autos, DIY, computing). Lack of advertising finished others, such as the illustrated weeklies *Picture Post, Everybody's* and *Illustrated*.

Advertising revenue helped shape national dailies – literally, by justifying the switch to a smaller tabloid format in which a 'full page' consumed less paper without a proportional decrease in revenue earned. It forced the closure of particular titles – the *News Chronicle, Daily Herald* and many other national and provincial papers with millions of satisfied readers. Once paper rationing ended in 1956, the size of papers swelled and slumped as fluctuations in advertising revenue paid for more or fewer pages. Within a paper, it influenced the space for different subjects. The big financial sections in the dailies owed more to the growth of appropriate advertising in the 1960s than to a surge of reader interest.

What was very difficult to prove – but was much suspected, especially in the late 1940s, at the time of the first Press Commission – was that advertisers used their leverage to get favourable coverage and dampen criticism. Crude threats to withdraw advertising might at any time have been counter-productive. *The Observer* and *Guardian* were popularly believed to have lost revenue because of their opposition to the Eden government's Suez policy at the end of 1956, but other such cases are difficult to find. The Distillers' Company, makers of the deforming drug thalidomide, withdrew their advertising from *The Sunday Times*, in which they were currently the largest advertiser, when *The Sunday Times* began its campaign in 1972 for better compensation for the drug's victims. This was presumably more in protest than in expectation that the campaign would be stopped (Evans, 1983, p. 93). Easier game for advertisers were feature subjects such as motoring, travel and holidays, where the latest models and resorts were hyped throughout the 1960s and 1970s. In those years, too, 'special supplements' became common among national dailies, in which articles about the special subject sat side by side with advertising matter.

In the provincial press, and especially the local weeklies, it is more difficult to believe that direct influence was rare. Would a local weekly, for example, launch an attack on the estate agency business or the standards of the second-hand car trade? The local press tended to be bland, and 'stirring things up', even in the angry years of the late 1960s, was the preserve of 'alternative' community newspapers.

The fear of direct influence by advertisers on programme content was one of the main planks in the opposition to ITV. Blood pressures rose at reports that US TV film of the Coronation in 1953 had been punctuated by ads featuring a chimpanzee, J Fred Muggs. The ITA was given tight control over the number, duration, placing and content of TV ads, which for most of the period were limited to an average of six minutes an hour. Sponsorship was excluded. Political parties, religious organizations, charities and various commercial products were banned altogether. So, from 1965, by a government directive, were cigarettes.

Most of that was straightforward. Since ITV had the TV monopoly of advertising and 'editorializing' was not allowed, few anxieties surfaced about advertisers' influence on programmes. The Pilkington Committee was more concerned, for example, with the fifteen-minute programmes known as 'admags'. In these, well known actors and comedians plugged a variety of goods in the familiar setting of a shop or pub. They had a deliberate soap opera quality. One, *Jim's Inn*, became so popular that its cast produced an LP. Pilkington disliked the impression conveyed that these friendly personalities just happened to be recommending products as though they were disinterested parties. The programmes were banned by the government in 1963.

The difficult problems came, both for the IBA and for the BBC, from the growth of indirect sponsorship. From the 1970s onward equestrians leaped improbable heights at Wembley on mounts more likely called Sanyo Music Centre or Everest Double Glazing than Foxhunter or Dobbin. Cricket boundaries were ringed with advertising boards. Grand prix motor cars were painted up like buses to advertise cigarettes and even contraceptives. Sports sponsorship was the indirect way in to TV advertising.

A final point about advertising revenue – and of major importance – was that media to some extent competed for it between as well as among themselves. As a proportion of national consumer expenditure, advertising more than doubled between 1945 and 1990, so they competed for a growing purse. But not all TV's advertising was 'new' expenditure. As Table 6.1 shows, the national press kept a remarkably steady share, in the region of 16–19 per cent. It was the magazine and provincial press sectors that suffered most, as TV's share wobbled upwards from 1 per cent in 1955 to 33 per cent in 1986.

Other 'continuities' from 1945 to 1990 are more briefly stated. *The division of the national press into 'quality' and 'popular' papers* was one of content as well as circulation, and it was itself largely a result of the higher advertising rates chargeable by the papers with readers who had more money to spend (not necessarily their own). In content, the difference was in range and detail, as well as in the proportions of the various subjects. Thus the 'qualities' covered a wider range of sports but gave them proportionately much less space overall than the populars. With foreign news the populars did less well on both counts. Such differences became even sharper with the contraction of the popular broadsheet papers after the death of the *Daily Herald* and *News Chronicle*.

Table 6.1 Distribution of advertising expenditure

	1948 (%)	1952 (%)	1956 (%)	1960 (%)	1964 (%)	1968 (%)	1972 (%)	1976 (%)	1980 (%)	1984 (%)	1986 (%)
National newspapers	14	16	19	20	21	20	18	17	17	17	16
Provincial newspapers	32	31	30	24	24	24	27	28	25	23	21
Consumer magazines	13	19	16	12	11	10	8	8	7	6	5
Business etc. magazines	16	16	11	10	9	9	9	9	8	8	7
Directories	–	1	1	1	1	2	2	3	3	4	5
Press production costs	8	6	7	5	4	5	6	5	5	5	5
Total press[a]	82	89	84	71	69	69	70	68	66	63	61
Television	–	–	6	22	24	26	25	26	27	31	33
Poster and transport	14	8	8	5	4	4	4	4	4	4	4
Cinema	4	2	2	1	1	1	1	1	1	*	*
Radio	–	1	*	*	*	*	*	1	2	2	2
Total[a]	100	100	100	100	100	100	100	100	100	100	100

* 0.5 per cent or less.
[a] Percentages are rounded and may not sum correctly.

Source: Advertising Association.

The quality—popular distinction reflected also the characteristically English *divisions of social class* in newspaper readership. Throughout the period, each paper was read by two or more people in addition to its purchaser, depending on the definition of 'read'. This contributed also to persistent *readership duplication*, with the average middle-class reader in the 1960s still reading about 1.25 national dailies. There was also much overlap between the nationals and the provincial mornings and evenings.

Divisions of social class were less sharp than the size and format differences of the quality and popular papers. Until the decline of the 'middle market' broadsheets (*Daily Express, Daily Mail*, and so on), readership and social class matched quite tidily. In 1966, for instance, the class distribution of *Daily Express* and *Daily Mail* readers, the two dominant middle market papers, with nearly two-fifths of the total readership, reflected very closely the class distribution of the population as a whole (see Table 6.2). The quality broadsheets were heavily skewed towards the wealthier social classes with more formal education, and the tabloids were skewed in the other direction. Readership duplication and the extremes of circulation size add a surprising twist to these class divisions. Far more AB (upper middle class) people read the *Daily Mirror* than *The Times* or *Guardian* even though they were a tiny proportion of the total *Mirror* readership.

Similar comments could be made about the national Sunday press. Further differences between individual papers and periods can be seen in Table 6.3. In general, there is no doubt that through the entire post-war period the readership of the national press reflected divisions of social class and eduction more distinctly than anything else — age, gender, religion, political attitude and so on. In discussions about 'choice', for instance, it would thus have been unrealistic to think of the number of alternative daily papers as growing from nine in 1945 to twelve in 1990. The well educated and well to do AB readers, 12—17 per cent of the population, were most likely to choose among some half a dozen papers. The much larger group of semi- or unskilled working class DE readers, 33 per cent of the population, plumped overwhelming for three or four.

Class differences also affected TV-watching. From 1955

Table 6.2 Readership of national daily papers: class profiles, 1956–86

| Newspaper | Date | AB^a | Percentage of each paper's readers in social class | | |
			$C1^b$	$C2^c$	DE^d
Financial Times	1966	56	29	11	3
	1976	47	34	11	8
	1986	56	30	9	5
The Times	1956	52	18	14	15
	1966	54	23	16	7
	1976	51	31	11	6
	1986	61	24	8	8
Daily Telegraph	1956	51	28	13	8
	1966	42	33	17	8
	1976	43	36	13	7
	1986	54	29	11	7
Guardian	1956	46	27	16	11
	1966	47	27	18	8
	1976	40	39	13	8
	1986	50	30	9	12
Daily Mail	1956	21	23	29	27
	1966	19	24	30	27
	1976	15	34	28	22
	1986	26	30	24	20
Daily Express	1956	17	20	34	29
	1966	12	22	37	27
	1976	13	30	31	26
	1986	20	30	28	23
Population Aged 16+	1956	14	18	34	34
16+	1966	12	19	36	33
15+	1976	12	24	32	32
15+	1986	17	23	28	32
Today	1986	19	29	32	20
News Chronicle	1956	12	21	34	34
Daily Sketch	1956	9	19	38	33
	1966	8	14	43	35
Daily Mirror	1956	6	14	41	39
	1966	4	13	47	36
	1976	4	19	41	36
	1986	7	18	36	38

Table 6.2   (cont.)

| Newspaper | Date | AB^a | Percentage of each paper's readers in social class | | |
			$C1^b$	$C2^c$	DE^d
Sun	1976	3	18	42	36
	1986	7	18	35	41
Daily Herald/Sun	1956	4	11	44	41
	1966	3	14	46	37
Star	1986	4	14	38	44

[a] AB — professional, administrative, managerial;
[b] C1 — other non-manual;
[c] C2 — skilled manual;
[d] DE — semi- or unskilled manual.

Source: IPA. Percentages are rounded.

onwards, working class people tended to watch more ITV programmes and middle class people more BBC. Similarly working class audiences were the heaviest listeners to BBC Radio 1 and 2 and ILR stations, and middle class listeners made up two-thirds of the audience for BBC Radio 3 and 4.

A different kind of continuity was in *the nature of news*. There is no reason to suppose people were interested by different kinds of things in 1945 than in 1990 — or 1890, for that matter. Sex, crime and sport were staples of the nineteenth century. Academic studies have confirmed the obvious: events make news if they are clear, unusual, unexpected or unpredictable; if they fit a medium's cycle (a daily paper, for example, or an hourly news bulletin); if they involve well known people or groups, places or countries; if they are close to home (literally or figuratively); if they are negative (accidents) or reach a certain volume (in terms of numbers hurt, for example, or goals scored).

In competing for readers, papers supplied not contrasting contents but remarkably similar ones. As in other kinds of market, the trick in increasing market share was to supply a product *slightly* different from the one with which a customer was satisfied. Thus although news executives continued to

Table 6.3 Readership of national dailies: sex, social class and age, 1966 and 1986

Newspaper	Date	Readership (m)	Percentages of: Men (%)	Women (%)	AB (%)	C1 (%)	C2 (%)	DE (%)	Gender: Men (%)	Women (%)	Age of readers: 15/16-34 (%)	35-54 (%)	55+ (%)
Daily Express	1966	11.2	32	24	29	32	29	24	55	45	3_	36	33
	1986	4.5	11	9	11	13	10	7	53	47	30	33	37
Daily Mail	1966	6.1	18	13	24	20	13	12	55	45	27	35	38
	1986	4.7	12	10	16	14	9	7	52	48	34	31	34
Daily Mirror	1966	15.5	43	34	14	28	49	42	54	46	40	38	22
	1986	11.0	28	22	17	20	32	30	54	56	39	30	31
Daily Sketch	1966	3.1	9	6	5	6	9	8	58	42	37	37	26
	1986	–	–	–	–	–	–	–	–	–	–	–	–
Daily Telegraph	1966	3.4	9	8	29	15	4	2	53	47	34	36	29
	1986	2.9	7	6	20	8	3	1	54	46	27	35	38
Financial Times	1966	0.4	2	1	5	2	*	*	73	26	31	44	24
	1986	0.7	2	1	5	2	1	*	71	29	41	41	19
Guardian	1966	0.3	3	2	8	3	1	1	60	40	38	39	23
	1986	1.5	4	2	9	4	1	1	62	38	47	35	18
Star	1966	–	–	–	–	–	–	–	–	–	–	–	–
	1986	4.3	12	8	2	6	13	13	59	41	51	27	21

Table 6.3 (cont.)

| Newspaper | Date | Readership (m) | Percentages of: | | | | | | Gender | | Age of readers | | |
			Men (%)	Women (%)	AB (%)	C1 (%)	C2 (%)	DE (%)	Men (%)	Women (%)	15/16–34 (%)	35–54 (%)	55+ (%)
Sun	1966[a]	4.5	14	8	3	8	14	13	61	39	31	37	32
	1986	11.4	28	23	10	20	33	33	53	47	46	30	25
The Times	1966	0.8	2	2	9	2	1	*	58	42	43	34	23
	1986	1.2	3	2	10	3	1	1	58	42	38	40	22
Today	1966	–	–	–	–	–	–	–	–	–	–	–	–
	1986	1.1	3	2	3	3	2	2	59	41	51	31	18
Total readership	1966	45.8	132	98	126	116	120	104					
	1986	43.3	110	85	103	93	106	95					
Estimated population 16+	1966	40.1	100	100	–	–	–	–	48	52	33	35	32
Estimated population 15+	1986	44.4	100	100	–	–	–	–	48	52	37	31	33

Percentages are rounded.
* Under 1 per cent.
[a] Not yet tabloid.

Source: IPA/JICNARS.

value 'scoops', Tunstall found in the 1970s that among journalists themselves, it was more important not to come *last* with the news than to be first with it (Tunstall, 1971). Similarly, Murdoch's *Sun* in 1970 was a close copy of the *Daily Mirror*, whose readers he sought to poach. Matthews' new *Star* was in turn a close copy of the *Sun* in 1978. Overall, as the 1974 Press Commission observed, newspapers stuck to the same basic 'components', such as editorials, letters, sports and 'personalities' (McQuail, 1977, p. 31).

Radio and TV did not change those news values. Early worries that picture availability would make a story newsworthy in itself on TV did not persist. What changed, obviously, were the people and events that met the criteria as the years passed. Moreover, TV and radio were not primarily *news* media, judged simply by the proportions of their output. They were increasingly good at breaking news fast, but their coverage was only a fraction of the newspapers', even measuring just the peak hours. The weight of TV output in practice was more comparable to the features content of the press.

Another way of looking at contents is by subject. Here, too, the *types of subject did not change dramatically*, considered in broad categories. The 1974 Press Commission noted a relative decline in the porportion of news in the national dailies between 1947 and 1975, but they attributed it to newsprint scarcity squeezing out features while rationing lasted. With certain exceptions, such as an increase in sport and a decline in foreign coverage, the more specific categories did not vary greatly either. In TV, the changes were greater (see below).

Difficulties of finding comparable data prevent detailed comparison of press contents from year to year. Tables 6.4., 6.5 and 6.6, therefore, present a patchy and summary picture. The pagination Table (6.4) gives a rough indication of national dailies' increase in size (new type faces and better ink eventually meant more words per page). The heavier news emphasis in the quality papers and the picture content of the tabloids are clear in Table 6.5. The news categories used by the 1947 Press Commission, which were followed for the 1975 analysis, were too general to show up many differences of detail, but are

Table 6.4   National daily newspapers: number of pages

Newspaper	1937	1947	1956	1965	1975	1983[a]	1987[b]
Daily Express	20	5	11	18	17	36[c]	41[c]
Daily Herald/Sun	20	4	10	14	–	–	–
Daily Mail	19	5	10	17	34[c]	36[c]	41[c]
Daily Mirror	22	9	18	26	28	32	33
Daily Sketch/Graphic	?	?	17	20	–	–	–
Daily Star	–	–	–	–	–	29	30
Daily Telegraph	25	6	12	26	28	32	37
Daily Worker/Morning Star	8	6	?	4	6	?	?
Guardian	19	7	14	19	23	27	33
Independent	–	–	–	–	–	–	30
News Chronicle	20	4	10	–	–	–	–
Sun (from 1970)	–	–	–	–	28	31	32
The Times	26	10	17	21	26	28	43
Today	–	–	–	–	–	–	44

[a] Figures for May/June only.
[b] Figures for May/June only.
[c] Format now tabloid.

Sources: Royal Commissions on the Press; Seymour-Ure, *The Press, Politics and the Public* (Constable, 1968); D. Butler and D. Kavanagh, *The British General Election of 1983* (Macmillan, 1984), *The British General Election of 1987* (Macmillan, 1988).

recorded in Table 6.6.

The 1974 Press Commission studied samples of provincial papers too. These generally had a larger proportion of advertising, and the higher the circulation, the greater was the amount of classified rather than display ads, which was the opposite of the nationals. The amount of local news varied from one-third in metropolitan papers (*Birmingham Post*, *Yorkshire Post*) to 60 per cent or more in East Anglia and the West Country. At least one-quarter of the local news was sport, with crime and police stories the next largest. Foreign news was 5–10 per cent. The evening papers relied even more heavily on local news – from 60 to 75 per cent.

Tables can give some measure of quality–popular, broadsheet–tabloid and subject differences, but they are no help in other ways. In the 1980s, for instance, colour became common

Table 6.5 National daily newspaper contents: 1947, 1965, 1975

| | Editorial space (%) | | | | | | | | | | | |
| | News | | | Features | | | Pictures | | | Other | | |
Newspaper	1947	1965	1975	1947	1965	1975	1947	1965	1975	1947	1965	1975
Daily Express	50	32	32	16	13	16	6	9	8	7	6	2
Daily Graphic/Sketch[a]	35	35	–	14	18	–	25	19	–	7	9	–
Daily Herald[b]	52	40	–	15	16	–	5	13	–	7	6	–
Daily Mail	49	32	30	15	16	24	7	9	9	8	4	3
Daily Mirror	40	29	28	11	11	20	10	15	11	19	10	4
Daily Telegraph	45	31	37	23	9	12	2	6	5	7	2	1
Daily Worker/Morning Star[c]	45	50	52	–	21	26	3	15	14	10	6	–
Financial Times	–	–	44	13	–	16	–	–	2	–	–	3
Guardian	–	38	37	–	14	25	–	6	7	4	4	4
News Chronicle	53	–	–	7	–	–	7	–	–	6	–	–
Sun	–	–	31	–	–	19	–	–	11	–	–	3
The Times	41	46	39	7	11	16	3	5	4	9	4	4

Table 6.5 (cont.)

Newspaper	Total Editorial Space			Total Advertisements			Total (each year)
	1947	1965	1975	1947	1965	1975	
Daily Express	79	61	58	21	39	42	100
Daily Graphic/Sketch[a]	81	81	–	19	19	–	100
Daily Herald[b]	79	75	–	21	25	–	100
Daily Mail	79	61	66	21	29	24	100
Daily Mirror	84	65	63	16	36	37	100
Daily Telegraph	65	48	55	35	52	45	100
Daily Worker/Morning Star[c]	81	92	92	19	8	8	100
Financial Times	–	–	65	–	–	35	100
Guardian	–	62	73	–	38	27	100
News Chronicle	79	–	–	21	–	–	100
Sun	–	–	64	–	–	36	100
The Times	60	66	65	40	34	35	100

[a] Renamed *Daily Sketch* in 1952.
[b] Renamed *Sun* in 1964.
[c] Renamed *Morning Star* in 1966.

Sources: Royal Commission on the Press, 1947; 1974–77; C. Seymour-Ure, *The Political Impact of Mass Media* (Constable, 1968).

Table 6.6 News in five national daily papers: 1947, 1965, 1975

Category	Daily Express 1947 (%)	Daily Express 1965 (%)	Daily Express 1975 (%)	Daily Mail 1947 (%)	Daily Mail 1965 (%)	Daily Mail 1975 (%)	Daily Mirror 1947 (%)	Daily Mirror 1965 (%)	Daily Mirror 1975 (%)	Daily Telegraph 1947 (%)	Daily Telegraph 1965 (%)	Daily Telegraph 1975 (%)	The Times 1947 (%)	The Times 1965 (%)	The Times 1975 (%)
Home news															
General[a]	25	26	18	27	32	20	24	32	17	32	36	24	30	28	25
Law, police, accidents	13	10	12	11	6	12	23	16	11	8	6	7	3	5	5
Sport	32	41	37	33	33	34	24	36	53	18	26	23	16	16	14
Other[b]	6	–[c]	8	9	–[c]	7	15	–[c]	8	6	–[c]	5	2	–[c]	3
Total home	76	77	75	80	71	73	86	84	89	64	68	59	51	49	47
External news															
Foreign	7	–[c]	5	6	–[c]	7	8	–[c]	3	7	–[c]	8	13	–[c]	10
International[d]	12	–[c]	11	10	–[c]	8	6	–[c]	7	19	–[c]	11	15	–[c]	13
Total external[e]	19	13	17	16	15	16	14	12	10	26	14	19	28	17	23
Financial, commercial, miscellaneous	4	10	9	4	13	10	*	3	1	8	17	21	20	33	30
Scientific and technical	1	*	*	*	*	*	*	*	*	*	1	*	1	1	*
Total[f]	100	100	100	100	100	100	100	100	100	100	100	100	100	100	100

[a] Includes political, social, economic, personalities, and so on.
[b] Included in 'General' in 1965.
[c] figures not calculated for this year.
[d] Includes international sport.
[e] Foreign and international news were not measured separately in 1965.
[f] Figures are rounded and do not all sum to 100. Pictures are excluded from the 1947 and 1975 figures.
* Less than 1 per cent.
Sources: Royal Commission on the Press, 1974–7; Seymour-Ure (1968) for the 1965 figures.

in the national press. Earlier, the colour magazine supplement to *The Sunday Times* (1961) was a landmark in Sunday journalism. (*The Observer* did not produce one until 1964.) Large Sunday papers, boosted by Thomson's classified ads drive at *The Sunday Times*, led to sectionalization, on American lines. It was adopted for some of the dailies too.

Changing contents

The changing character of journalism – a paper's distinctive 'voice' – is more difficult both to discuss and convey. Much has sometimes been made, for example, of the *Daily Mirror's* rapport with its working class readers in the post-war years – the press equivalent of a cloth cap image (the cartoon character 'Andy Capp', ironically, was introduced when the period was ending). Under the instinctive guidance of Hugh Cudlipp and others, with well established features and columnists, the paper was an articulate tribune for a class interest: 'Forward with the People!' said the mast-head. In the 1960s, long before its circulation dipped, that rapport had lessened, as the higher living standards and consumerist values of the 'affluent society' confused old certainties. 'The people had gone forward,' wrote Cudlipp. 'The question was, how to keep them there' (Cudlipp, 1962, p. 122).

The *Daily Express*, in contrast, had been the authentic voice of middle class England in the same period. In Arthur Christiansen it too had an inspirational editor and expert newspaper technician. His office bulletins became a fount of Fleet Street lore ('Always, always, tell the news through people,' for example). Editorially, the paper followed Lord Beaverbrook's idiosyncratic conservatism, but its columnists, cartoonists, sports commentators, share tipsters and foreign correspondents, all caught a mood of 1950s optimism.

It is not altogether fanciful to match moods to newspapers. To some extent, one is simply following circulation trends. While the *Mirror* and *Express* flourished, the *Herald* and its offspring *Sun* (pre-Murdoch) struggled, and the *Mail* lived in the shadow of the *Express*. On Sundays, the 1960s belonged to *The Sunday Times*. With circulation built on war memoir serializations, resources went into 'investigative journalism'. The other Sundays bounced in the wake. On weekdays, the *Guardian* thrived in a decade of Labour government reformism, while *The Times* struggled to modernize. In the 1970s, the *Sun* was the full-breasted leader. Later, the tabloids vied for market share with the kind of sensationalism and cheque book journalism that were the despair of quality journalists. The 1980s ended with the tabloids' confidence waning, and with the *Sun's* nudes moving to page five, perhaps to slip away for good.

Two further trends are worth including among such thumbnail sketches. In the quality press, first, the 1960s saw a great growth of specialization within public affairs journalism. Political, diplomatic and industrial specialists already existed. Not only did they multiply, with space now for reflection and analysis in addition to hard news, they were joined by education, economic, home affairs and social services correspondents, among others. Specific 'women's pages' were started: in the *Mail*, it was a 'Femail' section. The trend also belatedly reflected the increased scope of government intervention in the economy. The movement was not all one way. Foreign correspondents, for instance, dropped sharply. Papers relied increasingly on locally based stringers and news agencies. The very large costs of keeping their own staffers in foreign capitals were no longer justifiable, when British interests were a relic of their former importance.

The decline of anonymity, outside the leader columns, is also worth noting. Anonymity lasted until 1967 in *The Times* and for nearly as long in parts of the other quality papers. With a byline, an article becomes personal. How far the personality then intrudes and colours style and substance, is a matter of degree. In a world of TV, anonymous journalism probably could not have survived: when we see a face, we want a name (besides, print journalists were needed as guests on TV current affairs shows). At *The Times*, the change was signalled by the appointment as columnist of Bernard Levin, a writer whose highly distinctive voice, originally anonymous in the *Spectator*, could not 'unnamed' have stood regular exposure in a daily paper. Anonymity, like the uniforms of nurses, the police or soldiers, highlights the role, not the person performing it. In journalism, it therefore bolstered the idea of objectivity in reporting the news. Its disappearance fitted an era in which electronic media were taking over the 'hot' news role and papers were selling the personal expertise of their staff at interpretation, comment, analysis, more than for traditional hard news.

Other aspects of press content are best discussed in common with TV and radio. First, TV itself needs attention. Tables 6.7 and 6.8 summarize BBC and ITV programming at ten-yearly intervals. (Differences of definition and compilation make comparisons highly unreliable). The enormous increase in broadcast hours is easy enough to observe. The BBC started in 1946 with an average of 28.5 hours a week, generally from 3.00–4.00/4.30 pm and 8.30–10.00 pm. When ITV started, both channels were limited to 50 hours a week and not more than 8 on any one day. There were 'closed periods' from 6.00–7.00 pm on weekdays, Sunday mornings, and from 6.15–7.30 pm on Sunday evenings. These are a nice reminder of the anti-social intrusiveness attributed to the new medium (rather like Sunday lawn-mowing).

For the BBC, increased news did not mean more income. The cost of filling BBC2's hours, one must remember, had to be met from increased licence fees (controlled by the government), marginal economies and earnings from co-productions and sales abroad, and increasingly from the larger fee charged for a colour licence. Colour was introduced in 1967, on BBC2.

More hours did generally mean more advertising revenue for ITV, and the companies frequently pressed the government for expansion. In 1972 restrictions were lifted. ITV and BBC1 were both soon broadcasting some 13 hours a day (the main change being an extension of afternoon hours) – double the amount 20 years earlier. Breakfast time TV and Channel 4 doubled them again, so that by the late 1980s each network was putting out 200 hours a week. Viewers thus went from a choice of less than 30 hours a week in 1946 to more than 400 in the late 1980s. By 1990 you could watch TV round the clock.

Table 6.7 Weekly programming on ITV, 1956–86

	1956 (hrs/mins)	(%)	1966 (hrs/mins)	(%)	1976 (hrs/mins)	(%)	ITV 1986 (hrs/mins)	(%)	Channel 4 1986 (hrs/mins)	(%)
News and news magazines	3.15	7	4.39	7	10.01	11	11.01	10.5	4.02	5.5
Current affairs					–	–	–		16.35	22
Documentaries, arts	3.56	8	7.15	11	11.41	13	11.36	11	1.39	2.25
Religion	1.05	2	3.15	5	2.28	2.5	2.31	2.5		
Adult education	–	–	3.15	5	3.06	3	1.51	1.75		
School programmes	–	–	4.22	7	5.22	6	6.50	6.5	} 7.56	10.5
Pre-school programmes	–	–	–	–	1.42	2	3.35	3.5		
Children's 'informative'	1.08	2	0.50	1	1.33	1.5	2.12	2	–	–
Total 'informative'	9.24	19	23.36	36	35.53	39	39.36	37.75	30.12	40.25
Plays, drama series, serials, TV movies	13.05	28	16.17	24	21.35	23	26.21	25	16.05	21.5
Feature films	1.15	3	6.35	10	9.44	10.5	8.18	8	11.45	15.5
Entertainment and light music	14.36	31	7.38	11	10.03	11	14.29	13.75	11.00	14.5
Sport	2.13	5	6.12	9	8.38	9	9.00	8.75	6.07	8.25
Children's entertainment	6.27	14	6.21	10	7.02	7.5	7.24	7	–	–
Total all programmes	47.00	100	66.39	100	92.55	100	105.15	100	75.16	100
Breakfast TV (TV-AM)	–		–		–		21.0			

Sources: IBA Yearbooks. Figures are averages of the various ITV companies.

Table 6.8 Annual programming on BBC television, 1956–86

	1955–6 hours		1965–6 hours				1975–6 hours				1985–6 hours			
	hours	(%)	BBC1	BBC2	Total	(%)	BBC1	BBC2	Total	(%)	BBC1	BBC2	Total	(%)
News	149	6	172	147	319	5	232	156	388	4	410	51	461	4
Newsreel and documentation films/outside broadcasts	107	4	—	—	—	—	—	—	—	—	—	—	—	—
Talks, demonstrations & documentary programmes	634	25	483	265	748	13	—	—	—	—	—	—	—	—
Current affairs, features and documentaries	—	—	—	—	—	—	841	781	1,622	19	1,458	992	2,450	23
Drama	245	10	408	273	671	12	311	182	493	6	295	144	439	4
Light entertainment	332	13	277	126	403	7	335	154	489	6	518	217	735	7
Religion	33	1	145	5	150	3	126	11	137	2	156	10	166	2
Sport	301	12	682	264	946ᵃ	16	641	408	1,049	12	761	773	1,534	14
Entertainment films	115	5	—	—	—	—	—	—	—	—	—	—	—	—
British and foreign feature films and series	—	—	495	332	827	14	843	484	1,327	16	849	854	1,703	16
Children's	395	16	321	113	434	8	594	123	717	8	753	20	773	1
Music (including opera & ballet)	102	4	43	93	136	2	28	116	144	2	16	126	142	1
Schools	—	—	385	—	385	7	304	137	441	5	—	512	512	5
Further education	—	—	140	93	233	4	359	—	359	7	290	982	1,272	12
Other	113	5	369	278	647	10	304	137	441	5	184	198	382	4
Total hoursᵇ	2,526	100	3,920	1,979	5,899	100	4,857	3,624	8,481	100	5,690	4,879	10,569	100
Average hours per week	49		75	38	113		93	70	163		109	94	203	

ᵃ Includes outside broadcasts, not all of which were sport.
ᵇ Percentages rounded and do not add to 100.

The programme categories in Tables 6.7 and 6.8 reflect the broadcasters' need to demonstrate that they were 'informing, educating and entertaining'. The tables give an idea also of the kind of programming that was practical in the early days. 'Talks' and 'demonstrations' suggest the camera eavesdropping, as though in a lecture hall. 'Newsreels' copied the magazine style of the old cinema newsreels; they were not yet bulletins of latest news. 'Outside broadcasts' are reminders that for years TV was a cumbersome medium, happiest in the studio or on set piece occasions such as the Cup Final, which could be planned well in advance. There were very few feature films, because of competition with the cinema.

Ten years on, more of the familiar categories were in place. ITV's early schedules were dominated by 'entertainment'. 'Quiz shows with glittering prizes, fast-moving adventure series, drama series and soap operas and spectacular live variety, gave a new look to British TV,' recalled one IBA executive (David Glencross, 1985). The names resonate, even when their shelf life has finished: *Take Your Pick*, *Double Your Money*, *Emergency Ward Ten*, *The Avengers*, *Coronation Street* (still running in 1990), *Sunday Night at the London Palladium*. The differences in BBC and IBA programme categories do not conceal the contrast in those years between the 'serious' (equals 'less popular') scheduling of BBC TV and the 'entertainment' (equals 'popular') bias of ITV.

In retrospect, ITV justified its programmes, blatantly at odds with the intention of the policy makers, as the price necessarily paid to get the new system running. Certainly, as we have seen, it was no easy task, especially with a controlling body, the ITA, that *was* an Authority without as yet *possessing* authority. The regional bias of the system, too, worked against coordination in the early days. Nevertheless, these were years in which ITV helped TV as a whole to acquire the stigma of an 'idiot box'.

In 1962 the Pilkington Committee slammed ITV. Its criticisms could easily be dubbed 'elitist' (not in fact a vogue word at that time), but they boiled down to the traditional media dilemma about how far people know what they 'want' until they have been shown choices beyond their existing experience.

From the persuasive pen of Committee member Richard Hoggart, himself a working class man who had seized the opportunities of formal education, the critique flowed powerfully. The government not only gave the second TV channel to the BBC but slapped the excess profits levy onto ITV. The levy reduced the profit-maximizing incentive (thereby encouraging companies such as Granada to diversify out of TV) and in-directly helped the ITA to enforce the Television Act's requirements of programme quality and balance.

The Authority's grip grew progressively firmer. The result was a gradual convergence of programming between ITV and BBC. From the 1970s, ITV executives would note with a mixture of exasperation and glee that highly popular − but also esteemed and award-winning − ITV series were frequently mistaken for BBC products. *Upstairs Downstairs*, *World at War*, *Edward VII* (in the 1970s); *Brideshead Revisited*, *Jewel in the Crown* (1980s) − all were ITV programmes that set the elitists purring. They went out, of course, alongside the likes of *Opportunity Knocks*, *The Golden Shot*, *Crossroads* and *Emmerdale Farm*. By the 1980s the BBC too had *Blankety-Blank* and *EastEnders*. But, even so, viewers in 1987 still perceived ITV as better at quiz and game shows, entertainment and variety, adventure and police series, comedy and feature films; while BBC was the network for talk and chat shows, plays, science and nature, drama, documentaries and sport.

Even allowing for some massaging of programmes into 'serious' categories, ITV's progressive seriousness saw a halving of its 'entertainment' schedules. 'Informative' content was much boosted by the intrinsically serious nature of Channel 4. Much earlier than that, however, an important part was played by the rise of news and current affairs. BBC was traditionally strong in these areas (classic 'public service broadcasting' territory), but with the introduction of ITN's *News at Ten* on 3 July 1967, ITV broke new ground. This was TV's first half-hour news bulletin, and something of which Pilkington could have been proud, since research had shown in 1966 that 83 per cent of viewers were perfectly content with the traditional fifteen minutes at 8.55 pm.

News at Ten quickly became so popular that the companies built their evening scheduling round it. For TV news it was a symbolic moment. The BBC extended its own 9.00 pm bulletin. News was no longer an illustrated supplement to radio and newspapers. Newscasters worked as journalists and interviewers, not just announcers. Satellite transmission soon added immediacy and a much extended range of sources and material. 'The news' became less of a bulletin and more an integrated programme of 'reporter packages', capable of delivering large audiences in peaktime. In due course, colour, electronic news-gathering (an ITV innovation) and computer graphics would also add to the service. The growth of broadcasting hours made opportunities for lunchtime news in 1972 and an extended early evening news in 1976, with similar BBC expansion and a distinctive approach from Channel 4. More and more people came to see TV as their prime source of news.

A second factor drawing BBC and ITV together was the advance of programme people – producers and editors – into senior management posts at ITV, superseding the 'merchant venturer swashbucklers' of the first phase. The franchise changes of 1967/8 and 1980 confirmed this. Some of the talent were home grown, but others, including Michael Peacock of LWT fame and Jeremy Isaacs of Thames and Channel 4, came across from the BBC, where programmes such as *Tonight* (founded in 1957) had been famous nurseries of talent. ITV increasingly could pay better salaries too; but the movement, of course, went in both directions, and the 1980s ended with a Deputy Director-General of the BBC, John Birt, recruited from LWT.

One of the main differences between BBC and ITV programming envisaged in 1955 was an ITV regional bias. This was largely nullified by the almost immediate institution of the network system. This, again, was justified by necessity. The ITA was persuaded in 1956 that unless the four major companies had guaranteed access to a national market for so many hours a week, the whole system might fail. In essence, each of the four agreed to contribute a quarter of the programmes and to show the three-quarters contributed by the other three in its own region. The smaller companies took (and paid for) the network programmes, and contributed a modest share, but they had no say in programming decisions.

The only 'regional' element in the arrangement was that three of the network companies (Granada, Central and Yorkshire) out of the five (since Yorkshire joined in 1968) had a base outside London; so that Granada's *Coronation Street*, say, had 'authentic regional accents' (quite an innovation in their time) and escaped a metropolitan bias.

By 1985 the five network companies were producing 45.5 per cent of the ITV programmes, amounting to more than 40 peak or near-peak hours a week. The 10 smaller companies produced 9.25 per cent for the network and 7.75 per cent for showing in their own regions, where the IBA required up to 7 hours a week of 'local interest'. These companies' contribution lent itself to comparatively inexpensive, specialized programmes, such as science and religion. From the start Anglia specialized in drama and Southern in children's education (ahead of the BBC).

The network system evolved into a complex and allegedly acrimonious business of bargaining in weekly meetings of the five major companies and the IBA, under the umbrella organization of the Independent Television Companies Association. The IBA's increasing concern for programme standards and balance, plus pressure from the smaller companies that rightly felt they had more and more production potential to offer, added to the complications. Channel 4 eased the pressure for space, but also led to more programmes competing for it. At length, in 1987, the small companies were given greater access to the network and the number of network hours was reduced by about a quarter.

Many other features of TV programming, obviously, could be pointed out. Many of them would be as much a record of the times as of TV's part in them. TV missed the end of Empire, except for little bits like the Argyll Highlanders' steamy evacuation from Aden in 1967, but it caught the Vietnam War, the Nigerian Civil War, and so much as it was permitted in the Falklands. Colour TV transformed the fortunes of games such as snooker and transfixed the viewers of Wimbledon. The growth of controversy and public affairs programming is discussed below.

TV drama started with the BBC pointing a large camera at a small stage. Technical and financial improvement saw the virtual elimination of live performances (regretted by some people); immeasurable increases in the quality of settings, costumes and production generally; the commissioning of plays written specifically for TV (much encouraged by Sidney Newman's ITV 'Armchair Theatre' in the 1960s and BBC series such as 'Play for Today' and 'The Wednesday Play'); and the discovery, with the *Forsyte Saga*, that audiences would happily get hooked on serialization of literary classics (and not-so-classics). With film, similarly, TV at first was starved, then it did the deals bringing more feature films more quickly to the screen. Lastly, 'made for TV' movies developed.

All such developments, along with the increasing amount of airtime, put pressure on the capacity − and the justification − for limiting programme production to the BBC/ITV duopoly. By 1990 this was ending. The longstanding quota of 14 per cent on foreign imports was still in place, but Channel 4 was buying a quarter of its programmes from independent companies, and the BBC was moving in the same direction.

As TV poured over the surface of everyday life its programmes made fewer and fewer concessions to pre-existing forms, institutions, media, manners. TV made plays, told the news, taught school, increasingly on its own terms, not as a parasite, imitator or tolerated intruder concealed as a hatstand. As was pointed out earlier, it responded to popular taste, observing new taboos about racism and sexism, just as it helped demolish old ones of sexual modesty and obscene language. But common to all programming, on any channel, was an eventual confidence in the distinctive value of the TV medium. By 1990, TV did not need to make excuses for itself.

One unavoidable consequence was the impact of TV on the contents of other media. Some of the earliest TV 'panellists', who would later have been chat show hosts but were regulars on games like *What's My Line?* in the restricted TV hours of the 1950s, were well known columnists in the popular dailies. Gilbert Harding and Nancy Spain were two early examples. At first TV drew on established reputations in the press; later, the press wooed contributors from TV. The mingling of media personnel paralleled contents *about* different media. Soap opera characters, often blurred with the actors who played them, were a staple of the tabloid press. Programmes such as *What the Papers Say* dissected Fleet Street. TV rows with politicians, a growing practice, made newspaper headlines. TV criticism, initially a job for the plain man, became an important part of quality paper arts pages and attracted star journalists such as Clive James. Evening and weekend papers gave lots of space to programme schedules. Sporting stars pounded track, tennis balls or each other one minute and appeared on screen the next — or in celebrity quiz and talk shows later on. News stories overlapped: morning paper headlines took account of the previous evening's radio and TV stories, and the electronic media picked up items from the daily press (all these developments, indeed, applied to radio as well as to TV).

By the early 1970s mixed-media tie-ins and marketing of records, TV series and books were well developed and would increase. They had a major international dimension, as TV programmes were made for overseas markets, books were packaged for mass readership, feature articles were syndicated worldwide. They ranged from the modest puffing of his travel book by a visiting American author on Radio 4 to the screening of pre-launch films about the making of big budget movies such as *Gandhi*. Little in these practices was new, but they became endemic.

Audiences

Content analyses show only what was available. But how and why did people use the media? What difference did TV make? The short answer is that people's *motives* for using media do not seem to have changed much from 1945 to 1990 — whether to combat loneliness, find out what was going on or just relax. But people did not persistently use the same media in the same way.

How much time people spent watching TV depends on the definition of 'watch'. Until the Annan Committee knocked BBC and ITV heads together and made them run a joint system of audience measurement, ITV relied mainly on counting the number of sets switched on and the BBC used sample surveys and audience 'diaries'. Audience measurement was part of the duopoly's competition. The ITV figures were aimed at advertisers, the BBC's at programme planners and, ultimately, protecting the licence fee.

By any measure, obviously, TV-watching was the key development of the period, growing from nil to about 26 hours per head of the population per week (Tables 6.9 and 6.10). It grew in two ways: initially, as more people got TV sets, and then as programme hours increased. The growth was rapid, then gradual, and in the 1970s and 1980s it fluctuated. In 1970, 75 per cent of the population saw TV at some point during the day and in 1986 the figure had not risen much further to 78 per cent. This was fewer than the number of people looking at a daily newspaper. If viewing was considered by the week, however, TV was virtually universal: barely one person in twenty did not see something in an average week in 1986 (BBC, 1986).

Table 6.9 Time spent on TV and radio, 1961–86

Year	Hours/minutes per head of population per week TV	Radio
1961	13:30	7:00
1966	13:50	7:30
1971	15:34	8:48
1976	17:43	8:49
1981	18:08	9:17
1986	25:54	8:40

These averages conceal wide seasonal variations.

Sources: BBC; BARB/AGB.

Table 6.10　Time spent on TV, radio and newspapers: 1975

Average weekday time	TV viewing (%)	Radio listening (%)
None	3	16
Under 1 hour	7	29
1–3 hours	44	31
3–5 hours	32	11
5 hours or more	14	13

Average time per issue, by regular/occasional readers	National dailies (%)	Provincial mornings (%)	Provincial evenings (%)	Local weeklies (%)
Less than 15 minutes	16	15	16	13
15–30 minutes	22	26	22	18
30–60 minutes	34	35	35	35
1–2 hours	21	19	22	23
2 hours or more	7	5	5	11

Sources: Royal Commission on the Press 1974–7.
Respondents were aged 16 or over.

Viewing increased more with new broadcasting hours, such as afternoon TV in the early 1970s and breakfast time in the early 1980s, than with more channels and programme choice or technical improvements such as colour (colour licences overtook black and white in 1976). The idea of 'saturation' was implicit also in the fact that although multiple set households increased steadily through the 1980s (Table 6.11), only one set at a time was generally switched on. Typically, a second (or third!) set was in a bedroom or kitchen. They were a substitute for lugging the TV around, and they also reflected the growth of video games and home computers.

TV rapidly became the most time-consuming medium. This fact alone implies that it was not an exhausting activity but was used for relaxation and entertainment. In 1961 it was already overwhelmingly the nation's 'main activity' in the evening, and the BBC study establishing that fact produced much the same figures when repeated in 1975 (BBC, 1976). An ITV study in 1966 found TV easily the most popular leisure activity, followed

Table 6.11 Homes with more than one TV set

	1979	1981	1982	1983	1984	1985	1986	1987
Homes (%)	31	34	39	46	49	55	56	57

Source: IBA.

by 'entertaining friends' and 'reading newspapers and magazines'. Pubs, clubs and sport were right down the list. Watching televised sport was by far the most popular activity on Saturday afternoons (51 per cent of men, 34 per cent of women) (IBA, 1967). The government's annual *Social Trends* figures show sport the only serious rival to TV among the young, and gardening and DIY among the middle-aged (especially men).

TV stole its time from radio. Radio's peak hour audience (6.00 pm to 11.00 pm) dived from 35 per cent of the population in early 1947 to about 4 per cent in the early 1960s. The crossover year was 1955, when radio and TV each had half the audience, both with 15 per cent. Radio fluctuated thereafter more than any other medium. Within a generally low level, there were short-run increases in listening hours, from 7.5 per week in 1966 to 9.2 in 1972, for instance, and the amount stayed at about that level. But radio's 'reach' continued to decline. In 1970 52 per cent of the population listened at some point during the day, but only 43 per cent in 1986. Those who did listen tended to listen more. There were more radio sets than people in Britain in the 1980s (like sheep in New Zealand). Radio, in general, became *par excellence* the medium used while doing something else, mainly housework, preparing and eating meals and getting up or ready for bed. Fewer than a quarter described themselves as 'just listening' in a 1971 survey.

TV's effect on newspaper reading was less obvious. 'Reading' a paper is a varying and imprecise activity anyway. (Does doing the crossword count? What if you are watching TV at the same time?) Early studies suggested TV did reduce the time spent reading a paper. But researchers continued to show people spending large amounts of time at it. The average man read his paper for 69 minutes a day, according to an IPC survey in 1972–3, and the average woman for 47 minutes. Similarly, 4 per cent of *Sun* readers spent a heroic two hours or more reading the *Sun* every day, according to a 1975 study for the Press Commission. The same study found that people who read a daily paper were *more* likely to watch the news on TV than people who did not.

The newspaper readership tables produced for the advertising industry (Tables 6.2 and 6.3, for example) used rather generous definitions of 'read', along the lines 'Did you see a copy of this paper yesterday?' On that basis, TV was unlikely to damage the press. If radio had depended on advertising revenue to operate on its 1940s scale, TV would have killed it. TV arguably did help kill the *News Chronicle* in that way, and perhaps the London evening press. But TV's main effect was to change the way in which people used their papers, more than to reduce their use.

It was clear by the late 1950s that TV, like radio before it, would provide the 'main facts' and the latest news, and that people wanted to follow up the details in a newspaper. TV scored better than the national dailies for nearly all the categories of news listed in a survey for the 1974 Press Commission (Table 6.12). Its dominance over other media built up steadily through the 1980s (Table 6.13). Newspaper interest shifted, too, towards entertainment, and, as has been demonstrated, TV itself became an important item in the press. The single most important reason quoted to the Press Commission for reading a provincial paper was in order to find out what was on TV that night. As the press had found with radio between the wars, moreover, people liked to compare a newspaper account of, say, a televised play or football match with their own impression.

Did TV kill the cinema? It is natural to assume so. The weekly audience slumped from 25 million in 1955 to 2 million in 1976 (see Table 6.14 for annual figures). The problem is to know how far to link the rise and fall of the two media not to each other but to some independent factor. Docherty and others, for instance, argue that mass cinema-going fitted an era of large working-class urban populations with increasing leisure.

Table 6.12 Ranking of news subjects in TV and national daily papers, 1975

'A useful source of news about':	TV (%)	rank order	National dailies (%)	rank order
the government	66	2	50	1=
political parties	45	3	33	4
other countries	72	1	50	1=
trade unions	35	5	26	5=
business and industry	34	6	35	3
football	29	8	26	5=
horse racing	8	10=	11	9
fashions	17	9	16	8
people in entertainment	41	4	25	7
the local region	30	7	9	10
the local council	8	10=	2	11

Source: Derived from Royal Commission on the Press 1974–7. Respondents aged 16+.

Table 6.13 Sources of most news

	1980 (%)	1982 (%)	1984 (%)	1986 (%)	1988 (%)
World news					
Television	52	58	62	65	65
Newspapers	33	27	23	25	25
Radio	14	12	13	10	9
Talking to people, etc.	1	1	1	1	1
Local news					
Television	12	12	18	17	23
Newspapers	61	58	54	56	51
Radio	10	12	13	12	12
Talking to people, etc.	12	14	12	10	10

Source: IBA.

and a little spare cash. Late 1950s 'affluence' − cars, holidays, pop records, coffee bars, more comfortable and family-centred homes − turned cinema into just one more leisure pursuit

Table 6.14   Cinema admissions per annum

Date	(m)
1945	1,585
1950	1,396
1955	1,182
1960	501
1965	327
1970	193
1975	116
1980	96
1984	53
1985	70

Sources: Board of Trade/*Social Trends* to 1984. 1985 figure is a Marplan poll figure, reported in *Social Trends*.

among a range of alternatives. TV, on this analysis, was a beneficiary of those social trends and cinema a victim (Docherty, Morrison and Tracey, 1987).

The result, again, was a changed medium. Comedies continued to pull in the biggest audiences, followed by thrillers and adventure films. Profits were made by a small number of heavily promoted productions. Most people continued to go to the cinema occasionally, and about two-fifths of C2 and DE audiences in 1986 claimed feature films were their favourite TV programmes. It was cinema-going, not films, that changed. By 1970 the regular cinema audience had become disproportionately young, middle class and male.

In general, then, as TV percolated through social life, people accommodated their use of other media to it. This is not to say that TV was always dominant. The pattern of its use, like that of other media, was variable. TV-watching always dropped in summer, with differences of up to 20 per cent between winter and summer averages. People normally read fewer newspapers in summer too. Getting readers to renew the subscription cancelled on holiday in August had long been a challenge to circulation managers. Radio listening, on the other hand, was less variable.

Media use also varied during the week, being heaviest at the weekend. Sections of the quality Sunday papers, especially the colour magazines, were still being read well into the following week. Usage also varied, in ways one would expect, during each day. Peak time for radio, once it had reached its post-TV level, was in the early morning, when people were getting up, having breakfast and driving to work. Women continued to listen in quite large numbers through the morning. The afternoon audience steadily declined, built up for an hour or so in the late afternoon and then surrendered to TV, except for another late-night blip. For TV, subject to the pattern of broadcast programme hours, the peak was at the other end of the day. Newspaper reading, again, was fitted in round the working day, mostly in the morning and evening, with a mid-day blip. Media use varied significantly too with events. The Olympic Games, World Cup football, wars, royal weddings, natural disasters and accidents, could all distort a month's figures.

All those patterns and differences can be qualified by taking account of age, gender and social class. These changed least in the most stable medium of the period (in terms of usage), the press. Tables 6.2 and 6.3 have already illustrated the class skew of different papers, and the smaller age and gender skew. By comparison, radio and TV audiences were homogenous for most of the period, not least because there was only a limited choice for 10 years after 1945.

The war had seen some very large audiences. The nine o'clock news regularly held the attention of 50 per cent of the population, and comedy and variety 40 per cent. Four people out of five heard the D-Day Normandy invasion in June 1944 announced on the radio news. Tommy Handley's comedy classic, *ITMA*, with its cast of characters and catch-phrases (entirely lost on later generations), convulsed half the nation every week.

Peace immediately sent the news ratings down by one-third, but the pulling power of radio in its heyday is shown in the fact that 45 per cent of the people listened to the half-hour general election speeches in the 1945 campaign – feats of concentration (however imperfect) inconceivable in 1990. Successor to *ITMA* was Wilfred Pickles' comedy quiz and chat show, *Have A Go!*

This was attracting an average weekly audience of 54 per cent by 1948, a record for any regular light entertainment show on radio or TV ever since.

The gradual increase and specialization of radio channels disintregrated the audience. As with the peak-hours curve, it tended to go in the opposite direction to TV. In contrast to viewing, radio listening generally decreased with age, was highest among the higher social grades and had no female bias. The figures for 1986 (Table 6.15) show clearly the distinct appeal of each channel. Table 6.16 shows comparable figures for TV and Table 6.17 gives channel profiles. Channel shares had varied somewhat over the years, quite apart from the changes caused by the introduction of BBC2 and Channel 4 (Table 6.18). Regardless of fluctuations, BBC1 reflected closely the class composition of the population as a whole; ITV had a working-class skew right from the start; all channels (especially ITV) had a female skew; and all had an age profile considerably older than the population as a whole (in the 1970s, on the other hand 5–14 year olds had watched the most).

Compared with the press and radio, however, the TV audience remained very mixed: most viewers watched most channels for some of the time. TV-watching had become a relatively passive activity by the 1980s. In the early days it was like cinema in the home, watched with rapt attention. Now it was more of a cross between cinema and radio, sometimes watched intently, but sometimes left on in the background. Remote control and more channels meant people 'zapped' from one to another, often watching 'television' rather than television programmes. As Barwise and Ehrenberg (1988) argue, people came to have little involvement in their TV. Audience sizes were fairly steady from day to day; people tended to avoid demanding programmes; they did not worry about missing episodes of a serial or series; they often showed rather moderate levels of attention and appreciation.

Viewers were therefore happy with a mixed diet, rather as though, in a public library, they sometimes picked up *The Times*, sometimes the *Daily Mail*, sometimes the *Sun*. People typically watched a bit of many things instead of sticking rigidly

Table 6.15 Radio services: shares of listening, by age, sex and class, 1986

	BBC Radio 1	BBC Radio 2	BBC Radio 3	BBC Radio 4	BBC local	All BBC	ILR	Other	All radio
Age									
4–15	54	4	0	2	3	63	33	4	100
16–34	56	5	1	5	3	70	27	3	100
35–54	20	24	2	14	10	70	26	4	100
55+	4	33	2	19	19	77	18	5	100
Sex									
Males	33	18	2	10	8	71	25	4	100
Females	20	19	1	13	11	73	24	3	100
Social Class									
AB	20	19	5	31	6	81	16	3	100
C1	28	20	2	15	9	74	22	4	100
C2	36	17	1	6	10	70	26	4	100
DE	27	19	1	7	13	67	28	5	100
Total UK aged 4+	30	19	2	12	9	72	24	4	100
hours/minutes heard per head/week	2:35	1:38	0:09	1:01	0:51	6:14	2:06	0:19	3:39

Sources: BRD. Listeners to BBC regions are included in 'other'.

Table 6.16   BBC and ITV: shares of viewing, by age, sex and class, 1986

	BBC1	BBC2	Percent of each group viewing All BBC	ITV	C4	All ITV
Age						
4–15	41	9	50	43	7	50
16–34	37	12	49	42	9	51
35–54	38	12	50	41	9	50
55+	35	12	47	45	8	53
Sex						
Males	38	13	51	41	8	49
Females	36	11	47	45	8	53
Social Class						
AB	46	14	60	32	8	40
C1	41	11	52	40	8	48
C2	36	11	47	45	8	53
DE	34	11	45	47	8	55
Total UK age 4+	37	12	49	43	8	51
hours/minutes viewed per head/week	10.08	3.07	13.15	11.47	2.11	13.58

Sources: BARB/AGB

to films or sport or news. This did not, of course, mean that all programmes were watched equally. Audiences varied from the minuscule for further education, to 20–25 million for 'major events' like the Cup Final and Christmas Day programmes. Because of the decisive influence of the time a programme was scheduled, audience size was not a reliable indicator of actual popularity, and both networks researched audience preferences, eventually evolving a joint Audience Appreciation Index. In general, women, older people and the lower socio-economic groups were the most enthusiastic about what they watched.

The popularity of programme types did not change much, although there was always great variation within them and

Table 6.17 BBC and ITV: channel profiles, by age, sex and class, 1986

	Percent of each channel's viewing provided by each group				
	BBC1	BBC2	ITV	C4	Population UK
Age					
4–15	15	11	14	12	17
16–34	22	22	22	25	29
35–54	27	26	25	27	26
55+	36	41	39	36	28
Sex					
Males	44	47	41	44	49
Females	56	53	59	56	51
Social Class					
AB	17	16	10	13	17
C1	19	17	16	16	20
C2	29	29	31	31	28
DE	35	38	43	40	35

Source: BARB/AGB

Table 6.18 BBC and ITV: audience shares

Channel	1956 (%)	1960–1 (%)	1965–6 (%)	1971 (%)	1976 (%)	1980–1 (%)	1987–8 (%)
BBC1	38	46	45	45	49	39	37
BBC2	–	–	*	7	8	12	12
Total BBC	38	46	45	52	57	51	49
ITV	62	54	55	48	43	49	42
Channel 4	–	–	–	–	–	–	9
Total ITV	62	54	55	48	43	49	51

1956: evening viewing only; 1980–1 figures are from IBA handbook; others are BBC/BARB.
* The small audience with BBC2 available watched it for about 20 per cent of their viewing time.

overlap between them. In their 1958 diet (which did not yet include so many top feature films or so much news), men gave their highest preferences to sport, plays, news, travel, variety, documentaries, westerns and current affairs, and their lowest to serious music, religion and science. Women put plays, news and quizzes top, with sport roughly where men put religion, and science and serious music bottom (BBC, quoted in Tunstall, 1983, p. 112). Young people were more interested in films, crime and quizzes than their elders.

The different programme categories of the 1980s prevent exact comparison. In 1986 drama, series and serials, sport and documentaries all scored high on the Appreciation Index. Feature films, quiz shows, panel games, variety and the news were less popular. In sheer audience numbers, however, the programme rankings were less varied. Light entertainment, sport, feature films, soap operas and crime series got the highest regular audiences, followed by sport, drama and general interest series, chat shows, the news, documentaries, one-off plays and current affairs.

Newspaper readers' preferences are an equally complex business but cannot be dealt with here at length. One may argue indefinitely how far contents followed taste and how far they created it, but there is no doubt that the broad 'entertainment' appeal of the press increased at the expense of hard news and information. News itself became more entertaining, and technologies enabling better graphics and presentation made features more attractive.

The sheer quantity of matter meant that people did not read all their newspaper. Like the effect of programme scheduling on TV audience sizes, a story put on the front page was much more likely to be read than something buried inside, and 'page traffic' figures show slightly higher noting of items on right-hand than left-hand pages.

Readers' interests coincided generally with the news values listed at the start of the chapter. Home news was preferred over foreign, news about things familiar to the reader over the unfamiliar. Particular items like cartoons and horoscopes often had high readerships; leading articles did not. News about the government attracted attention; politics and parties were less popular. Sport attracted more men than women; fashions and women's features, obviously, more women than men.

Readers of quality papers wanted more 'serious' matter. Research for the 1974 Press Commission confirmed both that they enjoyed their paper less than readers of the populars and that they would miss it worse if deprived of it. This was interesting general confirmation that the element of 'serious' content that had been an important part of the deceased *Daily Herald* and *News Chronicle* was no longer something the non-quality reader was prepared to pay for in a daily paper. For the non-Conservative parties, too, it was melancholy news — blazoned every day in the tabloid approach of the *Sun*. The findings also supported this author's conclusion in a review of data in the early 1960s, that the further along the socio-economic scale one went, the more were entertainment and relaxation the motives for newspaper-reading (Seymour-Ure, 1968).

The entertainment role of the press was confirmed too by the Press Commission finding that most people felt their paper gave them as much news as they wanted. Among tabloid readers there was also a strong awareness of their paper's sensationalism, tendency to invade private grief and to print too many silly or trivial stories. The corresponding regular complaints against TV were about bad language, violence and sex (in that order). ITV viewers were most likely to be offended and BBC2 the least.

'Entertainment', of course, is an extremely general term. Over the years, many studies analysed people's motivations for media use in great detail, and many of the specific findings would count as 'entertainment'. Quiz programmes, for instance, appealed to people as a means of excitement and escape from worries, an opportunity to rate oneself in comparison with other people and possibly to learn something. Soap operas, naturally, provided endless scope for companionship, both with the fictional characters and as a conversation topic with friends and at work. Such studies resound with heartfelt quotations: 'I like to hear the sound of voices in the house'; 'The programme reminds me that I could be worse off than I am'; 'It sometimes helps me to understand my own life' (McQuail, 1972). Such motivations cut across different media and remind us again of the extent to which media permeate our lives. As with patterns of ownership, the impression of contents and media usage over the years is of an increasingly interlocking system, the user's version of conglomeration. Although it does not show up in the analyses, content surely also became more international, in source of origin, if not always in substance.

Within the system, finally, there were varying combinations of medium, content and audience interest. The world of rock and pop music — non-existent, virtually, in 1945 — linked radio, records, tapes, video and magazines, with a relatively small and specialized TV element. Sport was integral to the national and local press, TV and to a diminishing extent (except for cricket) to radio. Politics was the preserve of press, radio, TV and a few specialized periodicals. Fashion, 'life styles' and women's interests (an increasingly anomalous category) thrived in magazines and the press. Drama was strong in film, TV and radio; news, in TV, radio and press. Sex was featured most freely on film and, within the medium's limits, in magazines, with TV and newspapers inhibited by mass taste and public policy. These links all had several levels: financial, organizational, promotional, international, advertising, audience. The different patterns overlapped, linking, in a wide sense, to form the intricate media system as a whole.

7 Media, Government and Politics: the Intrusion of Television

Media observe and report the work of government and politics. Their decisions about how to do so inevitably make them offer an interpretation too − a judgement of the meaning and significance of what they see. Such judgements often go further and include criticism or approval.

That much could be said of most subjects in the media − football, for example. But media relations with government and politicians are distinctive for two reasons. First, the press and broadcasting provide important arenas or forums within which political argument is carried on. Second, the government can take powers over the media. Neither fact makes the relationship unique. For a dramatist, for instance, the TV studio *is* the stage − a new theatrical forum, requiring different skills from conventional theatre. Similarly other institutions, such as the courts and organizations controlling large capital, can exercise various kinds of power over media. But the government, as the instrument of the state, is in the strongest position of all to exercize power, either by making laws or by exerting the kind of informal pressures the Governors of the BBC have frequently endured.

Extra edge is given to the government's power to control media by the fact that, if it is used, the government interferes with an instrument of its own accountability. In constitutional theory, the accountability of the government lies through Parliament to the electorate. In practice, however, the rise of mass suffrage made the government dependent upon the media. Governments have naturally been jealous that media controlled the means by which most people got most of their information about government, and that media, in the 1945–90 period, provided almost no opportunities for governments to present themselves on their own terms. Media, equally, have traditionally suspected governments of itching to censor them. Whenever a government does so, media organizations believed in 1990 as strongly as in 1945, the major social force preventing unaccountable despotism is weakened, if not destroyed.

This historic tension between government and the press has never been much relaxed, and the decades after 1945 are no exception . The twangs could be unpredictable, like the snap of argument in a family row. In 1947, for instance, the MP Garry Allighan ruined his career by writing an article in a small newspaper trade journal, the *World's Press News*, alleging that MPs were 'lubricated into loquacity' by free drinks from journalists, in return for political titbits. Upon inquiry, the only journalist who could be found to admit to the practice was Allighan himself (journalism was his profession) . The Commons expelled him and censured the magazine's editors. (Allighan made a new life in South Africa.) The Suez crisis of 1956 saw a similar episode. When petrol rationing was announced, the *Sunday Express* appeared to allege that MPs were giving themselves unfair shares. The editor, John Junor, was summoned in pomp to the bar of the Commons and made to apologize.

While specific cases were unpredictable, there was perhaps a general rule about government/media tension. Political crises, as Jeremy Tunstall put it, commonly had a 'media sub-plot' (Tunstall, 1970). The Allighan case was a sub-plot of a more general crisis in relations between politics and the press in the post-war years, reflected in the appointment of the Royal Commission on the Press in 1947. The *Sunday Express* case was part of a sub-plot of government/media rows throughout the Suez crisis.

Those two incidents of tension were in the parliamentary forum. For most politicians, Parliament and political parties were the context in which their relations with media were carried on. For journalists, too, these were convenient benchmarks by which to judge the importance of personalities and events. The number of candidates fielded by a minor party at a general election, for instance, was the normal test of whether to give that party free broadcasting time. A frequent source of tension between media and politicians (in or out of government) was their differing views of whether Parliament and parties were getting the right amount and kind of media coverage.

The relative importance of particular parties, and of Parliament itself, changed between 1945 and 1990. Many people claimed the influence of Parliament was in decline. But parties, Parliament and Cabinet remained the dominant political institutions. On the media side, by contrast, TV progressively grew to match, and in some ways to supplant, the press as the chief political medium. This chapter, therefore, explores the intrusion of TV as a force in politics. The following chapter deals with the changing relations of media, parties, and prime ministers.

The intrusion of television: four stages

Parties made much of the running in the development of political broadcasting until the coming of ITV. Broadcasters often determined the style — how to interview a minister, what to ask about and so on. But many of the advances in getting *access* to the medium were driven, not surprisingly, by the spur of competition. This was sharpest in general elections, and when advances came between elections, they often did so with the next election in mind. The watershed year in the period 1945–90 can thus appropriately be regarded as the election year of 1959.

We are rapidly losing the capacity to imagine what general elections were like before TV. Until 1959, there was no radio and TV coverage of the campaign at all, beyond bulletins about the dissolution of Parliament and the weather on polling day.

This led to absurd situations where overseas listeners to the BBC World Service could hear reports of a major international speech by Winston Churchill in 1951 but British voters could not. (They could read about it, of course.) This 'Trappist' policy had one exception: the series of party election broadcasts produced quite independently by each party, with technical production assistance if required. These broadcasts had been numerous in 1945 — 26, totalling over 10 hours. In 1950 there were half as many, totalling half the length. Each party made one fifteen-minute broadcast in 1951 as well, but still in 1955 the radio broadcasts outnumbered the televised. Similar party broadcasts happened between elections, at the rate of three or four a year for the major parties, on each of radio and TV. But there were very few political interviews and discussions, and party managers kept tight control on who broadcast. Government party members needed clearance from Number Ten.

In 1959, on the initiative of ITV, the broadcasters held their breath and jumped into the electoral pond, to describe the froth and eddies of the campaign. This was arguably the single most important moment in the history of political broadcasting. Hitherto broadcasters took politicians almost entirely at the politicians' own value. Their main exercise of judgement was how much time to make available for the parties' own broadcasts. From now on, broadcasters were to make qualitative judgements about the news value of election campaigns; the relative importance of issues, personalities, minor parties; and how they should all be treated. Broadcasters increasingly took politicians at the *broadcasters'* value. Parties had to earn their coverage; to sell themselves, first to the broadcasters and through them to the electorate. The best portent of the future in 1959 was the invention of the daily campaign party press conference, introduced by Labour to catch the broadcasters' attention, and instantly copied by the Conservatives. The same shift of emphasis took place in the coverage of politics between elections.

This intrusion of TV may be divided loosely into four periods — two before 1959 and two afterwards.

Inauguration: TV at the heels of radio

Before 1959 TV news and 'current affairs' (the description, and the BBC department, which covered most political broadcasting) was in its infancy. The BBC still had a monopoly, and the best date with which to mark the end of the period is the end of the TV monopoly in 1955. ITV brought a breath of fresh air both by the stimulus of competition and by its own willingness to innovate.

TV in the early years was radio with pictures, and it followed exactly the same rules established over the previous quarter century for the treatment of 'controversial' subjects on radio. Applied to politics and government, the principles of 'public service broadcasting', agreed between successive broadcasters and party managers, could be reduced to a few simple ideas. First, there should be no editorializing by the BBC. Second, political coverage should be balanced. Third, the BBC should retain the right to decide who could broadcast, subject to the statutory power of the responsible minister to require the broadcasting of a particular communication. The operation of these principles caused continual difficulty, especially because they came under most strain in times of political tension. They were also capable of infinite refinement and the refinements themselves could be informally glossed.

The principle of 'balance' was not as contentious in the post-war years as later on, partly, no doubt, as a hangover from the wartime coalition mood and partly because the Conservative and Labour parties so dominated the political scene. 'Balance' meant treatment appropriate to a party's strength, which was measured by its parliamentary representation. The annual allocation of party political broadcasts was settled on this basis by a committee of party leaders and BBC executives. Parties got their proportionate share of coverage in the daily parliamentary report and the news bulletins. Careful count was kept of how many parliamentarians gave 'talks' (a disappearing genre by the 1980s) or had appeared in the comparatively few discussion programmes such as *Any Questions*, which began in 1948. Occasionally, MPs would ask in the Commons for details of these tallies.

If balance caused problems, they were either for groups that were simply beyond the pale — excluded from consideration by their failure to seek or achieve parliamentary success — or for the party managers. Good broadcasters, like good cartoonists, often turned out to be individualists or dissidents. The *Tribune* wing of the Labour party, under Aneurin Bevan's leadership and including gifted broadcasters such as *Tribune's* editor, Michael Foot, was a constant irritant to the Attlee leadership. Foot was part of a popular weekly TV programme, *In The News*, made up of disputatious conversationalists. But balance *within* parties was not the BBC's concern, except indirectly. It involved them in frequent negotiation about individual broadcasters, but it was clear that the parties themselves were in charge.

More delicate for the broadcasters, and fraught with the possibility of rows that might do long term damage to the BBC, was the issue of broadcasts by government ministers. Clearly, if ministers could command the microphone at will, BBC 'independence' would amount to nothing. Ministers must therefore appear only 'by invitation'. In what circumstances, if they sought an invitation, might it be refused? If granted, must the invitation be extended also to the Opposition, so as to maintain the principle of balance? If so, should minor parties be included (which, in this period, meant a tiny Liberal rump)? Here was a minefield indeed, and obviously it was in everybody's interest to define precise rules. These were set out in 1947 in a short *aide-mémoire* between the government, the Opposition and the BBC — one of the key texts in the history of relations between broadcasting and the State (Goldie, 1977, p. 341–4).

The note distinguished four types of political broadcasts. First were *uncontroversial ministerial broadcasts*. These could be made at the request of the government, to explain policy or legislation in a 'purely factual way', or to appeal to the nation on matters requiring public help (such as fuel economy). These broadcasts were to be as impartial as possible. The second type were *controversial ministerial broadcasts*. These were likely to be more tricky, because it was the Opposition that would claim they were controversial — regardless of the government's view — and would want a chance to reply. This opportunity should be sought from the government through the normal party channels, but the BBC reserved the right to make its own decision either way, if the parties did not agree within a few days. The third type were *party political broadcasts*, allocated annually by agreement between the parties and the BBC on the basis of parliamentary arithmetic, and put together by the parties themselves. The fourth were *controversial discussions* in which two or more parliamentarians on different sides took part.

Those arrangements were clear in themselves. But they promised little joy for the BBC, which was bound, sooner or later, to be caught in a row between government and Opposition about rights of reply, or in a row with the government about a ministerial broadcast being made at all. The 1956 Suez crisis provided both.

The *aide-mémoire* also reserved the BBC's right to let parliamentarians of 'outstanding national eminence' broadcast, if they might otherwise be shut out by having become 'detached' from their party. This was a sop to the argument that Churchill should not have been kept off the air in his pre-war wilderness years. As Asa Briggs points out, however, the BBC continued to play safe by not inviting Aneurin Bevan to the microphone, for instance, after his estrangement from the Attlee leadership in 1951 (Briggs, 1979, p. 615).

The agreement reflected, of course, an era in which political broadcasting of any kind was extremely rare and such notions as a 'right of reply' were prizes to be fought for. Finally, the note included the rule which most perfectly conveys the status of political broadcasting until the mid-1950s: the 'Fourteen-Days' rule. This was included at the request of the BBC, which had invented it in 1944 so as to avoid pressure from ministers who wanted to broadcast about current legislation which, as the wartime coalition began to strain, might be controversial. The rule now consisted simply in an agreement not to broadcast discussions or statements on any issues during the fortnight before they were debated in either House. As a result, programmes were frequently being replanned or withdrawn. On the BBC's estimate, 'some hundreds' of items in various stages of preparation were potentially vulnerable, and producers tended to sideline 'risky' subjects.

The ministerial broadcast provisions of the *aide-mémoire* had in fact removed the need for the rule at all. In 1951 the Beveridge Committee disapproved of it, and by 1953 the BBC was pressing hard to drop it. But by now the party leaders themselves had got used to it. After much argument, the BBC insisted that responsibility be clearly taken by the government, so it was issued as a formal ministerial directive (covering ITV too) in 1955. It survived until after the Suez crisis the following year.

The story of the 'Fourteen-Days' rule showed the broadcasters as subservient, in a strict sense: deferring to a crudely literal notion of the sovereignty of Parliament. But it had a kind of beauty, for it reflected in an extreme form the fact that in those post-war years, when radio still treated politics on a small scale, the BBC adapted its own needs very largely to the people, the institutions, the manners, the values and the style of discourse that it sought to report. In style, this was symbolized in the hushed tones for which the commentator Richard Dimbleby became famous on such occasions as the Coronation and the State Opening of Parliament (such tones were due to the need to speak quietly but sounded like deference). Physically, it meant a policy of inconspicuousness, epitomized in the practice of hiding the microphone in a vase of flowers when the Queen broadcast her Christmas message (first televised in 1957).

Inconspicuousness was more of a problem for TV than for radio: bright lights and big cameras were two of the reasons regularly quoted by MPs from the 1960s onwards in opposing televised debates. But this early period of inauguration saw TV gradually following radio's lead. In 1950 TV first covered the general election results. In 1951 came the first televised party election broadcasts (the BBC offered time in 1950 but the parties turned it down). In 1952 R A Butler was the first

Chancellor of the Exchequer to appear on TV. In 1953 the Conservative party produced the first TV party political broadcast. From 1952 onwards, ministers began to take part occasionally in the interview programme *Press Conference*, and in 1953 the first *Panorama* appeared. In 1954 the first Budget broadcasts by the Chancellor and Opposition spokesmen took place, and in October the Conservative party's annual conference was televised.

Adjustment, exploration, initiative

On the broadcasting side, the start of ITV marks a new period. Among the politicians, the corresponding change is the succession of Churchill by Eden in 1955. Differences between prime ministers are discussed in chapter 8: the essential point is that Churchill, 80 in 1954, belonged to a political era of print and live oratory, while Eden, Prime Minister at 57, was still adaptable and had already shown in election broadcasts that he could use TV effectively. Between 1955 and 1959, then, with the number of TV licences surging ahead, the broadcasters began to be aware of their muscle and of more welcoming surroundings. The balance started to tip: politics began to adapt to broadcasting, as politicians became keener to use it, by opening their arenas (the Conservatives' annual conference was a forerunner) or by using the arena of the TV studio.

Eden was content to see the 'Fourteen-Days' rule lapse. The Commons voted by 271−126 in November 1955 to retain it; but it could not withstand the national clamour of the Suez crisis, and it was suspended, supposedly for a 'trial period', in December 1956. Eden gave the first 'ministerial broadcast' in April 1956, when the Russian leaders Bulganin and Khrushchev paid a State visit. He was furious to discover during the Suez crisis that he could not address the nation by radio and TV at his own discretion, and that the Opposition leader Hugh Gaitskell might have a right of reply if the BBC agreed to invite him. He gave two such broadcasts, one on 26 August and the other on 3 November, when British and French troops were preparing to occupy the canal. Gaitskell broadcast on 4 November.

To Grace Wyndham Goldie, a leading BBC executive in the development of political broadcasting, Eden's use of TV in the crisis was the beginning of TV's primacy over sound. This was reinforced by the introduction of current affairs 'magazine' programmes such as the immensely popular early evening weekday programme *Tonight*. This trained new generations of producers to think specifically in TV terms. Interviewing, to give an instance of the difference, became, as Mrs Goldie put it, more journalistic and less reverential. This was even more true at ITN, which looked for its style to the United States rather than the BBC. ITN hired crisp young men like Robin Day and Chris Chataway, who stayed on the right side of brashness but were discouraged from calling ministers 'sir' or ducking hard questions. 'By 1956–57,' Mrs Goldie noted, 'the questioning of political leaders on TV by impartial interviewers had become established custom' (Goldie, 1977, p. 208).

In 1958, TV covered three significant political events, each quite distinct and each representing a kind of 'intrusion' by the medium. Together they heralded the watershed year of 1959. One, the latest and the most ceremonial, but important symbolically, was live coverage of the State Opening of Parliament. More important than the constitutional symbolism of the Crown and Parliament, with the Queen reading a speech prepared by her ministers, was the symbolism of the event as expressing the politicians' willingness to take a risk. The risk, hardly a great one but much vaunted, was that TV, by relaying a ceremony hitherto rather private and well understood by everyone involved, might make the viewing multitude wrongly believe that the partisan legislative proposals in the speech necessarily had the Queen's personal support. This programme, in its way, was a milestone.

Entirely different was the first CND Aldermaston march at Easter, 1958. Though it was not planned on these lines, the march can be seen as the start of 'visual politics' in the postwar era. In 1958, marchers walked *to* Aldermaston. Thereafter, because it made so much better a climax, not least in publicity, they marched *from* Aldermaston, ending with a rally in Trafalgar Square. The march was massively televised. Until the decline of CND it remained a superb instrument of pressure group publicity – visually varied; sustained over several days in a dead news period (a bank holiday weekend); embracing both ordinary people and several kinds of social and political elite; combining the predictable and the unexpected and culminating in spectacle and oratory in the greatest public space of the capital.

The iconography of marches and demonstrations, and their adaptation to secure the best TV coverage, became matters of professionalism – for example in the USA during the Vietnam years and the civil rights movement. When CND revived in the early 1980s, the simplicity of marches was replaced by more complex visual symbols. These were well suited to TV coverage, like the encirclement of a nuclear base by protesters holding hands. In 1958, surely, that would have seemed a rather strange idea.

In 1958, thirdly, came the pioneering coverage of a by-election by the Granada ITV company and ITN, with the BBC Northern Region in tow. Broadcasters had previously feared flouting the Representation of the People Act if they covered elections. The Act forbad anyone but a candidate's agent to spend money getting him or her elected. The press were exempt, but not broadcasters. News programmes cost money, so a programme which reported one candidate in a constituency but not all, or not on an equal basis, might break the law. ITV was also cramped by the Television Act of 1954, which appeared to limit party coverage to balanced discussions and debates and not to allow, say, a report from the hustings. ITV decided to test these restrictions. It covered the progress of the by-election campaign at Rochdale in March 1958. The heavens did not fall. Having successfully set this precedent, the broadcasters went on to cover subsequent elections in Kelvingrove, Torrington and Northern Ireland, and then the general election of October 1959.

Political broadcasting comes of age: 1960–1974

The fall of Edward Heath's government in February 1974 may be taken as the nominal end of the third period of TV's intrusion into politics (and radio's too, on a minor scale). This is not because TV played a conspicuous and decisive part in the election campaign and the miners' strike that led Heath to call it, but because Heath was visibly uncomfortable with TV, especially compared with his predecessor Harold Wilson. It is tempting to see his years in office as the time when politicians were no longer able to avoid coming to terms with TV. The question could now be seriously asked: which is 'bigger' – TV or politics? The broadcasters extended the range of their political coverage, though the cameras did not quite get into Parliament itself. Politicians adapted their behaviour more closely to the conventions of the screen. Formal rules, such as the *aide-mémoire* and the Representation of the People Act, were liberalized. TV's own political arenas – current affairs and discussion programmes such as *Panorama* and individual documentaries – began to be valued as such in their own right. Backbenchers in particular saw the advantages of a brief TV or radio appearance over a Commons speech that got no coverage.

Examples of all these changes dot the years. The Conservative party annual conference, for instance, used to meet for its first few days in the absence of the leader. On a Saturday morning, as a finale, he would arrive to make a rousing speech. Heath, elected Leader in 1965, with the party's fortunes to restore and his own authority to build, began the practice of attending throughout the conference, so that no opportunity of TV coverage would be lost.

Heath had been chosen as leader by a formal system of voting. Previous Conservative leaders had always 'emerged' – a euphemism for selection by a senior clique on the basis of 'soundings' within the party. In 1963 these soundings had to be taken during the annual conference, as luck would have it, since Harold Macmillan decided impetuously to retire as a result of sudden illness. In measured privacy, 'soundings' might be a dignified and justifiable method of selecting the right successor. In the glare of TV, they looked disorganized and unedifying, even if Lord Home, who 'emerged' (jettisoning his peerage), proved a popular choice. The procedure was quickly reformed, and TV had played a part in making that happen.

Election campaigns changed in this period, each one seeing further adjustment to new opportunities of TV. The timing and venue of speeches changed to fit the convenience of TV news and relay systems. So did their style. Heath commented in 1966 that TV coverage made his jokes stale more quickly. Wilson found in 1964 that to make repartee with hecklers effective on TV, he must repeat a comment before demolishing it. Leaders went on 'walkabouts' for the cameras, more than on extended hustings tours. Coverage focussed increasingly on the party Leaders, not least because of limited camera resources. In 1966 and 1970 more than half of *all* the radio and TV news coverage went on Heath and Wilson. The daily party press conferences became an important fixture. Candidates now came into the TV studios as well, for a growing variety of interview and discussion programmes.

The monarch too unbent to TV. The listening public heard Prince Charles' voice when he gave an interview to the early morning Radio 4 *Today* programme in April 1969. A few months later, 23 million viewers watched a uniquely 'natural' BBC documentary film of the whole royal family at work and play. This was a landmark in royal public relations. It took some of the mystery out of majesty. In the daily round of queenly duties, its equivalent was the development of the walkabout – spontaneous contact taking the royals off the red carpet (but still on the opposite side of the cordon) as they talked to people in the crowd that came to see them on public occasions. Walkabouts, of course, made good human-interest television.

These years also saw expansion of political programming. In this the satire shows of the 1960s should be included, for politicians were a ready butt of the irreverent brand of young mimics and humourists. *That Was The Week That Was*, anchored by the youthful David Frost, provided a Saturday night cabaret based largely on people and events in the news of the previous week. This was ground more homely to malodorous bog plants and stinging nettles than to clean, undeviating rows of 'balanced' runner beans. It came under the watchful eye of the 'Talks and Current Affairs' department, the BBC's experts in managing 'balance'. It had the backing of a Director-General, Hugh Greene, new in office, who knew as a young man the fizz of cabaret in the Berlin of the early 1930s. An emphatic sign of its political nature was that the show was taken off the air in the run-up to the 1964 general election. But it had successors with similar snappy names, like *Not Only But Also*. The actor John Bird became famous for his imitations of Prime Minister Harold Wilson.

The satire programmes were not easy for politicians to attack, for a complainant ran the risk of making himself ridiculous by looking pompous and thereby underlining the satirist's point. The programmes therefore tended to build up resentment. This might then explode. Most famous was Harold Wilson's explosion over the BBC documentary *Yesterday's Men* (1971). This had been intended as an innocent enquiry into the feelings and doings of ministers unexpectedly thrown out of office by the electorate. Wilson thought it tendentious, malicious, biased and quite contrary to the virtues of 'balance'. This very vulnerability, however, illustrates the underlying strength of the broadcasters by the mid-1960s: they might lose battles, but the TV medium was now too entrenched to lose the war.

Part of such entrenchment was the provision of new services. BBC 2 had started in 1964, with a remit to include 'serious' programmes of a kind with which politics tended to be lumped. In 1973 the first commercial radio stations went on air. One by-product of these in the two general elections of 1974 was the first election radio phone-in programmes, for phone-ins were a characteristic commercial radio device.

The idea of ordinary citizens giving voice over the air in an election campaign would have been entirely implausible in the 1950s. But the rules of access were substantially eased by changes in the Representation of the People Act in 1969. These were chiefly prompted by a law case following the 1964 general election, when the defeated Communist in the constituency of the Conservative leader, Sir Alec Douglas-Home, sought (without success) to unseat him, on account of his broadcast coverage. The new Act gave broadcasters the same immunity as the press already enjoyed, and it allowed candidates to broadcast freely on matters that did not concern their own constituency. This confirmed the legality of the front bench 'confrontations' and discussion programmes, which had been a feature of the 1966 campaign.

The 1947 *aide-mémoire* was also changed in 1969, to reflect the new realities of TV and political broadcasting. The category of 'explanatory', uncontroversial ministerial broadcasts was, in effect, abolished by the BBC undertaking to fit them into its regular programmes when required. The controversial or infrequent 'appeal to the nation' broadcasts, on the other hand, were now to be available to the prime minister (or a colleague designated by him) as a right, without the fiction of a BBC invitation. The Opposition were given an automatic right of reply. Third parties, if big enough, were entitled to join in a subsequent broadcast discussion with senior Cabinet and Opposition representatives. All these changes took the heat off the broadcasters.

The last point about political broadcasting in this period is that it produced in Harold Wilson the first TV prime minister. Eden and Macmillan had been sensitive to TV's potential, and Macmillan developed a fine TV manner. But Wilson was the first to build the medium into the prime minister's armoury. This was true in details of performance: talking quite frequently and informally in interview programmes, strengthening the Yorkshire accent, using pipe not cigar on screen. But his approach went also right across the board, to manipulative devices like punishing broadcasters by the selective denial of interview requests or appointing Lord Hill to be Chairman of the BBC Governors from the corresponding position at their arch-rivals, the ITA. These techniques continued, of course, in Wilson's second term of office, 1974–6, which falls in the final period of TV's intrusion. In 1964 the priority he gave to TV was a significant innovation. Heath suffered by comparison most noticeably as a performer. But henceforth all prime ministers must be 'TV prime ministers'.

TV ascendant: 1975–1990

The fourth stage in the intrusion of TV involves changes of degree rather than of kind. Among open political institutions (which excludes the Cabinet and civil service), only the courts still denied entry in 1990 to the cameras, and even the possibility of televised trials was not considered to be in all circumstances inconceivable. In 1989 the Commons, with much dragging of feet, decided the principles that should govern the televising of their proceedings. Regular radio broadcasting had started in 1976 after a short experimental period the previous year. The Lords had let in the cameras in 1985 and seemed to enjoy stealing a march on the Commons. The general elections of the period, in 1979, 1983 and 1987, saw TV ever more dominant over campaign substance and style. To say that 'TV *is* the campaign' was no longer novel, let alone shocking, but a truism.

TV performance was a major factor in decisions about the choice of parliamentary candidates and party leaders. Where Alec Douglas-Home was the first leader to be ditched by his party partly because the decision-makers in 1965 believed (perhaps wrongly) that he was an electoral liability on TV, Neil Kinnock was the first of whom telegenic qualities were said to be a main factor in his selection as Labour leader in 1983. By 1990 politicians shaped their appearance, their style and their rhetoric to the needs of TV.

The range of channels, hours of programming and types of programme proliferated. Channel 4 (1982) and Breakfast Time TV (1983) provided new outlets. Access to the airwaves became easier, for citizens as well as politicians. It was widely remarked that Mrs Thatcher was more troubled by a Bristol housewife on a talkback programme in the 1983 election than by any professional interviewer. Radio 4's *Today* programme was an almost daily forum for ministers and politicians in general.

In the late 1980s a minister took part for the first time in Radio 4's *Any Questions*. After his sensational and unexpected resignation and walkout from a Cabinet meeting about the future of the Westland helicopter company in 1986, Michael Heseltine made 17 broadcast appearances within 24 hours. The depiction of politicians in satirical programmes went a step beyond mimicry with the animated puppets of *Spitting Image*, a translation of caricature to the screen that would have delighted the great newspaper caricaturists of the 1930s and 1940s such as David Low. The royal family were guyed with a lack of restraint unimaginable even in the 1960s.

Living politicians were portrayed by actors also in a genre new to TV — the reconstruction as drama of recent historical events such as the Suez crisis. What was truth and what was fiction? In the 1940s, BBC executives would have agonized interminably, but such plays would, in fact, never have been contemplated. Now, politicians welcomed them, if it suited their purpose. A row about a Falklands War play, for example, centred on complaints that the BBC had cancelled it for being too sympathetic to the government's policy.

The old stopwatch approach to balance and non-partisanship seemed increasingly unrealistic. A glance at the future suggested that balance would be more and more difficult to maintain, if satellites were beaming programmes that did not even originate within British government jurisdiction. The Thatcher government's philosophy of 'market forces' in broadcasting, steered only with a 'light touch', sat uneasily with the old ideas about balance, although these could obviously still be maintained within particular programmes and series. The Conservative party, indeed, established a 'monitoring unit' to check for what it considered bias in TV and radio programmes.

What all this amounted to was that TV had reached political maturity. The generations of politician and of viewers who had to 'learn' TV — how to behave on it, how to watch it — were a vanishing minority. TV behaviour would continue to change, of course. But it was a medium with which nearly everyone in society had grown up and was no longer self-conscious. Even if some of them were no good at it, every politician knew how to use TV by 1990, just as any of them knew how to make a speech or write a piece for the local paper. TV, in sum, was no longer an instrument to be applied *to* politics: it was part of the environment *within* which politics was carried on. Whether it was 'bigger' than politics is a complicated and perhaps fruitless question. Certainly TV was shaped by politicians and governments, among other forces. But equally, politicians and governments could not escape the influence of TV any more than of their native language. TV had become, in a general sense, a forum of political accountability.

The division between these four stages in the intrusion of radio and TV into politics should not be made too sharply. But the stages help to emphasize how great that intrusion was, and how rapid, and to show how much the scope for argument about the forms and extent of broadcasting accountability increased.

Arenas, access and attitudes

This chapter concludes by looking briefly at the development of political broadcasting in a different way. Successive sections deal with the *arenas* in which politicians were seen and heard by broadcasters, the *rules of access*, and the *attitudes* of politicians and broadcasters to each other. Each was affected also by the developments in broadcasting technology, which steadily increased TV's capacity to cover politics in a more flexible, detailed and unobtrusive way.

Broadcasting arenas

'Arena' is here used to mean either a kind of activity, such as a broadcast interview, or a particular place, such as a TV studio or the chamber of the Commons. Many places in which politics is conducted are deliberately public. The arenas in which the broadcasters made their earliest and biggest intrusions were naturally those in which the politicians' own chief purpose was public communication. The negotiations involved were more about details than basic principles. Thus a daily radio report of parliamentary proceedings began in 1945, and *The Week in Westminster* went back to 1929. Election campaigns are intense and concentrated efforts in competitive publicity, and it was predictable that they should have eventually been affected more than any other arenas by the intrusion of the broadcasters, even if the start was timorous for fear of the law. The party annual conferences were another arena which was obviously well suited to TV. On the other hand, the Cabinet, which has no political role of public argument and persuasion as a collective body independent of its members' individual parliamentary roles, imposed the same system of secretiveness and non-attributability upon broadcasters as upon the press.

The general calculation determining a political institution's willingness to let TV into its arenas was whether the results would affect the institution's performance of its proper tasks. The hesitations of the Commons best illustrate the point. As a popularly elected representative and deliberative body, it needed publicity. Yet if this were gained by methods which might diminish its ability to act according to members' views of the best interests of their constituents, such methods would be rejected. Critics feared TV would reduce the quality of debates and encourage exhibitionism and superficiality, and they argued that the primary purposes of the Commons should not be distorted in that way so as to achieve the secondary purpose of publicity.

While existing political arenas gradually adjusted to TV, a number of new arenas developed, which TV was also able to use. These were often designed for the purpose of publicity, taking advantage of convenient moments and locations. Their use became routine over the years. They included airport lounges, aeroplane steps and in-flight interviews, and the routine business of election press conferences, summit briefings and the like. Their routinization was shown by the provision of permanent TV interview rooms in likely locations from London Airport to the House of Lords.

The third type of arena whose growth can be traced through the years was the broadcasters' own programmes. Alongside the intrusion of the broadcasters into the politicians' arenas (including their airplanes) came the politicians' intrusion into the broadcasters'. The development of political TV can be traced in the expansion of programmes from pioneer efforts like *In the News* (1950) and *Press Conference* (1952) through *Panorama* (1953), *Tonight* (1957) and many others with interchangeable self-explanatory names, joined after 1955 by their ITV equivalents (*This Week, World in Action, The World This Weekend*). Some were radio retreads, such as *Question Time*, modelled on Radio's *Any Questions*. Others incorporated formats popularized in the 1970s, such as phone-ins and chat shows.

Rules of access

Use of those various arenas – who might appear on programmes, how often, what they might say – was influenced by a kind of continuous negotiation between government or party managers and broadcasting executives. First, formal rules would be defined. Next, their application to particular cases required a gloss or interpretation. Then circumstances and personalities changed; new understandings would be reached. One day there would be a spectacular row. The air would clear. Then the formal rules would be redefined. There was not something as regular as a cycle, but part of the tension discussed at the start of the chapter was adjusted and kept in bounds by some such process.

The tendency between 1945 and 1990 was to relax controls that at first were tightly imposed. Party managers, in or out of government, did not want their members going on the air at will. Broadcasters, knowing their monopoly depended upon governments, did not wish to court interference through indiscretion. Citizens themselves counted only as audiences not as potential broadcasters.

The history of the *aide-mémoire*, the 'Fourteen-Days' rule and the Representation of the People Act, for instance, punctuated by crises such as Suez, the Falklands War and Northern Ireland, was one of greatly increased opportunities for nearly all kinds of politicians to broadcast, with more frequency and fewer restrictions of 'balance', and for citizens to make their own voices heard in a studio audience or on a phone-in. Of course, the change was only relative, and a few politicians, such as Irish extremists, found their opportunities actually decreased by a formal ban in 1988. For a party leader, the airwaves were more open in 1990 than in 1945 − but more open too for friends and foes, on terms that the leaders could not so firmly control as formerly.

Attitudes of politicians and broadcasters

Changing attitudes are difficult to capture. During most of the period 1945−90, the political decision-makers about broadcasting − ministers and party managers − were people adjusting to the new medium of TV in their maturity. At first, politicians used TV as an extension of radio. The face-to-camera address was typical. Gradually, executives like Mrs Goldie taught them the implications of the visual medium: to realize, for example, that 'vision is part of argument', and that on TV words may be in the service of pictures, not the other way around. Younger party politicians often provided the pressure to make their elders adapt, especially as the younger MPs regularly included a number of broadcasting professionals from the 1960s onwards, mainly at first in the Conservative party.

On the broadcasters' side, the historic shift was to accept TV on its own terms. In the early post-war days, a not untypical attitude was that TV news should be strictly limited − perhaps banned altogether − lest the integrity of the spoken word, and of news priorities related to intrinsic social values, might be defiled by the irrelevant charm of pictures. The underlying belief that politics *ought* to be about words, arguments, verbal and statistical facts, rather than about felt emotions charged through the eye, endured right through the 1980s and was strongly shared by many politicians. Some of the minor rows in the 1960s and 1970s, sometimes conducted in the letter columns of *The Times*, were about precisely such invasions of the linear flow of verbal information (in an interview, for example) by the techniques of a visual medium. The older politician might resent the use of voice-over commentaries superimposed on pictures, or the editing and transposing of sections of an interview to fit a picture sequence or create a 'dialogue' between interviewees; or the simple cuts made to fit a time slot and eliminate a slip of the tongue or a visual infelicity like a yawn. These were the kind of techniques which, as they developed, required the glossing and revising of the formal rules.

Early TV interviews and documentaries later looked stilted because audiences too learnt to receive programmes in the conventional forms gradually derived from the visual character of the medium. For a politician to talk face-to-camera for more than a few minutes, unrelieved, became unusual.

The history of political broadcasting, in terms of attitudes, was thus of changing expectations by politicians, broadcasters and audiences alike about what sort of behaviour would appear on the screen, what would look stilted, old fashioned, brash or unmannerly. Only if all three groups happened to apply broadly similar standards simultaneously, could there be lulls in the otherwise steady rumble of complaints, by viewers, politicians or among broadcasters themselves.

8 Media, Government and Politics: Prime Ministers and Parties

Prime ministers and the media

'The War Between Fleet Street and Downing Street'. That phrase made a good subtitle to the book by a veteran *Sunday Times* reporter, James Margach, about prime ministers and the press before and after the Second World War (Margach, 1978). The main title was *The Abuse of Power*: and it applied to prime ministers. News media typically saw themselves as victims of Downing Street, but prime ministers, equally, saw themselves as victims of the media. Chapter 7 viewed politics from the perspective of television. This one views media more from the perspective of politicians. The same functions are observed, but in a different light.

The media made work for prime ministers, whether they were 'victims' or not. Most of them seem on the whole to have found it tiresome. As the years went by after 1945, the work became harder, too, due chiefly to the growth of television. Prime ministers had to spend more time dealing with media: it became a more important part of the prime ministerial job description. This was partly a matter of personal performance, partly of management. Prime ministers had always been performers, but in Parliament and on the hustings. From the 1950s, as chapter 7 pointed out, they had to perform in the new studio arenas of TV and to adapt old hustings techniques to the cameras. Management involved a correspondingly more important press office at 10 Downing Street, and tactical decisions about the endless permutations of when and how often to broadcast, on what programmes (hence to what audience), with what interviewers, and so on.

By 1990, the development of TV had arguably had three effects upon the premiership. First was the shift in the job description towards more time on media work. Second was a similar increase in the prime minister's role as an opinion leader or mobilizer. General elections, again, highlighted it. Prime ministers dominated their parties' news coverage from the elections of the 1960s onwards. In 1987, 44 per cent of all Conservative mentions in the news on TV and BBC Radio 4 were of Mrs Thatcher. The runner-up, party manager Norman Tebbit, got 15 per cent. Even two out of every five photos of Conservatives in the national dailies were of Mrs Thatcher (Butler and Kavanagh, 1988).

The third effect was to draw the prime minister away from his or her natural parliamentary base. The overdue entry of the cameras to the Commons in 1989 might brake this trend but not reverse it. Indeed it might confirm it, if the cameras and the viewing figures chiefly followed the prime minister. For a specific kind of behaviour, designed for TV, might develop for 'prime minister's question time', for example, while the less newsworthy proceedings carried on much as they had in pre-TV days. In that way 'question time' might move figuratively away from Westminster even if the cameras had moved literally in there. It would become a kind of modified American presidential press conference, with MPs playing the part of journalists.

Compared with her predecessors, Mrs Thatcher spent less time anyway on the floor of the Commons. She also resisted the idea of open press conferences, except occasionally at international meetings where joint or competitive briefings by different leaders were not uncommon. Heath had tried grand, set-piece televised press conferences in the early 1970s. But these were unpopular, not least with print journalists who felt themselves stooges for the cameras, and they were soon abandoned.

Thatcher developed the 'doorstep' session outside Number

10, especially for announcements like that of South Georgia's recapture in the 1982 Falklands War. But these were quick question-and-answer – and picture – opportunities more than detailed briefings. The claim that prime ministers were being drawn away from Westminster rests not on such specific examples but on the cumulative effects of TV coverage in all its forms outside Westminster. Its implications – wholly intangible – concern the nature of the prime minister's authority; the part contributed to it by public reputation and by colleagues' estimates of this; the methods open to a prime minister for managing Parliament and cabinet (whose support, of course, is a precondition of office); and, ultimately, the kind of career people must follow if they seek ministerial office. (Two successful Commonwealth prime ministers of the 1980s, Bob Hawke in Australia and Brian Mulroney in Canada, had spent very little time indeed in Parliament before becoming prime minister.)

Many of those factors themselves affect judgements about the possible 'presidentialization' of the premiership. American presidents are constitutionally excluded from the legislature, so the comparison cannot be made too closely. But just as presidential power, lacking a secure legislative party base, is conventionally described as 'the power to persuade', so it is plausible to argue that the 1970s and 1980s saw an increasingly presidential *style* almost pressed upon prime ministers by TV. Labour's choice of Neil Kinnock as leader for his communication skills, even though he had no great parliamentary reputation and experience, also supports the argument.

Prime ministers' individual relations with TV were touched on in the previous chapter and need little elaboration. Table 8.1, showing the age of post-war prime ministers when TV restarted and when each first took office, is a reminder of the extent to which the 'inaugurator' prime ministers – Attlee and Churchill – had to 'learn' TV when they were already at or beyond normal retirement age. In fact, of course, neither bothered to learn. Attlee had no need, since TV was in its political infancy, and he refused to appear at all. During Churchill's premiership, however, TV took off. Churchill therefore appeared in news bulletins and at the first televised

Table 8.1 Prime ministers and television

Prime minister (party)	Born	First took office	Age on first taking office	Age when TV re-started (7 June 1946)
C. R. Attlee (*Lab*)	3 January 1883	26 July 1945	62	63
W. S. Churchill (*Con*)	30 November 1874	[10 May 1940] 26 October 1951	76	71
A. Eden (*Con*)	12 June 1897	6 April 1955	57	48
H. Macmillan (*Con*)	10 February 1894	10 January 1957	62	52
A. Douglas-Home (*Con*)	2 July 1903	19 October 1963	60	42
J. H. Wilson (*Lab*)	11 March 1916	16 October 1964	48	30
E. G. Heath (*Con*)	9 July 1916	19 June 1970	53	29
[J. H. Wilson (*Lab*)]		[4 March 1974]		
L. J. Callaghan (*Lab*)	27 March 1912	5 April 1976	64	34
M. H. Thatcher (*Con*)	13 October 1925	4 May 1979	53	20

Conservative annual party conference in 1954. He declined, however, to take part in a party political broadcast, even when pressed by party managers.

Eden, as we have seen, was the first prime minister to welcome television. He was judged an excellent TV performer, though still in a face-to-camera format. In the 1955 party election broadcasts, very shortly after becoming prime minister, he won the top audience ratings. Macmillan, succeeding him early in 1957, had an equally positive outlook, with several years of familiarity as a TV performer behind him and, as it turned out, nearly seven years ahead to refine his skills. He was a ready student of technique, winning plaudits from BBC professionals, and had been a keen participant in the first televised party political broadcast in 1953. He broke new ground with a televised Downing Street conversation with President Eisenhower − stilted by later standards but fascinating at the time. His premiership also covered the important political broadcasting innovations before and during the 1959 general election.

Alec Douglas-Home came to Downing Street in 1963 unexpectedly, as a result of Macmillan's sudden illness. But for recent legislation promoted, paradoxically, by Labour's Tony Benn (himself an inheritor of a peerage), Home would not have been able to renounce his earldom and enter the Commons anyway. He had little of Macmillan's taste for TV, nor his aptitude (for example, he proved unable to master the autocue machine). Chiefly he is important in this context as the first party leader whom TV helped to destroy. Whether his TV performances actually contributed to the extremely narrow electoral defeat in 1964, when Labour won an overall majority of four, is difficult to judge. But parliamentary colleagues thought so, and this weighed in Home's decision to stand down as Conservative leader in 1965.

The prime ministers during most of what Chapter 7 called the period of TV's political maturity were Harold Wilson and Ted Heath. Wilson, as Chapter 7 argued, deserves the label of 'first TV prime minister' because more than anyone before him he met TV on its own ground. He had plenty of opportunity by now, of course, to observe his predecessors, to get TV experience in opposition – and also to study the Kennedy TV skills in the USA. Not only did he use the medium skilfully as a campaigner, but he introduced informality by 'breakfasting' on TV with David Frost (at that time mainly on the 'showbiz' side of TV) and by letting the cameras follow him, in shorts and shirtsleeves, on holiday.

Wilson obviously made mistakes. One of the most notorious was a face to camera address about devaluation of the pound in 1967 (when there was still a fixed exchange rate against the US dollar). This contained a damaging claim, technically correct but open to misconstruction, that the purchasing power of the pound would be unaffected. For his successor Heath that kind of mishap was all too typical. Heath almost never looked relaxed on camera. Crucially, he failed in February 1974 to impose through TV his own view of the central issue of the general election that had been provoked by a long miners' strike. Intended as a 'Who Governs?' election, it was seen by voters in fact as about economic issues, and Heath narrowly lost.

Callaghan as a performer proved adept at handling interviewers but was associated with no particular TV developments. The Thatcher decade up to 1990, on the other hand, was important in a variety of ways, all reflecting the extent to which broadcasting and political events had become interwoven. As a performer Mrs Thatcher had many triumphs. Her manner with interviewers, including the formidable and experienced such as Robin Day, often lost them the initiative and reduced them temporarily to silence – yet without apparently alienating viewers. She listened to advice from experts such as Gordon Reece (knighted for his efforts) about how best to dress and groom herself for the cameras, how to pitch her voice. Political campaigns, not only in the three victorious general elections up to 1987 but during the Falklands War of 1982 and the year-long miners' strike of 1984–5, were planned and orchestrated with the help of marketing specialists, pollsters and advertising agencies (notably Saatchi and Saatchi). A BBC *Panorama* programme after the 1983 election was aptly titled 'The marketing of Maggie'. The veteran journalist and TV executive Geoffrey

Cox summed her up as 'an extremely effective screen figure who uses actions as an alternative to words' (Cockerell, 1988, p. 255). She popped up in Ulster in a red beret and flak jacket, and in the Falklands soon after victory — always providing good pictures, demonstrating her concern and commitment.

Much of what was involved had become the bread and butter of political broadcasting. In North America, as Wilson observed, they had got there first. Labour, learning the lessons after a disastrous TV campaign in 1983, ditched Michael Foot (ironically, one of the most exciting current affairs broadcasters of the early 1950s), and set about grooming and presenting Neil Kinnock in comparable ways. Round the globe, indeed, politicians were doing the same thing.

The extra dimension in the Thatcher decade was the growth of controversy about broadcasting. Mrs Thatcher, like many of her colleagues, was ready to blame the broadcasters for bad news. Many of the crises she faced involved a sub-crisis about the media. In the Falklands, it was about the broadcasters' insistent evenhandedness and their counterclaims about aggressive news management. In the miners' strike it was, inevitably, about 'bias' (but this was a classic industrial dispute where all sides were bound to make that complaint). In the Westland crisis of 1986, ostensibly about a helicopter company but in fact about Mrs Thatcher's authority in the Cabinet, the row was about the legitimacy of leaking documents as a method of news management. Above all, there were rows about the reporting of Northern Ireland — generally about when and whether Republican extremists should be broadcast.

Previous governments long in office had had fewer rows. In the Conservative governments of 1951–64 there was less broadcasting to have rows about. The Suez crisis did indeed produce a major row, but the Macmillan years were largely trouble-free. 'Media sub-plots' in the prolonged Profumo crisis of 1963 — another that was implicitly a crisis of political authority, despite its call-girl context — chiefly involved the role of the press, more than of broadcasting, in the initial exposures.

Next to Thatcher, Wilson was the prime minister who had most rows with the broadcasters — and whose length of office, though split, came closest to hers. Apart from the day to day niggles, one programme in particular reflected his sensitiveness. This was *Yesterday's Men*, a serious but not sombre look at the after-effect upon Labour ministers of being unexpectedly tumbled into opposition by the 1970 election. Wilson resented especially being asked what fee *The Sunday Times* was paying for his memoirs. He sought to 'punish' the BBC when back in office. But Mrs Thatcher, 10 years on, set about making the broadcasters accountable with more determination and as part of a wholesale restructuring of the broadcasting system.

Some of the tension between Mrs Thatcher and the media was concentrated on the Number 10 press office, headed by an outspoken Yorkshireman, Bernard Ingham. The work of the office was closely connected with the group of Downing Street reporters known collectively as 'the Lobby'. This had grown up as long ago as the 1880s, when reporters were increasingly keen to supplement their accounts of parliamentary debates, observed from the press gallery, with background stories about the ins and outs of party policies and personalities – which meant mingling with MPs in the lobbies and corridors outside the Commons chamber. In return for this privileged access, including an early sight of official documents, the journalists became the embodiment of discretion, keeping their sources of information anonymous or 'off the record'.

The Lobby correspondents were from the start a collective group: there were informal rules and a committee, and membership was strictly limited to one reporter per paper (and an extra ticket for the editor of *The Times*). Between the wars they began to meet for regular collective briefings – off the record – from ministers and other parliamentarians. Many stayed in the lobby for 20 years or more, barely distinguishable from longtime MPs, and operating both in competition with each other and as colleagues chasing the same sources (Tunstall, 1970). It was understandable that particularly important and sensitive wartime stories, such as Dunkirk and D-Day, were fed by the government through the Lobby.

With the massive growth of government legislation after 1945, the balance of lobby work began to shift further towards policy and away from personalities and the immediate context of debates. As the reporters were not specialists, except in the business of Westminster and cabinet politics itself, they became more reliant too upon the collective briefings. At these, ministers might be accompanied by senior civil servants, to help explain, say, a forthcoming White Paper on anything from defence to agriculture. The Leader of the Commons and the Leader of the Opposition gave weekly briefings, too.

The key figure orchestrating the briefings (apart from the Opposition Leader's) was the prime minister's press secretary. He also briefed the lobby himself twice a day — once for the evening papers and once for the mornings. Pressure to increase the membership grew. The intimacy intrinsic to the system had led to an 'inner Lobby' of morning paper journalists and an 'outer Lobby' of Sunday, weekly and overseas papers. All the latter were excluded from the briefings and often from the lobby itself except once a week.

Membership became steadily diluted. First came the provincial evening papers in the 1940s; then 'alternate' members (that is to say, more than one, but not simultaneously). The Sunday papers became full members in 1961, the weeklies 10 years later, and finally the broadcasters. Multiple membership eventually followed. The 'inner/outer' distinction survived till the 1970s. But by 1990 the system was a much looser version of the elite corps of intimates in 1945.

Yet the principle of a mutual exchange between reporter and source remained. It was personified in the increasingly important Number 10 press secretary. British prime ministers themselves had no strong tradition of personal contact with journalists. This was partly a matter of class. They might mingle with editors and publishers — have known them at school or university, even — but rarely with reporters. This was as true for Churchill, who earned his keep by his pen, as for a patrician Old Etonian publisher such as Harold Macmillan.

The tradition was also an accident of personality and career. Eden, with a lifelong interest in foreign affairs, was certainly comfortable with diplomatic correspondents, who were perhaps a less earthy bunch than the Lobby. Attlee was hopeless about all aspects of news media. He only took to the news agency tape machines at Number 10 when he found they reported the cricket score. In Wilson journalists of all kinds for the first time found a prime minister who prided himself on knowing about deadline times and news routines. This made his disillusion with the media when things went badly all the worse.

The decline of patrician prime ministers and the growth of unavoidable personal contact with journalists once the broadcasters moved in, brought prime ministers closer to the media. But it did not necessarily make them more regularly accessible. In particular, and compared with their counterparts elsewhere and with American presidents, they avoided the regular press conference. Even private meetings with the Lobby were rare until Wilson's time – and still rare after it.

The Number 10 press secretary was thus a key intermediary. Mr Attlee created the post out of a previously rudimentary information officer role. He appointed Francis Williams in 1945, to interpret to the press the brave new world of the Labour government. Attlee wanted someone in 'broad sympathy' with Labour, but not so obviously partisan as to alienate the Lobby. Williams, a substantial figure in every sense, who at length became a Peer, had been editor of the *Daily Herald* before the war and senior Ministry of Information official thereafter. He stayed two years and was a great success.

Like him, almost all of Williams' successors were journalists turned civil servants (including Ingham). A few became civil servants only for the duration; and one of these, Joe Haines, suspended an open partisanship only temporarily. He joined Harold Wilson's Downing Street office in 1969 from the old Labour *Sun*, stayed with him in opposition through the Heath years, and went back to Number 10 in 1974 for Wilson's two-year second term. Haines' predecessor, Trevor Lloyd-Hughes, was a provincial Lobby correspondent who in contrast became a permanent civil servant.

The importance of a press secretary in the post-war world was confirmed by the unsuccessful attempt of Winston Churchill to do without one in 1951. Eden needed no persuasion and made an imaginative appointment in William Clark, a diplomatic correspondent and early TV journalist. The sensitiveness of the secretary's position as an intermediary, interpreting the government and the press to each other, became clear in the Suez crisis. Clark was unsympathetic to Eden's hawkish line and the planned invasion of Egypt. Eden therefore found him increasingly ineffective, while the Lobby, on their side, found it difficult to know how far he spoke with his master's voice and how far with his own. In a difficult situation Clark resigned.

Ted Heath, like Eden, chose press secretaries with a foreign affairs bias. Both his appointees were senior career diplomats with experience in the Foreign Office news department. The choice reflected Heath's priority of legislating Britain's entry to the EEC. What they lacked in direct press experience, they made up in organizing skills and Whitehall know-how.

From Heath's time, the press office became larger, though even in 1990 Bernard Ingham had only five assistants plus secretarial backup. The work diversified. With Harold Wilson – and bigger jets – the Lobby journalists began to globetrot, and the press office was drawn into the logistics. The growth of TV brought a new medium, a faster rhythm, the need for new kinds of advice. The post developed four clear roles: *spokesman*, *adviser on media relations*, *agent* (or intermediary) dealing with news organizations, and *coordinator* of information services in all the Whitehall ministries. The latter became a bigger task in the 1960s, as the press employed a greater range of specialist correspondents, somewhat on the Lobby model, to cover social services, education, home affairs – most of the areas of government activity.

From the late 1950s, too, the Lobby and Number 10 system became occasionaly an issue *in* politics. An early example was the sensation caused in 1959 when *The Times* splashed an unattributed story claiming Mr Macmillan had taken his Foreign Secretary's arm in a paternal grip and, in effect, warned him to expect the sack. The story appeared during a meeting of Foreign ministers in Geneva, preparing for a summit conference; and *The Times*' reputation overseas meant the story was bound to be thought inspired. *The Times* had to write a calming leader ('Back to Sense'). The Foreign Secretary (Selwyn Lloyd) stayed put. Years later *The Times* reporter admitted Macmillan himself had been the source.

The tribunal conducting a post-mortem on the Vassall spy case in 1962 exposed the flimsy factual base on which unattributed stories could easily rest. Harold Wilson's disillusion with the Lobby, after an early honeymoon and a misguided attempt to treat them as reflective columnists rather than hard news reporters, led to unprecedented public discussion about the pros and cons of the system. *The Sunday Times* tried to institute a 'Whitehall Correspondent' to get beyond Westminster-based journalism into the civil service seats of policymaking, but Wilson was able to squash the experiment. In his second administration, relations between the press office and the Lobby became so strained that Joe Haines suspended the daily collective briefings. They were restored by Mr Callaghan.

These briefings became more and more the focus of criticism in the Thatcher decade; less for their collective character than for their unattributability. This had become especially vulnerable as the anonymity of broadsheet journalism itself virtually disappeared in the 1960s. Critics claimed the system now gave Bernard Ingham too much scope to fly kites, put his own spin on the news agenda, dodge responsibility, exploit the Lobby tendency to 'pack journalism' – in short, privily to *manage* the media. As time went on, moreover, Ingham was criticized for behaving virtually like a minister. After 10 years of close understanding with Mrs Thatcher and speaking in her name, could the principle that he was simply a civil servant be sustained, even if he deliberately stayed away from party occasions and electioneering?

Wilson avoided such problems by employing a separate 'Parliamentary Press Liaison Officer', paid from party funds and working independently of Lloyd-Hughes and Haines (this was the future Labour minister, Gerald Kaufman). Harold Macmillan's way had been to appoint a Cabinet minister to look after political media strategy (including regular briefings). The first was Charles Hill, post-war favourite as 'the Radio Doctor', who became Chairman of the ITA (1963–7) and was impishly appointed by Wilson straight from there to the BBC.

After him came Bill Deedes, already a veteran journalist, who later edited the *Daily Telegraph*.

If Mrs Thatcher had adopted either expedient, Bernard Ingham might have avoided some of the flak, not least from MPs. MPs especially resented the way in which he more than once sounded a ministerial death-knell with a remark about someone having become a 'semi-detached' member of the Cabinet. Ingham operated in a TV era. Compared even with Haines, he could not avoid being caught by the camera, popping up on the screen at Mrs Thatcher's shoulder, or briefing the media at summits. His job's visibility reflected its increased importance and the tensions inescapable in a prime minister's relations with media. James Margach wrote about 'the War between Fleet Street and Downing Street' as a print journalist. TV had simply increased the number of battle fronts. Clearly prime ministers had to adjust to the needs of the media – and to beware them. But so too, as the experience of the Downing Street press office suggests, were they able to manage them.

Political parties and the press

The close historical links between parties and the press make a startling contrast with the isolation of the parties from broadcasting. Papers of all kinds – national and local, daily and weekly, newspapers and journals of opinion – have a natural affinity with parties. Politicians and voters have traditionally expected, and often banked on, press partisanship. Yet broadcasting has been hedged with non-partisanship, and party programmes have been stuck in the ghettos of the party political broadcasts.

Between 1945 and 1990 the press became less predictable and manageable for the parties, and therefore less satisfactory to them. This was true both for individual parties and for the party system as a whole. For the press, the result was an increasing risk that frustrated politicians, tempted rightly or wrongly to blame the press for their failures, might interfere with traditional rationales of 'press freedom'. For the political system as a whole, there was less certainty that party politicians could reliably communicate with the electorate on the politicians' own terms. Where newspapers once were the clients of parties and were owned or subsidized by party financiers, politicians by the 1960s were the clients of the press. Clement Attlee could command the *Daily Herald*, which the Labour party controlled, in a way that Harold Wilson and his successors could not command the *Daily Mirror* (the only Labour stalwart after 1970). Wilson instead had to feed them Honours: there were at one point four or five peers in the Mirror Group. Mrs Thatcher had to flatter Conservative papers in the same way.

How well can a democracy work if the people cannot be sure they hear the authentic voice of their leaders? If the press did not play the party tune, if might not matter, provided that the broadcasters' stopwatch approach to political balance endured. But by 1990, as we have seen, this had been diluted and supplemented by the intrusion of political controversy. The relation between the parties and the press was therefore an important aspect of the general issue of media accountability.

The affinity between parties and newspapers is easily stated. People form parties to seek a common goal. Organization and campaigns require communication, and newspapers are a highly suitable medium: cheap, and easy to distribute. They are verbal, and politics is a verbal activity. Their contents tend to be broad, and parties are potentially concerned with the whole of a society's problems. The same social forces that find expression in a party tend to find expression also through the press. Parties are therefore bound almost by definition to be concerned with, and about, the press. Politicians across the board, from Lenin to Hitler, have vouched for the importance of newspapers as a focus of activity and a rallying voice for a party at the point of departure.

In general, then, we might expect to have found in 1945 a rough fit between the press and the party system. The policies of each party would be echoed in the columns of one or more national papers, with an overall balance between the strengths of the parties and of the press as a whole. But the fit was already imperfect. Table 8.2 gives a summary impression. Using general election years as benchmarks, the table can serve as the basis for an outline of how and why the pattern changed across the years.

For a start, there was an imbalance in the *number* of party papers. In 1945 this was not bad: four Conservative, two Labour, two Liberal (including the *Manchester Guardian*) and the Communist *Morning Star* (omitted from the table). It became worse first as a result of the death of the *News Chronicle* in 1960, which removed the only mass circulation Liberal daily. Then the replacement of the Labour *Herald/Sun* by the Murdoch *Sun* — a successor only in name — made the Conservative/Labour balance more lopsided in the early 1970s. The foundation of the *Star* and late-1980s papers confirmed it.

Taking *circulation figures* into account (which means the quality–popular distinction too), the imbalance looks even worse. Table 8.2 shows that the Conservative share of general election votes was always lower than the total Conservative circulation. Until 1964 the difference lay within roughly 10 per cent. From then on, it was usually higher. The Labour party, in contrast, continually campaigned in the knowledge that more of its voters than of the Conservatives were likely to be reading the 'wrong' paper; and by 1979 these were in a majority — that is, more Labour voters were reading a Conservative than a Labour paper. Only once, in 1970, did Labour circulation match the Labour vote (in percentage terms). This distortion among the major parties was accentuated because the Liberal circulation, while the *News Chronicle* survived, nearly always exceeded the Liberal vote. Clearly many *Chronicle* readers were not Liberal voters.

Those comparisons give a fair idea of the trend in partisan imbalance, but they oversimplify. At any time from the mid-1970s, for instance, it would have taken only the *Sun* to transfer its loyalty to Labour for the imbalance to have toppled sharply in that direction and against the Conservatives — although the number of Conservative titles would still have been greater. Apart from that, figures alone say nothing about the nature of *editorial partisanship*, nor that of the *readers' partisanship*.

Many readers, to judge by opinion surveys, did not have a

Table 8.2 Newspaper partisanship at general elections, 1945–87

| | Circulation (m) and party support | | | | | |
	1945	1950	1951	1955	1959	1964
Daily Express	3.30	4.10	4.17	4.04	4.05	4.20
	Con	Con	Con	Con	Con	Con
Daily Herald/Sun[a]	1.85	2.03	2.00	1.76	1.47	1.30
	Lab	Lab	Lab	Lab	Lab	Lab
Daily Mail	1.70	2.22	2.27	2.07	2.07	2.40
	Con	Con	Con	Con	Con	Con
Daily Mirror	2.40	4.60	4.51	4.73	4.50	5.08
	Lab	Lab	Lab	Lab	Lab	Lab
Daily Sketch/Graphic[b]	0.90	0.78	0.79	0.95	1.16	0.85
	Con	Con	Con	Con	Con	Con
Daily Telegraph	0.81	0.98	1.00	1.06	1.18	1.32
	Con	Con	Con	Con	Con	Con
(Manchester) Guardian	0.08	0.14	0.14	0.16	0.18	0.28
	Lib	Lib	Lib/Con	Lib/Con	Lab/Lib	Lab
News Chronicle	1.55	1.53	1.51	1.25	1.21	–
	Lib	Lib	Lib	Lib	Lib	
The Times	0.20	0.26	0.23	0.22	0.25	0.26
	None	Con	Con	Con	Con	Con
Financial Times[c]	–	–	–	–	–	0.15
						Con
Sun	–	–	–	–	–	–
Daily Star	–	–	–	–	–	–
Independent	–	–	–	–	–	–
Today	–	–	–	–	–	–
Total circulation	12.79	16.64	16.62	16.24	16.07	15.84
Total votes cast	24.08	28.77	28.59	26.76	27.86	27.66
Conservative: % Circulation[d]	52	50	52	52	54	57
% Votes	40	43	48	50	49	43
Labour: % Circulation[d]	35	50	39	40	38	42
% Votes	48	46	49	46	44	44
Liberal: % Circulation[d]	13	10	10	9	9	–
% Votes	9	9	2	3	6	11

[a] *The Sun* replaced the *Daily Herald* in 1964. It was bought and relaunched by Rupert Murdoch in 1969.

[b] Named *Daily Graphic* 1946–52.

[c] Not counted as a general interest paper before 1964.

[d] Includes papers with divided support. Percentage may therefore add to more than 100. In 1974 there were general elections both in February and in October.

Sources: Royal Commission on the Press, 1974–7; Nuffield College election studies by D. E. Butler and co-authors. Circulation figures are for the periods covered by the elections.

Table 8.2 (cont.)

1966	1970	Circulation (m) and party support			1983	1987
		1974	1974	1979		
3.99	3.67	3.29	3.26	2.46	1.94	1.70
Con	Con	Con	Con	Con	Con	Con
1.27	–	–	–	–	–	–
Lab						
2.46	1.94	1.73	1.76	1.97	1.83	1.76
Con	Con	Con	Con	Con	Con	Con
5.02	4.85	4.29	4.26	3.78	3.27	3.12
Lab	Lab	Lab	Lab	Lab	Lab	Lab
0.84	0.84	–	–	–	–	–
Con	Con					
1.34	1.39	1.42	1.42	1.36	1.28	1.15
Con	Con	Con	Con	Con	Con	Con
0.27	0.30	0.35	0.36	0.28	0.42	0.49
Lab/Lib	Lab/Lib	Con/Lab/ Lib balance	More Lib influence	Lab	Not Con landslide	Lab
–	–	–	–	–	–	–
0.25	0.41	0.35	0.35	Not	0.32	0.44
More Lib	Con/Lib	Con/Lib	Con/Lib	published	Con	Con
0.15	0.17	0.20	0.20	0.21	0.25	0.28
Uncommitted	Uncommitted	Con	Con	Con	Con	Con
–	1.51	2.97	3.15	3.94	4.16	3.99
	Lab	Con	Coalition	Con	Con	Con
–	–	–	–	0.88	1.31	1.29
				Uncommitted	Con	Con
–	–	–	–	–	–	0.29
						Uncommitted
–	–	–	–	–	–	0.31
						Coalition
15.59	15.08	14.60	14.76	14.88	14.78	14.82
27.26	28.34	31.34	29.19	31.22	30.67	32.54
55	57	71	69	67	78	74
42	46	38	36	44	42	42
42	43	32	50	27	22	26
48	43	37	39	37	28	31
3	5	5	26	–	–	2
8	7	19	18	14	25	23

strong sense of the partisanship of their paper at all, and 'politics' ranked low on the scale of interest. In 1963 the first major British voting study found that only about half the sample named the party support of their paper correctly (for the loyalist *Daily Telegraph* and *Daily Herald* the figure was three-quarters) (Butler and Stokes, 1971). Not until 1983 did the majority of *Sun* readers realize their paper was now Conservative (Butler and Kavanagh, 1984, p. 215). It is no surprise that pollsters generally found that papers had at least a plurality of readers supporting the same party as their paper, but that there was no overwhelming dominance. The exceptions, again, were the superloyal *Daily Herald* and *Daily Telegraph*, and (when it started to count as a national daily) *The Financial Times*.

The degree of party support fluctuated, of course, with changes in voters' preferences. With the 1970s these became more volatile, culminating in the challenge of the Liberal/SDP Alliance party that in 1983 won almost as many votes as Labour. In 1983 and 1987, most Alliance voters read a paper supporting a Conservative or Labour victory. The correspondence between a paper's partisanship and its readers' thus became even less in the 1980s than earlier and was less consistent. How far papers contributed to this volatility and *shaped* voting opinions remained extremely difficult to establish (Harrop, 1987). Party leaders were probably wise to assume at least some connection.

Trends in *editorial partisanship* can be measured by content analysis: laborious work of limited value unless it can be matched to reliable information about what people actually read and digest. Again, the simplest measures of trends are election campaigns, when partisanship is likely to be strongest.

For 30 years after the war the trend was away from full-blooded party bias. A study of the four general elections from 1966 to 1974 showed that papers consistently gave more space to reporting the party they supported editorially (Seymour-Ure, 1977). The same was doubtless true in earlier years. But *qualitative* bias is more difficult to judge. Some of it could be unintentional. For example, the way a paper chose to cover a party's campaign might not suit that party. The press disliked 'quiet' elections, preferring plenty of substance and excitement. They liked clear-cut issues, that differentiated the parties and were 'real' (that is, consistent with media's view of political priorities). Yet parties — especially when in office — sometimes wanted a 'quiet election', like the Conservatives in 1955 and 1959 ('business as usual' kinds of campaign) and the 'Crisis? What crisis?' style of Callaghan in 1979 after the 'winter of (industrial and climatic) discontent'. Equally, parties' views of what were the important issues might differ from each others' and the press'. Labour in 1983 and 1987 had nothing whatever to gain from highlighting defence, a policy minefield for them. Press coverage of the Alliance in the 1980s was unlikely to please either of the established parties.

Deliberate partisanship certainly changed, and almost as certainly declined, for 30 years after 1945. Many factors played a part, and most of them affected partisanship between elections too. There was a decline, first, in 'official' party loyalty. The hallmark of this, according to a 1950 commentator, was that all the paper's 'themes and leader subjects seemed to be raised first in speeches or party declarations' (Nicholas, 1951, p 175). Such papers were represented best by the *Daily Herald*, because of its TUC control; but party ownership was not in fact a necessary condition. In 1945, the *Herald* arranged a great Labour election rally at the Albert Hall and its entire coverage was geared to securing a Labour victory. Even so loyal a Conservative paper as *The Daily Telegraph* could not have been as committed in its sympathies — following the party leadership and preaching orthodoxy, rather than taking initiatives of its own. The only papers in a comparable position to the *Herald* were the *Daily Worker*, whose fortunes declined fairly rapidly, and the *Reynolds' News/Sunday Citizen* owned by the Co-op branch of the Labour movement.

In the 1950s papers virtually abandoned election 'stunts', a traditional device intended to scare voters away from a party. In 1951, for instance, the *Daily Mirror* ran a crude 'Whose Finger on the Trigger?' campaign designed to discredit Winston Churchill, then in opposition, as a warmonger. Instead, election coverage became more balanced. By 1966, the *Mirror* was making a virtue out of 'First the Inquest — Then the Verdict', delaying its (predictable) declaration of Labour support until late in the campaign. From 1955 it became common for papers to feature articles contributed by leaders from each of the parties.

The expansion in the size of newspapers in the late 1950s gave much more space, too, for increasingly sophisticated analysis of the electoral process. Concepts like 'swing', 'marginals', 'image', became widely understood and did not fit easily into partisan polemic. Nor did opinion polls, and in the 1960s these became increasingly prominent. Previously, Gallup had the market virtually to itself, sponsored by the *News Chronicle*. The change came partly by an increase in competitors and partly by papers ceasing to treat them as valuable, copyrighted 'exclusives'. Instead, polls were milked for their publicity value, and other papers and broadcasters were encouraged to quote them.

Polls became the barometer of an election campaign. Papers often found themselves headlining polls showing a clear lead for a party they opposed — as did *The Daily Telegraph* in the landslide Labour election of 1966 or the *Mirror* in 1983. They had to gear their coverage to independent and increasingly reliable estimates of the electorate's mood, not to their own wishful thinking.

The prominence given to polls also increasingly made them a part of the campaign itself, since politicians obviously had to respond to them. In 1966 11 per cent of election headlines in the national dailies were about polls; in 1970, 25 per cent, and in February 1974, 18 per cent. The figures would not always be so high, but from the 1970s TV joined in too, with the broadcasters commissioning polls and using them to help structure their own coverage of issues in interview and discussion programmes. The broadcasting requirements for 'balance' clearly fitted the objective information of the polls very tidily. By the 1980s, parties themselves were using polls — both published and private — to fine-tune their campaigns.

Other influences making papers less partisan are more speculative. The spread of TV may have been one, for instance, but it is difficult to pin down. Arguably it was a bit more difficult to paint opponents in lurid colours, like Churchill in the 'Whose Finger ...?' campaign, when readers could see them on TV most nights. More subtlety, at least, was needed. Again, the tabloid tendency in the press was accompanied by a decline in detailed political coverage: the shift towards entertainment and feature items reduced the relevance of partisanship. Similarly, the proprietors of the 1960s and beyond were less committed to a party (and especially a political career) than the Beaverbrooks and Kemsleys of earlier years.

This last generalization needs treating with particular care. Murdoch, Maxwell, Stevens, Rowland – the later owners – certainly came off the party fence. But they had no personal political career in mind. Often, they did not control their organizations' capital. Running conglomerates, they had more complex (and international) goals than the singleminded aims that enabled Beaverbrook to boast mischievously to the 1947 Press Commission that he ran his papers for propaganda and for no other purpose. In effect, party politicians had to *court* the loyalty of the later barons: it was, in principle, unreliable.

With the opening up of divisions between the radical Conservative party of the Thatcher era and the post-Wilson/Callaghan Labour party, the trend in press partisanship moved the other way again. The position was complicated by the centrist appeal of the Alliance parties. These attracted much support from journalists and broadcasters, many of whom were professionally inclined to 'a middle way'. But as Table 8.2 shows, news and feature column even-handedness was not reflected in editorial support. Moreover, the tabloid style and format of the 1980s suited the kind of graphic, assertive, unqualified partisanship reminiscent of the 1940s. The *Daily Mail* and *Daily Express* in particular rediscovered the 'scare' story. Because TV had become the dominant source of news in election campaigns by 1979, one commentator suggests, 'straight news virtually vanished from the press, to be replaced by accounts that explicitly contained impressions and opinions' (Craik, 1987, p. 77). These were likely to reflect the Conservative sympathies of their organizations. In 1987 the weight of election coverage in the Conservative press favoured Labour – but much of it was knocking copy (Butler and Kavanagh, 1988).

The predicament of the Alliance parties – plenty of coverage but not on their own terms (in the sense of having a paper supporting them editorially) – illustrates the lack of responsiveness in the press to changes in the party system. Could a new movement have got so far in the early 1900s without being in a position to start or buy a newspaper of its own? Probably not. Similar examples can easily be quoted. CND, the major mass movement of the post-war decades, never enjoyed the support of a national daily. The issues of Scottish and Welsh nationalism were continually restricted to regional media, except in by-elections and for a short period around the early 1970s. Northern Irish problems were perhaps improperly understood on the mainland because the metropolitan press and readers were for too long uninterested. The strength of popular feeling against British membership of the EEC in 1966 had no voice in the national press except, for a while, in the idiosyncratic Commonwealth-hankering *Daily Express*. In the 1975 national referendum on continued membership, there was no serious editorial opposition at all, beyond the tiny *Morning Star*. Minor parties (mainly the extremes of left and right) found themselves at anytime more likely to get coverage on the basis of general news interest than of their manifestos. Most coverage for the Workers' Revolutionary Party in the 1979 election, for instance, came because one of its candidates was the actress Vanessa Redgrave. A right-wing party such as the National Front, lacking star appeal, got blow-up photo-publicity from its policy of mass marches (widely perceived as racially threatening): tabloid politics for a tabloid press.

By 1990, then, the press had become more detached from the party system in a variety of ways than in 1945. Parties had to work harder to get attention of the kind they wanted, and it was less reliable. For the press, the detachment raised in yet another form the question of accountability: who was responsible for the consequences of their political opinions? This question is examined in greater detail in Chapter 10.

9 Media Accountability: Government Policymaking

Mass media may easily be taken for granted, since they are so much a part of everyday life. But if we are tempted to assume that, say, the spread of TV was therefore 'inevitable', we need only recall that in the mid-1950s many shrewd financiers thought ITV too risky to invest in.

It would be extremely difficult to give an exact answer to the question *why* media developed in the way they did between 1945 and 1990. Many social, political, economic and technical factors played a part. The developments themselves also varied widely. Some consisted in the creation of new examples of existing kinds of product using old technology – such as new national newspapers or TV channels. Others took the form of an 'old' type of product made by a new technology. Recorded music, for instance, was revolutionized first by the LP, then by stereo, audiotape and compact discs (Table 9.1 gives a very rough indication of dates and changing terminology). In other cases again, entire new media were produced by new technology – notably TV.

Those broad categories were blurred in practice by numerous detailed changes: colour TV, colour in newspapers, high quality colour in books; the replacement of open spools by tape cassettes; the growth of wide-screen film and the decline of black and white; the virtual eclipse of the hardback novel by the paperback.

The scale and scope of development make judgements of cause and effect depend very much upon one's general view of

Table 9.1 Recorded music: changing technology, changing names

1940s	1950s	1960s	1970s	1980s
'Gramophone' (wind-up) →	'longplayer' / 'record player' →	'stereo system',		
		{ 'record deck' / 'amplifier' / 'speakers' } →	'music centre' →	'CD player' / 'midi system'
	'tape recorder'		'tape deck'	
'Record' ('disc') →	{ '78' / 'EP' / 'LP' } →	'single' / 'album' →	'cassette' →	'CD'
	'tape recorder' →	'cassette recorder' / 'cassette' →	{ 'personal stereo' / 'Walkman' }	
'Radio' / 'Wireless' / 'Radiogram' →	'portable' →	'transistor' →	'personal stereo'	

the nature of social change — how far it can be influenced by individuals rather than impersonal forces, how far controlled and fashioned deliberately. Among media people themselves, especially in the baronies of press and TV, 'great man' theories of history may well seem more persuasive than analyses of trends in education, leisure time, disposable income, world newsprint prices and distribution networks.

This chapter therefore concentrates more on how than why. In particular, it looks at the role of governments in media policy and innovation, for this is one of the means by which the media system in general may be held accountable to the public.

A policy of no policy?

At the end of the Second World War there was probably a general belief that British governments do not have media policies. A 'free press', after all, was the kind of ideal the Allies had been fighting for, whereas the Nazis burnt books and censored newspapers. A 'free press', for the British (certainly for its dominant classes), meant a press free from direct government control and shaped purely by market forces. Broadcasting, too, was deliberately organized at arm's length from government and presented as a public good, the servant of no one interest and particularly not of government.

Governments seemed to have, in other words, a traditional policy of no policy. The semblance was reinforced by the absence of specific press laws; by the emphasis in English law upon freedom of speech rather than freedom of inquiry; by the lack of a codified constitution in which a free press might be guaranteed (like in the USA) or limited; and by the lack of a Ministry of Communication (compare also the lack, equally uncommon elsewhere, of a Ministry of Justice). The Ministry of Information in the Second World War was unpopular both with politicians and public; it was dismantled as soon as possible, and its residual functions were put under Foreign Office responsibility in a harmless-sounding Central Office of Information. Similarly the minister with responsibility for broadcasting was the seemingly innocent Postmaster-General (until 1969), with an image of whistling friendliness and bicycle clips (and without even a seat in the Cabinet).

Popular belief in a policy of no policy very likely remained as strong in the 1980s. But of course the semblance was false. It is true that, as Jeremy Tunstall argues, British governments had a 'hostility towards a single media ministry, or a single set of strategic national media goals' (Tunstall, 1983, p. 238). Instead, policies were generally uncoordinated, reactive, expediential, partial and indirect; a matter of broad objectives and attitudes ('freedom of the press', 'an independent British film industry', 'public service broadcasting') rather than of detailed programmes and plans. The whole thus added up to less than the sum of its parts. At one time or another, however, every aspect of media was the subject of policy – the structure and organization of whole industries (film, TV) or of particular parts (Channel 4); finance (no VAT on newspapers); content (official secrets and contempt laws); and audiences (compulsory TV licence fees). The more media organizations became conglomerate, the more likely they were to encounter government policy in one of its forms.

Governments were least ready to make policy directly affecting content and audiences. This may do much to explain the popular belief that they had no media policies at all. Moreover, the content/audience policies were often of general application, such as the laws on copyright, official secrets and libel, and they therefore did not seem specifically *media* policies. Even so, there were obvious and important government controls on a citizen's right to use a radio or TV receiver and to record programmes and make copies, or to sell and buy books below the publisher's fixed price, or to deal in obscene publications at any price.

This point can be taken further. So pervasive are media that many types of government policy affected them without that having been the exclusive aim. Industrial relations are a good example. Labour government legislation in the mid-1970s, designed to help trade unions by facilitating the closed shop, threatened the freedom of newspaper editors to hire and fire. Ministers such as Michael Foot, an ex-Fleet Street editor steeped in journalistic tradition, anxiously sought ways to avoid this by such devices as a non-statutory journalists' charter. This conundrum disappeared in 1979 with the Labour government. Under its successor, conversely, management was strengthened. The introduction of new technology into Fleet Street by Eddie Shah and Rupert Murdoch was less difficult because of Thatcher government legislation limiting union rights, including the power to picket firms not directly involved in an industrial dispute ('secondary picketing') and the right of immunity from fines and the seizure of assets.

Similarly, in organization and finance, media were subject, of course, to the same vagaries of taxation, laws on fair trading, monopoly, foreign exchange and so on as everyone else. A late example of an unusually direct and unanticipated effect was the abolition of capital allowances against tax in the 1984 Budget. This threw out the financial calculations of the 30 companies that had just been awarded franchises to develop cable systems. The venture now looked far more risky, and the companies did indeed make slow progress.

Government policy affecting media, then, was often *indirect* in its motive but *direct* in its effect, and it was mainly about the structure and organization of media, their finance, and the development of technology, rather than about the content of what was communicated and the uses people made of it. A third general feature was governments' preference, as Tunstall puts it, for 'minimalist legislation and the voluntary principle' (Tunstall, 1983, p. 237). This was true both of Conservative governments (in office for about three-fifths of the period 1945–90) and Labour. Specific policies, clearly, were different from the decisions the other party would have taken if in office. A Labour government of the mid-1950s would not have introduced ITV; nor would Channel 4 have taken exactly the same shape under a Labour government in the 1980s. But Labour did not attempt to reconstruct the ITV system when it had the chance in the 1960s and 1970s (not surprisingly, in view of ITV's popularity with Labour voters); nor did the Conservatives give the third TV Channel to ITV in 1962. Similarly, Labour governments were as non-interventionist about Fleet Street after the Royal Commissions of 1947−9 and 1974−7 as the Conservative government after that of 1961−2.

Neither party, in other words, was doctrinaire in its treatment of media, and neither yielded to the temptation to legislate in detail and take direct powers. 'Direct powers' may sound implausibly authoritarian in the context of British media history, and certainly one may doubt that any post-war British Labour government would have felt such powers brought benefits worth the furore involved in legislating for them. But the term could include no more, say, than a broadcasting system financed directly by an annual parliamentary grant out of taxation. This was exactly how the Australian equivalent to the BBC was financed, yet the ABC (admittedly attracting a regular audience about the proportionate size only of BBC2) did not feel itself, therefore, a tool of government; on the contrary, it shared the same mystique of public service broadcasting as the BBC.

A Labour government that did try to intervene directly or in detail with either broadcasting or the press, in the sense of imposing direct statutory controls over structure and organization, would indeed have faced almighty opposition. Moreover, obvious expedients such as government press subsidies in the lean 1970s would paradoxically have kept Conservative papers flourishing at the cost, possibly, of the Labour *Daily Mirror*, which was profitable without subsidy. Why should a Labour government keep a predominantly Tory Fleet Street going? In the early 1960s, when the Labour *Daily Herald* could have done with a subsidy, Labour was not in power.

Subsidies discriminating on party grounds, furthermore, would have been a crude device and have created immensely risky precedents. From the perspective of the Cabinet room, the prospect of a successor government doing to you what you have done to them presumably encouraged forbearance. Harold Wilson, prime minister in 1964, no doubt knew, for instance, that if the Attlee Government had taken powers to enable the prime minister to broadcast to the nation at will, Anthony Eden would have done just that during the Suez crisis of 1956, without the BBC necessarily being able to give the Opposition a right of reply.

Reduced to its simplest terms, the position was that the Conservatives did not need to intervene directly, since the heart of the press beat in the right place (at the times when it mattered) and a public service broadcasting system was intrinsically conservative (with a small 'c'); while for Labour in office there were higher priorities, the electoral and political risks and costs were too great and the possibility of a successor government turning the precedent against them was an added disincentive.

In practice, as has been seen in previous chapters, every government used the ample opportunities within the limits of 'minimalist legislation and the voluntary principle' to try and steer broadcasting and, to a lesser extent, the press, along desired lines.

The broadcasting organizations provide the most prominent examples of 'minimalist legislation', the major difference between them (in this respect) being that the IBA regulated franchise holders and the BBC made programmes itself. The Cable Authority set up in 1985 followed the IBA model, but with a 'lighter touch' on programme standards (the authority's functions were given to the new Independent Television Commission by the 1990 Broadcasting Act).

Standards – particularly complaints about them – were also handled by voluntary self-regulation. The Press Council, Broadcasting Complaints Commission, British Board of Film Censors and Advertising Standards Authority, were all set up by the industry concerned, either spontaneously or under legislation giving them generally weak powers. In areas of potential political controversy, too, governments left the broadcasting authorities to operate the policy of 'balance' themselves, however much in practice the politicians put pressure on them.

Fragmentation and unevenness

A fourth feature of government policy-making was its fragmented and compartmentalized quality. Over the years and at any one time a variety of ministers and departments were concerned.

This was only to be expected. given the social prominence of media and the range of activities and purposes involved, say, in broadcasting. The Annan Committeee pointed to the difficulties:

> Broadcasting is not an easy responsibility to place within the present structure. The Department of Industry seems unsuitable for such a highly cultural and politically sensitive activity. In the Department of Education and Science there might be a tendency to treat broadcasting as another branch of the arts or education and sacrifice its interests accordingly: how would its capital programme fare in competition with school buildings? Or the recently exhumed Department of Transport might become a Department of Communications, particularly if broadcasting were again linked to telecommunications (Annan, 1975, p. 50–1).

To trace the changes of departmental responsibility over the years would be complicated, for departments themselves were frequently reorganized and renamed. Table 9.2 refers to the early 1980s but has longer application, for the general pattern is unlikely to have changed greatly, allowing for the shifting importance of old and new media. If public corporations and other statutory authorities are included, Tunstall calculates that there were at least 30 public bodies involved in the making and implementation of British media policy by the end of the 1970s (Tunstall, 1983, p. 244). Few departments, one might feel, are left out, especially if 'indirect' media policy is included. Nor, of course, did they always see eye to eye on policy developments, so that the differences had to be resolved through yet more institutional machinery, such as interdepartmental committees.

One simple measure of the fragmentation of policy is the way that the periodic major inquiries into the press and broadcasting went side by side but not hand in hand. Late in 1989, in belated recognition of at least some of the implications of concentration and conglomeration, the government started an investigation of the use of one medium to promote another in the same ownership. This was provoked by complaints of his press interests plugging Murdoch's Sky satellite channels. The Office of Fair Trading also had in hand a general study of media concentration.

Table 9.2 Selected departmental responsibilities for media policy: 1987

Medium	Department
Press	
Competition	Trade and Industry
Industrial relations	Employment
Radio and television	
General policy	Home Office
Finance	Treasury
Overseas services	Foreign and Commonwealth Office
Film	Trade and Industry
	Education and Science
Cable	Home Office
	Trade and Industry
	Treasury
	Environment
	Employment
Satellite	Home Office
	Trade and Industry

The departments of Trade and Industry were separate until combined under one minister in 1983.

Table 9.3 lists the press and broadcasting inquiries. These illustrate also the typical policy-making method for the main media. A suitably distinguished figure, acceptable to the government of the day but not actively partisan, headed a committee balanced in regional, political and occupational terms. Evidence was canvassed and oral hearings held. Publication of the report was followed by a period of digestion, during which interested groups could lobby the relevant departments to try and get the recommendations adopted or changed. Eventually, government action might follow.

Publication of the committee's report thus looked like a culmination, but in practice the process was much more of a continuum. This was particularly true of broadcasting, since action was almost bound to follow in one form or another: the BBC Charter and ITV franchises came up regularly for renewal, new channels became available, and decisions had to be taken.

Table 9.3 Main government inquiries into press and broadcasting

(*Date; chairman; number of submissions of evidence; scope*)

Royal Commissions on the Press	Committees on Broadcasting
1947–9 Sir W. D. Ross (Academic) 163 Performance, control, management and ownership of the press, including finance and monopolistic tendencies	*1949–51 Lord Beveridge* (Administrator; academic) 120[a] Constitution, control, finance and other general aspects of radio and TV
1961–2 Lord Shawcross (Lawyer; Labour politician) 168 Economics and finance of the press; their effects upon its numbers and diversity	*1960–2 Sir H. Pilkington* (Industrialist) 503 Future of broadcasting; whether additional services should be run by a different organization from the BBC/ITA
1974–7 Prof. O. R. McGregor (Academic) 247 Independence, diversity and editorial standards of the press; including economics, management, labour relations, concentration; the Press Council	*1974–7 Lord Annan* (Academic) 758 Future of broadcasting; constitution, organization, finance
	1985–6 Prof. A. Peacock (Academic) 842 Alternative methods, including advertising, of financing the BBC; their implications

[a] Organizations only. Number of individuals not specified ('a large number').

Besides, those grand public deliberations happened within a system in which the departments and the broadcasting authorities were in a continuous dialogue (about details of finance and engineering, for example). 'Good broadcasting is a practice, not a prescription', commented the Pilkington Committee. The formation of policy thus merged into its implementation; much of the process was organic and evolutionary.

The press inquiries were rather different. Unlike broadcasting, the press had no parent department and no franchises for periodic renewal. The press inquiries were triggered by political hand-wringing about the prospects and consequences of concentration and contraction. Not much came out of them: they may have caused a ripple of public awareness and forced journalists to reflect upon their industry. They epitomized governments' continuing policy of no policy. Only one, the McGregor Commission, brought itself to recommend public subsidy, to help Fleet Street introduce new technology and cut through the tangle of union resistance, but the Callaghan Government declined to be drawn in. Earlier, in 1965, the Wilson government followed up a Shawcross Commission recommendation for legislation to check press mergers, through the Monopolies Commission. But this did nothing to prevent takeovers by *non*-press groups (that is, conglomeration) and left ministers with wide discretion over whether particular cases should be referred to the Commission at all.

A fifth feature of governments' media policy was the unevenness of their interest. This was an aspect of their focus on technology and organization, rather than on use and users. Broadcasting policy, for instance, was determined at root by the limitations on available airwaves; while such policy as existed for the press had more to do with content, since there was no problem in principle of a finite number of possible papers. From the viewpoint of users, there was an element of arbitrariness in this practice. Policies on film and on TV were substantially different, yet increasingly, with the decline of cinema-going, the two overlapped (most films being seen on TV). Again, the Thatcher government's policy imposed few restrictions on the contents of cable, treating it more like the press than TV, even though cable programmes would be putting out familiar film and TV material. A further example might be radio and audio-tapes/discs. These were overwhelmingly used for music; yet there was scarcely any policy about records at all, while radio was subject to careful regulation.

What these anomalies surely reflect is a characteristic politician's view that some media — especially those concerned with news — were, so to speak, 'for' politics while others were not. The press, radio and TV were a continual preoccupation of politicians: film, books, audio-tapes and records were not. The preoccupation stemmed chiefly from the importance credited to the former as major influences over the formation of popular opinion and as media through which public and politicians communicated with each other. Media that only 'entertained' (rather than 'informed') seemed less significant. Thus the sport, education and showbiz elements in broadcasting were able to carry all manner of political undertones without being subject to 'balance'. Policy about film, books, tapes and pop music was concerned not with politics but with social values and taste (obscenity, pornography) or economic and industrial goals.

Government media policy, further, generally failed to distinguish between the non-political and the non-partisan: 'politics' meant 'party politics'. The distinction is best illustrated by TV drama. It was easier in the 1970s and 1980s to make a radical political statement — about unemployment, racism, Northern Ireland, nuclear weapons and so on — in a TV play than in a documentary or current affairs programme. Similarly, pop music increasingly acquired political content; yet apart from a few Labour enthusiasts, parliamentary politicians failed to see pop music as 'for' politics. In the broader world of showbiz, the 1983 general election saw a greater involvement than before by leading personalities with party campaigns, but on no great scale. Again, while sport became a growing issue in international politics in the 1970s, sport in media was left alone by politicians. Overall, media policy throughout the period reflected a view that the political media — which need regulating in some way to avoid or ensure certain political qualities — were those with a clear partisan interest.

The results of these fragmented, compartmentalized and uneven polieies can be summed up in the ease with which inconsistencies may be paired off, like tricks in a card game:

- For much of the post-war period there were twice as many TV organizations as Fleet Street proprietors. The former were 'publicly controlled'; the latter were treated as in a 'free market'.

- The sale of newspapers could be subject to approval by the Monopolies Commission; the sale of book publishers was not. The sale of a TV franchise was forbidden.
- Print media were subject to the Obscene Publications Act; broadcast media (until 1990) were not.
- Broadcasts had to be politically non-partisan; newspapers were traditionally expected to be partisan.
- Churches and political parties were excluded from holding cable franchises; there was no bar on them owning newspapers.
- Cable, under Thatcher policy, was to be 'entertainment led'; broadcast TV was statutorily obliged to 'inform, educate and entertain', in that order.
- Newspapers and books were zero-rated for VAT; records, tapes and TV sets were not.
- The film production industry was subsidised; Governments persistently refused to help Fleet Street even in the black period of the early 1970s.
- Book publishers were permitted to enforce resale price maintenance; record and tape manufacturers were not.
- Foreign investment and programmes were limited in TV; no comparable rules restricted the press.

Innovation and reaction: protectionism and competition

In addition to those contrasts, media policy can also be characterized by two more general sets of opposites:

- active/innovative versus reactive
- protectionist versus competitive

Policy on the press was mostly reactive. Each of the three Royal Commissions was set up when political anxieties had reached a certain pitch. The 1961 Commission was inspired specifically by the death of the *News Chronicle*, and the legislation subjecting press mergers to Monopolies Commission scrutiny came in direct reaction. The guarantee to the local press of investment opportunities in ILR companies when the commercial radio system started was in reaction to fears that the press might be badly damaged by loss of advertising revenue.

Parts of broadcasting policy were reactive too. Radio 1 and local radio owed much to the initiative of the pirates and, later, to clandestine community stations. The Department of Trade and Industry reluctantly started issuing satellite dish licences to private citizens in 1985 when it was clear that people were erecting them anyway. The Peacock Committee on BBC finance was provoked by the increasingly vulnerable licence fee system. The very introduction of ITV, it might be argued, was in reaction to an extremely well organized lobby. The BBC itself was set up, initially as a joint stock company, in reaction to the growing activities of Marconi and other private broadcasters and receiving-set manufacturers.

Broadcasting in general, however, must be judged an 'active' policy area. The establishment of the BBC was a major creative act of social and cultural policy. As the medium developed from radio to TV and then by the proliferation of channels, policy became a mixture of initiative and response. As Howkins puts it, 'Government has intervened at certain turning points but in each case has been notable for listening to and agreeing with the constituency of professional broadcasters rather than imposing its own ideas and interests' (Howkins, 1982, p. 63). With cable and DBS (direct broadcasting by satellite) in the 1980s, the Thatcher government was more interventionist, seeing these developments through very rosy spectacles as instruments of industrial and employment policy and seeking to move ahead at a great pace compared with the deliberation that preceded the introduction of BBC2 and Channel 4. Later, the reconstruction of the entire broadcasting system in the 1990 Broadcasting Act was the most 'active' policy since the 1920s. This was a determined break with the attitudes Howkins describes. The Act enshrined the 'auction principle', according to which franchises for the existing ITV channel and for a new Channel 5 were to be awarded to the highest bidder (offering the highest fee, that is), subject to a minimum 'quality threshold'.

In response to criticism, the government gave more weight to this threshold as the Bill went through Parliament; but it was greeted with general gloom by established public service broadcasters.

On the protectionist/competitive dimension, film was the best example of protectionism. From an early date it was clear that a British film industry would not survive without import quotas against Hollywood (imposed in 1927) and, later, a positive subsidy. This was engineered through a combination of a levy on cinema seat prices (made statutory in 1957 but long predating that), which was fed back into the industry, and — for a time — a system of capital funding through the National Film Finance Corporation, founded in 1949 but later abolished.

Minor examples of protectionism include the previously mentioned press entitlement to ILR shares; the net book agreement forcing booksellers to retail new books at the price fixed by the publisher; import quotas in TV programming; and the 'must carry' requirement obliging cable stations to transmit the four BBC and ITV channels. In contrast, policy towards press mergers aimed to stimulate 'competition', with few signs (apart from zero-rating for VAT and exemption from its predecessor, purchase tax) of the financial cushioning of the press in general against competition from other media, or of measures to maintain any particular number or type of national newspapers. Competition, similarly, was forced on British Telecom by the Telecommunications Act of 1981, both in minor matters such as the sale of telephone sets and major ones such as the provision of an alternative service (very slow to get going) by the Mercury consortium.

Fragmented, compartmentalized, anomalous, uneven. But how far is it really fair to call government media policies 'inconsistent' or, as Curran and Seaton do, 'contradictory' (Curran and Seaton, 1988, chapter 18)? The question depends on the context of policy and directs attention back to the issue of media coherence. Media policy could be consistent, surely, only if there were a common or consistent set of purposes media fulfilled — if they were all *news* media, for instance, or were all in a market that (unlike TV) could in principle have unlimited suppliers. During the post-war period, however, media did not in fact have such common features. Media were popularly defined in differing ways, as suggested in chapter 2: film, by location (the cinema); newspapers and magazines, by the physical product and distribution cycle; books and tapes, by the physical product; radio and TV (indirectly, perhaps) by a receiving apparatus; cable and satellite, by a means of distribution; video and sound records, by their uses. Implicit in those differences (liable to change, and not always clear cut) were varying purposes, as illustrated in chapter 6: news, entertainment, education, information. Governments imposed no unity of social purpose upon them, nor treated them consistently either as economic or as technical goods. Without such consistency of approach, as there was towards what constituted defence, social services or transport, for example, there could be no department of media and no deliberate consistency of policy. Governments certainly had plenty of media policies in 1945–90, but they were no nearer a single policy in 1990 than at the start.

10 Media Accountability: Markets, Self-Regulation and the Law

If government policy about media was so spotty, how and where else, if at all, could media be held accountable? The question might lead in a variety of directions. The big media organizations were not monoliths: they had internal lines of accountability. A Fleet Street editor, for instance, used to have great authority over his staff (though the completely 'sovereign editor' was always largely a myth). Then, in the increasingly cost-conscious 1970s, financial managers took more control. In either case, there was a line of accountability from bottom to top of the organization.

Looked at differently, journalists always had a large measure of autonomy, irrespective of charts. They were accountable simply to their consciences for the truthfulness of their reporting, and editors had to take them on trust. On the other hand again, for 30 years from the mid-1950s the entire editorial enterprise was arguably subordinate to the production unions. Trade union power was only very occasionally used to black specific articles, cartoons and advertisements (on subjects such as industrial relations and South Africa), but it was a looming presence in all calculations about investment, modernization of plant and general planning. By the late 1970s, in one editor's phrase, 'Fleet Street was an industry at war'. Stoppages were commonplace, and on some papers disputes were taking up to 80 or 90 per cent of middle management's time (Jenkins, 1979, pp. 69, 108). In ITV, the unions successfully enforced unnecessarily high manning levels (judged by international standards) in studio and camera crews, right through the 1980s.

Yet another claim could be that newspapers and ITV companies were chiefly accountable to the needs of advertisers for media audiences that fitted their product markets. As Curran and Seaton put it, 'Commercial television produces audiences not programmes' (1988, p. 193). Of this, there could be no more striking example in the national press than the viability of *The Financial Times* with a low six-figure sale in 1960 and the contrasting unprofitability of the *News Chronicle* and *Daily Herald* with sales over a million. The media barons may have looked like autocrats to the outside world, but often that cannot have been how they felt.

To pursue those arguments, however, would be to take a very wide view of 'accountability' — to identify it virtually with any type of influence over media people and output. On a narrower view, accountability refers not to the internal power relations of media but to the arguments and arrangements through which they justified themselves externally to the public. The issue is legitimacy. The question is, therefore, not whether, say, newspapers were in the pockets of their advertisers but how, if they were, they could account for what they published.

The natural preference of media was understandably for *self-regulation* — independence from any kind of external accountability beyond the market. Apart from that, there were the courts, with laws such as libel and the Official Secrets Act, which media found a continual thorn in the flesh. In between, a kind of halfway house developed over the years after 1945. Typically this took the form of a body exercizing *collective*, industry-wide self-regulation, such as the Press Council and the Advertising Standards Authority. These bodies may be viewed as outposts in the media defences against regulation by complete outsiders. By 1990, for the press and broadcasting at least, they were badly bomb-damaged. 'Right of reply' legislation was a real possibility, and a new Broadcasting Standards Council was being set up, on a statutory basis and quite outside the control of the broadcasters.

This chapter follows these distinctions by dealing first with the courts, secondly with industry-wide regulation and thirdly with the rationales of self-regulation.

Media and the law

People in media would fret about the law. Schooled to believe in 'free speech', they tended to think themselves the best judges of what, when and how things should be said and to resist the idea that courts were superior judges of the public interest. They looked with envy at the USA, where a free press was guaranteed in the constitution and libel laws were weak.

The general problem for media throughout the period 1945 – 90 was the *uncertainty* of the law, its occasional *severity* and the *inhibitions* these caused. From the media viewpoint, the position got worse as the years passed, especially in the second half of the 1980s.

The range of legislation that could affect media contents was always bound to be wide. It included laws about trade descriptions, race relations, the rehabilitation of offenders, the prevention of terrorism, the police and criminal evidence, and data protection. These affected the flow of information in various ways, including personal rights to privacy (about health or criminal records, for example) that went far wider than publication of stories in the news media.

Even in the obvious media areas, such as libel, the range of laws affecting media was wide. It included fairly arcane examples like 'Crown Privilege' and Parliament's power to punish damaging criticism of MPs. The fact that such measures were rarely used after 1945 simply added to their unpredictability if they were. Moreover, like the H-bomb, an inhibiting sanction need not actually be used in order to influence day to day events.

Four kinds of media contents were most at risk. One kind was the potential *libel*. Another was books, films, plays, magazines – mainly fiction, whereas libel dealt with claims of fact – that offended laws about '*morality*'. This chiefly meant obscenity and once or twice, to general surprise, blasphemy. Third were contents making *disclosures*, which the courts thought were premature (information prejudicing a defendant's fair trial, for example), or which revealed secrets, usually about defence. Finally there were a few cases involving the *refusal of journalists themselves to disclose sources of information* – usually, again, leaks about defence and security.

The law thus affected both sides of media work: not only publishing things, but finding them out beforehand. Some of the best one-liners reflect this duality: 'The law emphasizes freedom of speech more than freedom of enquiry', 'the law protects the individual interest over the public interest', 'the law places the right to a fair trial above the right of free speech', and so on.

Little of the uncertainty followed changes in the law, for these were few. The libel laws were slightly relaxed in the Defamation Act of 1952, which made justification easier as a defence. But 10 years later Cecil King, *Daily Mirror* chairman, could easily back his claim that libel was still 'an absolute nightmare', and the former Attorney-General Lord Shawcross could grumble that the operation of the law was at fault even if its substance had improved. The Official Secrets Act, whose notorious section 2 was fit to be 'pensioned off', said a judge in 1971, was reformed only in 1989.

Those were the laws that set leader writers thundering about the 'fourth estate'. In addition, a new Obscene Publications Act was passed in 1959, and the unsuccessful prosecution of *Lady Chatterley's Lover* the following year in a plum pudding of a trial, showed it could have liberal effects. That reform, however, made the law no more certain: cases still turned on decisions about the vague criterion of 'a tendency to deprave and corrupt'. Contempt of court, too, was reformed in 1981. This is a good example of a law having direct influence on the day-to-day behaviour of media yet without many cases arising in the courts.

Uncertainty was due to less tangible causes. One was simple chance. Would an unwitting libel be spotted? Would the victim choose to sue? How would the jury jump? With official secrets, would the government decide to make an issue of a leak?

Would they prosecute the paper that published it, or just the leaker? Again, would a litigant resort to some cobwebby piece of legislation like the Blasphemy Act? This was used by the Christian moralist Mrs Mary Whitehouse to prosecute the magazine *Gay News* in 1977. The editor, who was fined £500 (and the paper £1,000), had published a poem describing the emotional response of a Roman centurion to the crucifixion of Christ. The financier James Goldsmith, similarly, sought to bring a highly unusual charge of criminal libel against the magazine *Private Eye* in 1976 for allegations linking him to the unexplained disappearance of Lord Lucan. Unlike civil libel, the normal kind, truth was no defence to criminal libel. It was judged by intention and results (would it cause a breach of the peace?) and the object of the prosecution was punishment. *Private Eye's* editor could have gone to prison if the case had come to court. Goldsmith changed his mind, however, possibly because he was currently interested in becoming a Fleet street proprietor himself (Ingrams, 1979).

Secondly, uncertainty came from changing public attitudes. 'Taste' changed, of course. By the standards of 1990, most of the inhibitions about the language and depiction of sexuality at issue 30 years before in the *Lady Chatterley* case looked ludicrously prudish. Pornography, on the other hand, was still safe for official censorship in 1990. So was the sado-masochism of video-nasties, banned under legislation of 1985.

In other areas the implications of changing attitudes were more complicated. The balance between secrecy and privacy might cause difficulty, for example. 'Privacy' was valued, 'secrecy' in general disapproved. Did other people have a right to know whether you had a record of mental illness or imprisonment, or whether you were HIV positive? The conflict between a collective public interest and an individual private interest is endemic in journalism. Assertion of the former was a frequent tabloid justification for prurient disregard of the latter.

Over the years, pressure groups pulled in opposite directions. A 'freedom of information lobby' fought unnecessary bureaucratic secrecy. Yet at the same time consumer and welfare groups lobbied for greater personal privacy. The Rehabilitation of Offenders Act of 1974, for instance, made it legal to suppress details of certain criminal convictions after the lapse of five years, and the Data Protection Act put strict limits on the disclosure of personal details held on computer.

The other side of the matter was changing fashion among media. This had a more direct effect upon the laws with which media clashed. The incidence of Official Secrets cases, for instance, varied roughly with media interest in defence. Wars and nuclear weaponry provided the benchmarks. More broadly, the fashion for 'investigative journalism', which was at its peak between 1967 and 1979 and was epitomized in *The Sunday Times*' long campaign to expose the full story of the deforming ante-natal sedative drug thalidomide, was bound to produce cases of libel and contempt, injunctions against publication, appeals to the 'confidence' laws, charges under the Official Secrets Acts, and the many refinements shaped by clever lawyers backed by large corporate resources.

The thalidomide story went back to the early 1960s. The drug was taken off the market in 1961 after some 450 British families had been affected. After 10 years, only about 60 claims against the company had been settled. *The Sunday Times* wanted to find out how the drug had come to be marketed and also to campaign for better compensation. The problem with this was that since dozens of law suits between Distillers and the families were pending, the paper's articles might prejudice legal proceedings, until the last claim was settled.

The paper published one article in 1968 and got away with it, because it was about the European developer of the drug. Another, in 1972, led to a High Court ban on what had been planned as the next in a series – and had been sent to Distillers in draft, by agreement. The compensation campaign, meanwhile, was a great success, once parliamentary momentum and media interest had worked up. Distillers raised their compensation from £3.25 million to £20 million, and eventually the government helped. But *The Sunday Times* article on the cause of the tragedy was still banned. The ban was overturned in the Court of Appeal – and then reinstated in the House of Lords. Because it used Distillers documents acquired without the company's consent, it was also banned under the law of confidence. Not till 1976, when nearly all the families' claims had been settled, did the High Court lift the original injunction. But *The Sunday Times* wanted to prove its point about the 'public interest' nature of the issue and took the case to the European Court of Human Rights. There it won a gratifying victory, when the Court declared the House of Lords ruling had infringed the European Convention on Human Rights clause on free speech. This judgement led to the liberalization of the law on contempt of court in 1981. The whole legal effort, the campaign, and the essential background research, had been massive, and massively expensive, yet clearly justified in the end (Evans, 1984).

In the 1980s the competitive edge went out of investigative journalism. The focus shifted to tabloid competition, in which truthfulness often took second place to sensationalism and sums up to £1 million changed hands in libel actions. The big secrecy trials came less from media resourcefulness than from the whistle-blowing enterprize of civil servants such as Clive Ponting (acquitted, 1984), Sarah Tisdall (six months sentence, 1984) and Peter Wright (*Spycatcher*, out of reach in Tasmania, 1985−8).

An impression of these fluctuations and uncertainties can be gained by tracing cases through the years. A spicey libel case was always good media copy: running story, strong on human interest, outcome uncertain till the last minute, with the denouement anything from a contemptuous 'farthing damages' to a tax-free sum rivalling a win on the pools. A large selection of these could be quoted. Those which attracted most attention involved people or events already in the public eye.

One of the earliest post-war cases of this kind was brought by Harold Laski, a well known LSE political science professor who was also chairman of the Labour party's National Executive Committee during the general election year of 1945. Laski played a prominent role (in some ways tiresome to Mr Attlee) in the campaign. Several papers, including the *Daily Express*, reported him as saying Labour would have to use violence if it could not win socialism by general consent. Laski thought himself libelled. He claimed to have said, in effect, that if Labour could not get socialism even when it had general consent, it would have to use violence. Laski lost. His costs were paid by public subscription. But politicians bacame wary of fighting 'political' libel cases, in or out of election campaigns. Another who lost expensively, right at the end of the period, was the Labour frontbencher Michael Meacher. He failed to convince a jury in 1988 that an *Observer* article cast unfair reflections on the genuineness of his working class credentials. His legal costs were reported to be £200,000.

Typically libel cases involving politicians were about their private lives. One that attracted attention in 1957 was a *Spectator* piece which suggested two leading Labour MPs, Nye Bevan and Richard Crossman, and the party secretary, Morgan Phillips, had got drunk at an international conference. The magazine had no hope of substantiating the claim and damages were awarded. But the case reverberated because it was quite widely believed that the claim was true and that the three leftwingers had merely seized the opportunity to milk a Conservative publication (Crossman in particular had close connections with the rival *New Statesman*).

Libels on entertainers predictably caught the public eye. A famous case in 1958 was brought by the pianist Liberace against the *Daily Mirror* columnist 'Cassandra' (William Connor), a powerful polemicist. Liberace, more notable for his jewellery and costume than his music, claimed Connor imputed homosexuality to him. Most *Mirror* readers had probably worked this out for themselves. But at this time homosexuality was still legally as well as popularly stigmatized and Connor lost. The case cost £8,000 with £27,000 in legal costs. It was great entertainment and was widely reported in the UK and in North America.

Another category, which declined with the years but could rouse strong feelings, was the libel about someone's war record. Lord Russell of Liverpool, author of horrific accounts of Nazi and Japanese atrocities (*The Scourge of the Swastika*, and others) was an early complainant against *Private Eye*, which referred to him as Lord Liver of Cesspool and eventually had to pay up

£5,000 in 1966. In 1964 the author Leon Uris was successfully sued by a retired Doctor Dering, for suggesting in his novel *Exodus* that Dering had carried out experimental sexual operations on prisoners in Auschwitz concentration camp. The doctor was vindicated: the number of operations was exaggerated. But a jury was hardly likely to feel generous, and he was awarded half a penny in damages. David Irving, author of *The Destruction of PQ17*, another war book, describing the fate of a naval convoy to Russia, was sued in 1963 by the escort commander, Captain Broome. Broome was awarded £40,000. Even in 1989, reputation in the Second World War could bring people to court. Lord Aldington, in a long, stupendously expensive case, successfully sued the authors of a pamphlet about the treatment of captives in the Balkans in 1945.

In principle, to pursue Lord Shawcross's comment, the libel laws looked quite reasonable. Why should not the courts protect people against defamatory statements reflecting upon their character or reputation and tending to lower them in the estimation of right thinking people, or to bring them into hatred, ridicule or contempt? The decisions on the libel and on damages were made by a jury of ordinary people, not by the judge. Truth was a defence (except in the rare cases of criminal libel). 'Qualified privilege' protected media which in good faith reported libels made by many categories of other people (MPs, for example). 'Fair comment on a matter of public interest' was also a defence. The plaintiff had to prove the libel. Groups (such as 'trade union leaders' or 'Tory backbenchers') could not be libelled; nor could anyone who had consented to a publication in advance.

On the other hand, in addition to the chanciness of a libel even being spotted and pursued, the defendant had to face the possibility of an expensive defence; belief in the truth of a libel was no defence (though it might be a mitigation); the plaintiff need not prove the extent of damage or loss; and statements might be found libellous not because of their explicit meaning but for their innuendo. Innuendo, of course, was even more difficult to prove or disprove, especially if the defendant had not intended it. Finally, jury trial, for all its abstract beauty, meant that 12 people, yanked from their everyday surroundings and set to value a reputation in the isolated cell of the jury room, tended to behave unpredictably. They sometimes went wildly over the top, by everyday standards, in the financial damages awarded.

In the 1980s, the size of awards was the main matter of interest about libel. It had a knock-on effect, too, in encouraging defendants to settle out of court and on generous terms. The first earthquake case had in fact happened in 1961. Short paragraphs in the *Daily Mail* and *Daily Telegraph* ('Fraud Squad Probes Firm'; 'Inquiry on Firm by City Police') were found by a jury to carry the inference that the firm of Mr John Lewis had in fact committed fraud, whereas everyone including the newspapers acknowledged it had not. Damages totalling £217,000 (£1,800,000 in 1989 prices) were awarded. Although a new trial was ordered on appeal in 1962, on a point of law and because those damages were excessive, the case caused a judder of concern. A distinguished working party of the pressure group Justice suggested liberalizing the law and reducing the role of the jury. Papers became even more cautious than before in vetting stories before publication and settling cases out of court. Litigants more readily issued 'gagging' writs, with the effect of bottling up a paper's stories about them but often with no real intention to follow up the writ with a court action.

In the late 1960s, as a result, there were no lush libel cases – and no reform. The government did, however, set up its own inquiry under the judge Sir Neville Faulks. His committee suggested extending legal aid for libel cases and ending the jury's power to set damages. None of that was done. Publicity in the 1970s focussed more closely on issues of contempt and official secrecy.

In the 1980s cases, juries appeared to be punishing the press for its supposedly increasing prurience, intrusiveness, deviousness and willingness to fabricate news. It almost seemed as though the tabloid press viewed damages as an advertising item in the competition for sales – just another form of sensation. The entertainer Koo Stark brought eight successful actions in four years, including damages of £300,000 from the *People* in

1988 for allegations of an adulterous affair with Prince Andrew after her marriage. The writer Jeffrey Archer won £500,000 from the *Star* in 1987 for allegations that he made payments to a prostitute. Pop star Elton John agreed an out of court settlement with the *Sun* of £1 million in 1988 for unfounded allegations ('Sorry, Elton', said the *Sun*). *Private Eye* was hit for £600,000 in 1989 by Sonia Sutcliffe, wife of the 'Yorkshire Ripper', because of an article suggesting she sought to profit financially from his notoriety as a mass murderer. On appeal, the sum was reduced to £60,000. The decade went out with a bang when the author Count Nikolai Tolstoy (a descendant of the Russian novelist) was found guilty of libelling a business man and former Conservative politician, Lord Aldington. Tolstoy and an associate had distributed a pamphlet – not even a publication freely on sale – to parents and others connected with Winchester College, of which Lord Aldington had been chairman of governors. It accused him in effect of being a war criminal. Despite a caution by the judge not to be too cavalier with the noughts, the jury awarded £1.5 million. Tolstoy planned to appeal, but had the funds only to conduct his appeal in person, and he was eventually refused leave.

The BBC did not escape these 'Monopoly money' awards. Esther Rantzen's popular *That's Life* series paid out a total of £1 million in 1985 for libel against an aggrieved doctor. The case was settled out of court, after six weeks during which costs piled up.

Contempt of court threw up a few dramatic cases – widely publicized not least because they placed judge and journalist so squarely in opposition, with a whiff of martyrdom for the journalist. In 1949 Sylvester Bolam, editor of the *Daily Mirror*, was imprisoned for three months in Brixton by Lord Chief Justice Goddard, last of the 'hanging' Judges. The paper was also fined £10,000. Bolam had published a sensational story about 'vampire' murders in London and linked it indirectly to a man in custody, John Haigh. Haigh, known for his method of corpse disposal as 'the acid-bath murderer', was indeed found guilty. But the *Mirror* of course had jumped the gun and technically prejudiced his chances of a fair trial.

Bolam's case became notable not as an 'issue' – he admitted the error of judgement – but as showing editors were not safe through status from strict punishment. More of an issue was raised by the imprisonment of two journalists in March 1963 for contempt of court. They had refused to disclose their sources of information about an Admiralty spy, John Vassall, when requested by the tribunal inquiring into the circumstances of the spying. Civil libertarians saw this as an attack on the confidentiality essential to a free press. Others (including the judge) argued that in matters of security the government had to be the judge of the national interest, and if this required the disclosure of sources, so be it.

The contempt law was reformed in 1981. Papers continued to fall foul of it, especially as there need be no intention to interfere with the course of justice. There were no spectacular cases, but that simply indicates the law's effectiveness in bottling up media comment. On one estimate there were at least 16 Old Bailey trials in 1982 that went entirely unreported as a result of judges applying the 1981 Act, which empowered them to prohibit reporting where this might pose a substantial risk of prejudice to the administration of justice.

The Official Secrets Act did not start seriously worrying the news media until defence policy became a more divisive subject with the decline of a cold war mentality and the growth of CND in the early 1960s. Journalists were more reluctant to keep the government's secrets and quicker to suspect the law was being used to hide political embarrassment rather than matters of genuine national interest. A series of spectacular cases, starting with the prosecution of *The Sunday Telegraph* in 1970, led to repeated backbench attempts to liberalize the Act through Private Members' Bills. The government made one attempts at reform in 1979 – but withdrew the Bill after opposition by its own supporters – and finally put a new Act on the statute book 10 years later. The 1989 Act narrowed the range of official secrecy offences and put the emphasis mainly on the prosecution to prove that unauthorized disclosures had caused harm. But critics saw the changes largely as a tidying-up job, very far from the freedom of information measures typical of the USA, Scandinavia and even of Westminster systems like Australia. A particular complaint was that the Act failed to allow defendants a 'public interest' defence.

The three problems with the old Act (mainly dating from 1911) were its breadth and unpredictability, and its inescapable political overtones (for it nearly always provoked, or was used in, a political crisis or controversy). It covered both those who published leaks and those who did the leaking. Media were thus concerned both for themselves and for their sources. In *The Sunday Telegraph* case two sources and the editor were charged. In the 'ABC' case of 1977 (about secret defence communication systems) one source and two journalists were charged. In the Sarah Tisdall case (1984), the source was charged but not the newspaper. The Ponting case (1984), though a culmination, involved a leak to an MP, and the press was not directly involved. In the Dennis case (1985), both source (a civil servant) and newspaper (the *Guardian*) might have been prosecuted, but because of the Ponting acquittal the government decided not to proceed.

The Act's breadth came from the wording of its sections 1 and 2, which, by the use of phrases such as 'the making of any sketch, plan, model or note which could be useful to an enemy' and 'for any purpose prejudicial to the safety or interests of the state', covered virtually any information in Whitehall. Section 2 was the bugbear for journalists. Anyone who knowingly received or passed unauthorized information committed an offence. Refinements in practice included the possibility that publicly available facts, harmless individually, might comprise a 'secret' when joined together, on the analogy of a jigsaw puzzle.

Critics enjoyed quoting ridiculous examples of technically secret facts, such as the number of cups of tea drunk in Whitehall or the usage of paperclips. The serious point was that media could not always tell which articles or programmes would bring the risk of prosecution and which would not. In a system of newsgathering which relied heavily upon confidential relationships in any field and at all times – epitomized in the 'off the record' practices of the lobby correspondents – the Official Secrets Act was a concealed landmine.

The need for guidance was so obvious that a mechanism for giving it had been set up as soon as the 1911 Act was passed. This was the D notice system, a quintessential British fudge based on Old Boy attitudes. 'D' (for defence) notices were issued by a committee (which almost never met) run by a secretary, who was a retired senior services officer and known to get on with the press. The committee consisted of very senior civil servants, chaired by the head of the Ministry of Defence, and media representatives. The notices were mostly in general terms and remained in force indefinitely — perhaps a dozen or so at any one time. Media knew that if they published stories contravening then, there was a risk — not a certainty — that they would be prosecuted. If in doubt the secretary would give further advice. Indeed he could be consulted on any matter, regardless of whether there was a D notice about it. Since services personnel tend by inclination to be distasteful of party politics, the secretary avoided suspicion of confusing 'genuine' secrets with those that might simply embarrass one of the political parties.

The system worked. President Kennedy wished he had something similar to ease the management of his Cuban missile crisis in 1962. In 1967 it came under strain, and the public at large heard of its existence. The reason was, at root, that Harold Wilson, still a comparatively inexperienced prime minister, doubted the loyalty of the secretary, Colonel Sammy Lohan, whom he believed to have connived at publication by the *Daily Express* defence sleuth, Chapman Pincher, of a story about security services vetting of private international cables. To Wilson, Colonel Lohan probably did rather look like a class enemy, being a bluff, bowler-hatted type. But as the high-powered committee set up by Wilson confirmed, his loyalty was rock solid. Pincher's story, embarrassing rather than damaging, was of the 'jigsaw' type.

The D notice system survived, with minor modifications in 1982 after a parliamentary inquiry. It worked satisfactorily in the Falklands War. Its long run authority was weakened less by the Lohan incident than by the increasing tendency of respectable publications like the *Guardian* and *Sunday Times* to ignore the notices and the secretary's advice (small and radical publications were already outside the system). For example, the name of the head of MI5 and the addresses of security service officers were published, on the ground that state enemies surely knew them already. One of the D notices warned against such publication. A particular blow came late in 1987, when a Radio 4 team loyally cleared its plans for a programme about the security services with the secretary, but then found that the government obtained an injunction to ban it anyway. The future of the committee under the reformed, narrower Official Secrets Act in the 1990s was unclear.

The *Sunday Telegraph* case in 1970 started the reform ball rolling. The case was about an official report on the Nigerian civil war, leaked by the British government 'observer', Colonel Cairns, to the *Sunday Telegraph* via the journalist (later MP) Jonathan Aitken. It was difficult to see how the British national interest was affected, especially as the war ended on the day after publication. The defendants were acquitted and a committee under Lord Franks (a non-partisan elder statesman) recommended reform. Section 2 in particular was 'a mess' and a 'catch-all provision'.

Little more than pious talk followed. The Labour party election manifesto in October 1974 pledged reform. But legislation never had a high enough priority, and there was no compelling reason why any government, possessed of the existing Act, should see advantage in weakening it − unless its own backbenchers complained. The Callaghan government got as far as a White Paper, generally judged a victory for hardliners, before losing office in 1979. The Thatcher government's own Bill, in October 1979, self-destructed when it became clear that the exposure − endorsed by the government − of the long retired spy Sir Anthony Blunt, would have been an offence under that Bill. In the next 10 years, Bills introduced by Conservative, Labour and Liberal/SDP backbenchers kept the issue alive. More than 100 Conservative MPs supported the Bill of their colleague Richard Shepherd in 1988, and this proved a catalyst for government action.

Meanwhile, Messrs Aubrey, Berry and Campbell were found guilty but discharged in 1978 (a moral defeat for the government) for publishing details in *Time Out* about British army signals intelligence. The Tisdall and Ponting cases followed in 1984. The bizarre *Spycatcher* saga ran from 1985 to 1988 but was an official secrets case without capital letters. That is, the Act could not be used to gag the author, former MI5 agent Peter Wright (writing through the pen of a ghostwriter) as he had wisely retired to Tasmania. Instead the government used injunctions, prior restraint orders, the law of contempt and the law of confidence. Attempts to quash publication overseas very largely failed, notably in the USA and Australia, and the government became a laughing stock in proportion to the sales of the book, its seepage into Britain (on sale beside the M4 near London Airport, at one stage) and the extravagance of the legal costs. In the Australian courts, gleeful pom-bashing counsel mauled one of Britain's top civil servants, the Cabinet Secretary Sir Robert Armstrong. Proceedings were closely followed at home. The government, chiefly concerned to avoid Wright establishing a practice of memoir-writing that his successors might imitate, finally threw in the sponge, and *Spycatcher* became freely available after the injunctions were lifted in 1987.

The inconsistencies and unpredictability of the Official Secrets Act were shown just as clearly in these years by leaks and publications that were not prosecuted. The welfare lobbyist Frank Field, later a Labour MP, published a leaked Cabinet paper about child benefit plans in the magazine *New Society* in 1975. He was not prosecuted, despite a furore. Duncan Campbell published articles about telephone-tapping in the *New Statesman* in 1980 but received only a warning letter from the D notice secretary. Similar incidents happened in 1984. The former MI5 officer Cathy Massiter gave information on surveillance methods against CND and certain trade unions to a TV programme called 'MI5's Official Secrets' in 1985. She repreated much of it to *The Observer* when the programme looked like being ditched. No prosecution followed. Over the years, several books of war memoirs and studies of intelligence were also published with impunity.

Even when there were prosecutions, it was difficult to know whom the net would snare. The MP Sir Hugh Fraser actually wrote to *The Times* in 1970 to ask why he was not being prosecuted with the other *Sunday Telegraph* defendants, since he was part of the chain along which the government document passed on its way to the newspaper. The answer, most probably, was his parliamentary status. For the ultimate irony (or hypocrisy) of the Act was that ministers and MPs operated a long established procedure of leaks through the lobby correspondent system, with effective legal (though not always political) impunity. As the *de facto* judges of 'the public interest' in this sphere, that was the ministers' prerogative. Their rule, in essence, was: 'I give guidance. You leak.'

The working of the 1911 Official Secrets Act had many sides that did not directly threaten the news media. These included such sensational cases as the jailing (in 1961) and story-book escape from Wormwood Scrubs (in 1966) of the Soviet spy George Blake. The government misused the D notice system to try and suppress embarrassing details of his treachery — and that of the spy at the head of the security services, Kim Philby (publicly exposed in 1967).

With all these laws — Official Secrets, libel, contempt, Obscene Publications — the general allegation was that they inhibited media. Things that did not happen are of course extremely difficult to measure and evaluate. It is tempting to blame an outside cause, too, as an excuse for laziness. For example, some journalists in the 1970s argued that the D notice system discouraged enterprize by providing an easy excuse for not chasing defence stories.

Certainly the inhibiting effect of the Official Secrets Act had declined by the 1980s, despite its continued use. In its old form, it no longer served the government's purpose of blocking leaks — though not for want of trying. Since libels, on the other hand, were mostly unintentional, and since media routinely employed lawyers to check pre-publication copy, the libel and contempt laws had an undiminished, cautionary, finger-crossing effect. The alternative was the *Private Eye* policy of high risk publication. This rested originally on the basis that sueing an improverished satirical magazine would make a plaintiff look even more ridiculous than did the original libel. As the magazine prospered, that logic vanished. From the 1970s, libel costs and out of court settlements cost the magazine a fortune, though some of it was no doubt recouped in increased sales, as well as by fighting funds supported by readers.

Collective self-regulation

The courts were a fact of life. Bodies like the Press Council and the Broadcasting Complaints Commission, media people probably felt, need not have been.

The attitude of the press towards the Press Council, from the start, was one of defensive resignation: it was a body to satisfy the public, not the press. The Council was set up at the suggestion of the 1947 Press Commission, but only after the threat of legislation. It began work in 1953 with vague terms of reference that suggested a mixture of trade association (dealing with recruitment), research institute (monitoring monopoly trends) and complaints tribunal. It soon became just the latter. All 25 members, including the chairman, came from the industry; so did the budget. The Council had common sense procedures (you must complain to the newspaper before complaining to the Council, for example), and it had no weapons beyond publicity and wounding criticism.

The next Press Commission tightened the screw. Grudgingly, the press accepted lay members from 1963, and a lay chairman. A succession of distinguished lawyers took the post, including Lord Devlin (a retired judge), Lord Shawcross (ex-Attorney-General and chairman of the 1961 Press Commission) and Sir Zelman Cowen (ex-Governor-General of Australia). The terms of reference focussed more sharply on complaints and the budget was pushed up. After the third Press Commission (1974), lay membership rose to 50 per cent − strictly, with the chairman, a lay majority.

Over the years, obviously, the case load rose from fewer than a dozen complaints at first, to nearly fifteen hundred in 1989. Papers generally published its adjudications against them, and it seemed to enjoy a certain respect. But it continued to lack clear authority. This was due, perhaps, to industry scepticism; lack of sanctions; lack of wide agreement on what 'the highest professional and commercial standards' ought to be; uncertainty about how far to be active, not just reactive; and the balance between individual cases and general issues.

Agreement on standards was surely a non-starter. Almost by definition, the kind of 'free press' with which such a Council could coexist involved the probability of conflicting views on the propriety of foot-in-the-door reporting, sneak photos of bikini-clad royals, and chequebook journalism. Yet to stick simply to hearing complaints about factual inaccuracy, quotations out of context or letters left unpublished by an editor, would have been to ignore issues of genuine public concern. So the Council did become increasingly active in stating views about such matters.

The Council itself was sometimes criticized not only for its decisions but for its procedures. For example, when it rebuked papers for publishing the four-letter words used in the *Lady Chatterley's Lover* trial in 1960 the editors involved complained that they had not first been given a chance to justify themselves.

One school, including Lord Shawcross, thought the Council's procedures should be very informal, for the sake of speed and simplicity, and that its principles should evolve through the accumulation of case law. Others thought there should be a tightly drawn code of practice. This would certainly have been necessary if sanctions were introduced, such as the fines and suspensions which were suggested to the 1974 Press Commission.

At the end of the 1980s, in response to public pressure, London editors agreed some rules of good practice and appointed their own individual ombudsmen. The Press Council itself was then unexpectedly transformed. From 1991 it would be a Press Complaints Commission − smaller, better funded, and applying tougher standards. The Government warned, too, that this was the last chance for self-regulation: if practice did not quickly improve, a statutory press tribunal would be set up.

The broadcasting complaints bodies were limited always to

hearing individual cases. The BBC set up a three-person Commission in 1972, headed by a former ombudsman (Britain's first), Sir Edmund Compton, but staffed, appointed and paid for by the BBC itself. The comparable IBA Complaints Review Board did not even have outside members. After scathing criticism by the Annan Committee, a single Broadcasting Complaints Commission with an independent chairman was established by the 1981 Broadcasting Act, to hear complaints about 'unjust or unfair treatment' and invasions of privacy. Results were published in the *Radio Times* or *TV Times* and on the same channel and at a similar time as the item of complaint. In 1988–9, the Commission's busiest year, there were 348 complaints and 39 full adjudications. The load was greatly limited by the terms of reference excluding most of the things subject to everyday grumbles: sex, violence, bad language, bad taste and inconvenient scheduling.

Compared with both the Press Council and the Broadcasting Complaints Commission, the Advertising Standards Authority was impressive because in practice it had effective sanctions. It started in 1962, in an attempt to make advertisements 'legal, decent, honest and truthful'. Like the other bodies, it was goaded by the threat of legislation. After 1974, with an independent chairman, a mixed lay/industry membership and a budget provided by a 0.1 per cent levy on display advertising, it was able to enforce its code of practice through an agreement by the press not to publish ads that it had banned. It had a much higher public profile than other bodies, monitored thousands of ads per year and received over 8,000 complaints in 1987–8. But the crucial press agreement and code of practice had no exact comparison with what could be expected of the non-advertising contents of the press.

For the *news* media, then, the semi-independent bodies seemed at best capable of helping individual citizens enforce accountability. They were little help in producing a more general accountability to the public.

Arguments for 'independence'

Media really just wanted to be left alone. The press in particular had a wide range of time-tested arguments to justify resisting unwanted interference by outsiders. Most simple was account-ability to the market place: 'If you do not like what is in my paper, read another or found your own'. By 1945 this should have been long discredited. In the early 1900s it had had some plausibility. Not everyone with something worth saying (es-pecially if radical) could even then find an outlet. But relatively well to do groups and individuals, usually with political aims, could afford to launch a paper and keep it going even at a loss without ruination.

In the first half of the century, however, the laws of market economics themselves destroyed the force of the argument. As we have seen, regional papers were linked in chains to each other and to the nationals; the nationals became dominant in circulation; the minimum viable economic size of a paper in-creased and the weakest were driven out of business. Already when Colonel Astor rehearsed the argument to the 1947 Press Commission, in justification of his ownership of *The Times*, the 'free market' claim was rusty. It had seized up so completely by the mid-1970s that the third Royal Commission proposed a public subsidy to keep existing national dailies afloat, never mind the question of starting up new ones. That was beyond the pocket even of the super-rich until Shah and Murdoch broke the power of the unions in the 1980s.

The 1947 Press Commission endorsed 'market accountability' not because it naively believed free entry was realistic but because it thought the existing range of papers covered enough points of view to meet the conditions of an informed democracy, and because intervention in the market would have been a cure worse than the disease. The Commission's arguments became the classic post-war statement bolstering the historic claim that a free press was a press free from government — regardless (implicitly) of the social and financial powers that might curb it. The two later Commissions shifted the emphasis but did not challenge the argument's essentials.

Part of the plausibility of the Press Commission view came from the traditional links between the press and the party system. The Commission thought 'all important points of view' should have an outlet. Most of the important issues and interests in society, the argument went, were represented in the various political parties. There is a natural affinity, as chapter 8 suggested, between parties and papers: a paper is a focus of activity and a means of building membership. Parties are as strong as their support, and a loyal party paper is therefore popularly accountable. Bias does not matter, provided that readers are aware of it and that rival papers exist in support of other parties. As the 1925 *Labour Year Book* put it, 'the falsehoods and mis-representation of one party [are] promptly exposed and refuted in the national organs of the other'.

The 1947 Press Commission defence of 'market account-ability' thus rested (implicitly, in fact) on an assumption that the post-war press and party system would continue roughly to parallel each other. This did not really happen, as we have seen. Papers became notoriously unreliable, from the viewpoint of leaders and party professionals who were involved in day to day policy and tactics. Party loyalty was always liable to clash with the rival journalistic belief in the importance of indepen-dence from government.

The idea of press accountability through links with the party system really belonged to an age when readers did not look to their papers chiefly for relaxation and entertainment. As the 'seriousness' of a broadsheet format gave way to tabloid values, and as TV expanded, the papers most people read stopped covering party politics like their predecessors – even though they continued to have strong political views.

While the *Daily Mirror* was steadily loyal to the Labour party leadership in the 1940s and 1950s and dealt with politics in a serious way, it could equally have justified itself not by 'party accountability' but by a populist appeal: 'We just give our readers what they want'. This was the natural defence of a mass circulation tabloid, whose values stressed entertainment and relaxation, with neither scope nor space for political detail and abstractions. It might be called the 'Page Three' theory of accountability. Although it dated back at least as far as North-cliffe, who used movements in his papers' circulation figures to justify shifts in the editorial line, its post-war use was most effectively signalled by the arrival of the Murdoch *Sun* in 1970, with its daily bare-breasted girl on page three. This was the newspaper as follower not leader: if people did not like nudes on page three, circulation would drop and they would be replaced. Within much broader limits than on the broadsheet papers, quantitative not qualitative judgements ruled (is it good for sales, never mind about souls?). Where the inter-war barons and the party papers aimed to carry their readers with them, while telling them what they 'ought to know', the populist tabloid was driven by market research and readers' known preferences, and was in this sense genuinely 'the voice of its readers'.

The populist argument had the uncomplicated appeal of boiled sweets. To some extent, it was true by definition that the larger was the circulation of the paper, the more it necessarily reflected the likes of the mass of its readers. The success of the 'soaraway' *Sun* in the 1970s and 1980s was difficult to argue with. The problem about it as a form of accountability was that of the excluded alternative. Notwithstanding readership research, how could one be sure people would not have preferred a more serious tabloid if it could compete on equal terms (rather than start from scratch), or if one grew up expecting something less frivolous in a newspaper? Maybe (though is it likely?) the *Sun* 'soared away' *despite* the nudes on page three, not because of them. The complaint, particularly from the left, was as old as popular journalism. The *Sun*, and to a less degree the *Mirror* before it, could be seen either as an enlivener of dull lives or, in the phrase radical critics used against Northcliffe, as 'polluting the pure river of enlightenment'.

The pure river of enlightenment was certainly fed by the springs of *The Times* − in the view of *Times* people, anyway, and of that part of the nation's elite known in the 1950s and 1960s as 'the establishment' (a usage coined, in fact, by a *Times* man). If Colonel Astor offered the accountability of the market place in 1947, his staff would surely have supplemented it by a

242 Markets, Self-Regulation and the Law

justification summed up in the notion of independence – the word chosen in 1986 for a new daily based substantially on the old *Times* idea (and drawing many of its older readers).

The Times, perhaps *The Observer*, and later the *Independent*, appealed for the reader's trust on the basis of a comprehensive disinterest or detachment. 'Independence' was indeed the key – from government, parties, pressure groups, advertisers, financial interests, profit margins. Even the cult of personality was avoided, by keeping the entire contents anonymous: only in 1967 were bylines introduced. (The one previous exception – and conceit – was 'Oliver Edwards', the pseudonym of Sir William Haley, the editor till that year, who wrote a weekly books column.) Freed from such constraints like no other institution (except perhaps a university), a paper could report and judge events supremely on their merits. *The Times* in the mid-nineteenth century had seen itself virtually as an estate of the realm. Northcliffe, who bought it in 1908, thought seriously of bequeathing it to the British Museum, not for embalming with the mummies but to secure its independence. In precisely that spirit it was bought by Colonel Astor on Northcliffe's death in 1922, specifically to secure it from party politicians such as Lloyd George.

Throughout the Astor ownership and that of the Thomsons from 1967 to 1981, *The Times* continued to claim a special kind of independence. It was institutionalized in the presence on the board of a handful of 'national' directors, such as the Governor of the Bank of England and the President of the Royal Society, as a protection against malign influences. Under Murdoch the arrangement continued; but it looked a sham, for it did not prevent him sacking the editor, Harold Evans, in an interventionist and most un-Astor/Thomson-like way. The last of the old, independent editors was thus William Rees-Mogg, in the chair for most of the Thomson years. The experience qualified him perfectly for chairmanship of the Thatcher government's Broadcasting Standards Council in 1989, which (on a generous interpretation) was intended to epitomize comparable 'independence'.

The Times' independence, it should be emphasized, did not

mean sitting on the fence or expressing 'all points of view'. Rather, it was a matter of the procedures by which a view was reached. The unique quality of these was supposedly that unlike even a statesman, who had to take account of public opinion and electoral calculation, the paper could judge dispassionately by a process of reasoned argument based on clear principles and accurate information. If its conclusions did coincide with a government's, that would be entirely fortuitous. The idea was summed up in *The Times'* letters column. This was a nationally unique forum, in which people whose worlds might otherwise never collide could hammer away at an issue. It was class-based, of course. But it was capable of wider resonance, since other papers from time to time quoted it or followed up letters as news items; and the voice of working class representatives, such as trade union leaders, was frequently heard, if not working class tones themselves.

In the years after 1945 two experiences gave force to *The Times'* claim to independence. One was the paper's beetroot embarrassment and guilt at having been so utterly wrong about the best way to handle Hitler and Mussolini in the 1930s. Its campaign for a policy of appeasement, it now conceded, was the result of the editor Geoffrey Dawson getting too close to ministers and playing the statesman instead of the detached observer. The second experience was the paper's startling enthusiasm — startling because it had seemed previously so conservative if not Conservative — for the welfare radicalism of the Attlee government. In the mid-1940s, under the guidance of historian-turned-leaderwriter E H Carr, *The Times* was politically pink.

The theoretical problem with this idea of 'independence' was that the paper's basic values obviously had to come from somewhere: in that sense it had a bias no less than any other paper. In practice this was 'constitutionalist', a concern primarily that things were done in the right way — whether in social policy, international relations, standards of public life or on the football pitch — and only secondarily with what actually was decided. The paper prided itself on being a 'journal of record', carrying detailed law reports, parliamentary coverage and various official announcements that were not easily justifiable by ordinary news values but that recognized the importance of the institutions concerned to the social order. Among these, naturally, was the monarchy. *The Times* published the daily Court Circular on its Court Page, and until well after the war a few copies of the paper were printed at the end of each daily run as a 'Royal Edition' on special high quality paper.

A second problem about 'independence' was that, if it was to be taken on trust, it had, like justice, to be seen to be believed. For how else could readers know it existed? Under the Astors, this was no problem, partly because no financial crisis raised the issue of profit versus journalistic values until the 1960s. But in the Thomson and Murdoch ownerships, *The Times* passed to multinational conglomerates, and Thomson had major holdings, for example, in North Sea oil. Anyone wishing to impugn the integrity of the paper could claim it was in the grip of sectional interests. *The Sunday Times*, moreover, had become a crusading specialist in exposure journalism under Thomson's ownership. What chance of an exposé of oil company profiteering? Perhaps there was no profiteering, but how were readers to know what subtle pressures might gag the editor?

Times-style 'independence', like party ownership of papers, belonged to an earlier age of smaller, self-contained organizations. Its logic remained intact, and new life was indeed breathed into it by the *Independent*. But it was necessarily precarious in practice, for it depended on financial security; and if at some future date the *Independent*, which lacked the backing of a conglomerate, found itself unprofitable, how long would its independence last? *The Observer*, similarly independent, lost credibility after it passed to Lonrho in 1981. The *Guardian* remained free of a conglomerate, but it was fortunate to survive the hard economic times of the 1970s at all. Besides, it did not take quite the same view of 'independence', being committed to a policy of radicalism by the terms of the trust that controlled it.

Papers that wished to show they were not the tool of conglomerate owners adopted in the 1960s and 1970s a notion of accountability that combined opening their columns to a variety of discordant opinions (made easier by the decline of anonymous journalism) with an editorial stance of scepticism or hostility towards powerful interests. This was the heyday of 'adversary journalism'. It chimed with (perhaps contributed to?) the anti-authoritarianism of the late 1960s, and it reached its international peak in the destruction of the corrupt American President Nixon by the *Washington Post* and *New York Times*. In Britain, it was led by *The Sunday Times*, under the editorship of Harold Evans, with its remorseless 'Insight' team, exposing the wicked and incompetent.

Adversary journalism invited people to believe that if a paper was against the big and powerful, it must be *for* the readers. It was an extension of the 'fourth estate' tradition. But it had two flaws. It was open, first, to the challenge. 'We know what you are *against*, but what are you in favour of?' The answer, for *The Sunday Times*, seemed to be a mixture of *Times*-style rationalism and a residual Tory partisanship left over from its Kemsley ownership. The second flaw, the distinctive vice of adversary journalism, was more subtle. It consisted in a confusion of the newspaper with the news. Time and again, what started as a *Sunday Times* campaign — whether about thalidomide or about excessive government secrecy stifling publication of an ex-cabinet minister's diaries — ended with the role of the paper itself as the news. Should the paper be allowed to publish an article critical of the drug company? Should it defy a government ban on the Crossman diaries? This confusion might not matter much. News anyway has traditionally included not only 'the story' but an element of 'how we got the story'. But in the context of accountability, the confusion suggests that if a paper justifies its role too prominently by reference to what it dislikes, it risks lack of proportion in its reaction to events, for its own involvement becomes a major criterion of their importance. It risks becoming hound not guard dog, bully not champion.

All those arguments trying to justify non-interference in the press by outsiders rested ultimately on the assumption that there was for the reader somewhere else to go. The listener and viewer, however, had initially no such choice. For that very reason, of course, the thread of broadcast accountability was spun strong. Broadcasters were held formally accountable to

Parliament through the intermediary body of one, later two, public corporations.

For day-to-day practice — whether a programme really did 'inform, educate or entertain' — those threads were gossamer thin. Only in the rare event of a massive row (someone drunk on air; frightful language or violence; a claim of political bias) did they prove strong. Even then, they could only bind for the future, since the rows almost always came *after* a broadcast, not before.

On a day-to-day basis the broadcasters gradually adopted the same range of self-justifications as the press. Thus 'entertainment' — the showbiz element of programming — appealed to the populist claim to give the viewers what they wanted. This created the massive audiences for soap operas, quizzes and chat shows, and it effectively reversed the old order of priority by putting entertainment first. For the BBC, the need to give higher recognition to this argument was one of the hard consequences of competition after the introduction of ITV and ILR.

Phone-in, talk-back and 'open door' or access programmes, all of which became commonplace after shaky and self-conscious starts in the early 1970s, represented the closest the broadcasting duopoly could get to the 'free entry' ideal theoretically available in the unlimited market of print. Party politics were treated scrupulously on the basis of 'paralleling' the parliamentary party system, with disputes limited mainly to the conditions of access for minor parties. Current affairs and documentaries trod a precarious line between party balance, 'adversary journalism' and claims to independence of judgement comparable to the old *Times* idea. BBC news used to be the quintessence of 'independence'. As we saw, the very introduction of TV news was opposed by traditionalists fearing picture value might adulterate correct news values. 'Constitutionalist' elements were represented in the reverential approach to broadcasting about royalty, in the privileged position given to the legally established religion of Protestantism compared with alternatives, and in the daily report of parliamentary proceedings, which was edited less by news values than by reference to Parliament's own objectives.

In general, broadcast programme categories and production groups did not overlap, so the danger that these different forms of accountability would clash was slight. But occasionally they did, in plays, for example. Drama production was involved in a perennial tension between the familiar or popular and the innovative. From the mid-1960s onwards the political play was a type that politicians periodically treated as appropriate to political accountability rules not 'entertainment' rules. The broadcasters, however, kept their customary rules of balance in mind when planning plays and usually resisted pressure.

The distinctive problem of accountability for the broadcasters by the late 1980s was that the number and diversity of radio and TV channels, hours of programming, production organizations and methods of finance meant that the simple principles effected through the public corporation model were increasingly inadequate. Yet the system remained a *regulated* market, with the result that the varied rhetoric of accountability developed for the press fitted broadcasting even less convincingly than it fitted newspapers. The Thatcher government's response was to set up the Broadcasting Standards Council as an instrument of programme accountability, while making broadcasting structures as much of a 'free' market as possible through such devices as guaranteed access for independent production companies and through auctioning whole ITV franchises.

Broadcasters were predisposed against the Standards Council partly because their internal machinery of accountability was elaborate and well established. In the BBC this included a large General Advisory Council, regional Councils and specialist advisory bodies for subjects such as religion, education and agriculture. All these were a supplement to, and originally a substitute for, detailed audience research. ITV had a similar structure, with the additional dimension of advice about the contents of advertisements. Backing these up were the broadcasters' codes of practice – symbols, again, of good faith and self-discipline. From 1964, for example, ITV operated a code on violence in TV programmes ('ingenious and unfamiliar methods of inflicting pain and injury – particularly if capable of easy imitation – should not be shown without the most careful consideration', and so on).

Press and broadcasters, then, relied eventually on very similar arguments to persuade the public, the politicians and the increasing number of interested pressure groups, that it was ultimately in everybody's interest for media to be accountable in general to some combination of their consciences and the market place. On the whole, they got away with it — even if that did not necessarily mean they carried conviction. But how long into the future would they continue to do so?

11 Conclusion

When people ask about the effects of media, chapter 1 suggested, they generally turn out to be interested in something else, of which media might be a cause, such as violence or political bias. A history of media could easily slip into being a history of society as a whole. This in itself reflects the centrality of media in our lives.

For the same reason, questions about the effect of media upon individual people often get unsatisfactory answers. Until you know why the questioners are asking — the question behind the question — you cannot be sure what to say. Are they interested in *intentional* influence or *unintentional*? *Short-run* influence (however defined), or *long run*? Influence over a person's *knowledge, attitudes, beliefs*? Or over the person's subsequent *behaviour* (many people are persuaded that tobacco and alcohol are bad for them, but they go on smoking and drinking, even so)?

A question about media and violence or pornography, then, would get a rather different answer according to which of those other questions someone was interested in. At the extremes, the general answers about media influence over individuals are a safe bet. People in 1945–90 were not the puppets of the media barons, jerking at every tug of the string. Nor, equally , can we seriously believe that popular attitudes were entirely unmoved by the media. The problem is to know where inbetween, in particular cases, the balance of influence and autonomy lay.

If we were to pursue the issue further, it would be most clearly done through a series of categories and distinctions. From previous chapters, it is clear that media had influence in some measure over elite individuals and groups. Media created and destroyed reputations – sometimes conclusively in politics, as with the scandals surrounding the Conservative minister John Profumo (1963) and the Liberal leader Jeremy Thorpe (1970s). Pop stars, as a class, were the creation of media. Media transformed the economics of sporting stardom, from football to snooker and darts. Formerly amateurs or poorly paid, the best performers advanced to superstar wealth. The royal family acquired a more complex kind of superstardom (and without any direct increase in personal wealth).

Another category of speculation could be media's effects upon the distinctiveness of regional and social class cultures. An early landmark in the period was Richard Hoggart's discussion of working class culture in *The Uses of Literacy* (1957), but the subject was part of a wider and continual sociological preoccupation with class in post-war Britain. A third category might be the effects of media upon political and social institutions of all kinds – schools, trade unions, the police and armed services, scientific and medical research laboratories, in addition to the institutions of Parliament and political parties discussed in chapter 8. Fourth might be our perceptions of the outside world. What did TV contribute to our grasp of the reality and moral issues of war, famine, race?

The triteness of such paragraphs illustrates again the difficulty of talking about media effects at large. Hence, too, the recurrent theme in this book of *accountability*. Assume that media *were* a major influence in 1945–90. We have analysed the arguments they used to justify self-regulation and the accountability of the market place, and have seen that their claims became increasingly rickety. Conglomeration, concentration and internationalization made them even worse. The post-war decades contributed no new solutions, beyond complaints machinery and the powers of the IBA and the monopoly laws (weak in practice) to limit cross-ownership and press concentration.

The case for accountability must not be taken for granted.

Lists and tables showing concentration and conglomeration are not in themselves an argument. If three or four large newspaper groups were not enough for popular accountability in 1945–90, what number would have been? What difference did it make, that the dominant groups changed periodically? Would lots of smaller groups necessarily have reflected and encouraged the variety of our culture more successfully? If governments had interfered with the media market more actively, what would that have implied for the accountability of governments themselves?

This last question is the critical one for the post-war period. No one argued a successful case that the need to hold an increasingly integrated media industry accountable to the public through the government was greater than the need to hold the government accountable through the media. But in practice, one did not have to be a cynic to argue that by 1990 Britain had reached the worst of both worlds: audiences who were not very interested in media that spent time and money on holding governments accountable; and governments that sought to manipulate the media but not to limit the excesses of concentration and cross-ownership.

Perhaps in the 1990s that might change, if true. Telling the future is no more reliable with media than with anything else. In 1913 the anonymous author of *Bohemian Days In Fleet Street* peered ahead to 1960. He visualized a suburban Mr Jones coming down to breakfast keen for news (including, presciently, of the reigning monarch, Queen Elizabeth). Beside his plate is a 'receiver and communicator' which 'sucks in from the ambient air the news sent circulating from the central depot'. Jones selects the subjects 'by a curious arrangement of "stops". There is the "City" stop, the "Parliamentary" stop, the "Courts" stop, the "Racing" stop ... Thus the news is gently murmured to Jones as he eats his ham and eggs.' The only thing seriously wrong with this fancy is what happens after breakfast. Instead of driving off to work by car, Jones unhitches his aeroplane from the aero-railings.

Appendix: Provincial Evening Papers

Listed by town, name of paper, owner and circulation (thousands) in 1945 (or at start) and owner and circulation (thousands) in 1987 (or at closure).

Papers existing in 1945

England

Barrow, *Evening Mail*; Westminster (19); Warm Welcome (22)
Bath, *Evening Chronicle*; Wessex (15); Westminster (27)
Birmingham, *Evening Despatch*; Westminster (138); closed, 1963
Birmingham, *Evening Mail*; Iliffe (200); Ingersoll (233)
Blackburn, *Evening Telegraph*; Kemsley (70); Thomson (55)
Blackpool, *Evening Gazette*; Grimes (40); United (52)
Bolton, *Evening News*; Tillotson (65); Reed (51)
Bournemouth, *Evening Echo*; Southern (45); same (56)
Bradford, *Telegraph and Argus*; Westminster (103); same (81)
Brighton, *Evening Argus*; Southern Publishing (42); Westminster (95)
Bristol, *Evening Post*; BEP/Associated (109); BEP (108)
Bristol, *Evening World*; BEP/Associated (60); closed, 1962
Burton, *Daily Mail*; BDM (18), Yattendon (Iliffe) (22)
Cambridge, *Evening News*; Taylor (17); Yattendon (Iliffe) (46)

Carlisle, *Cumbrian Evening News*; Carlisle Conservative News-
papers (12); Cumbrian (28)
Cheltenham, *Gloucestershire Echo*; Associated (18); same (29)
Coventry, *Evening Telegraph*; Iliffe (50); Ingersoll (91)
Darlington, *Evening Dispatch*; Westminster (13); closed, 1986
Derby, *Evening Telegraph*; Associated (46); same (79)
Exeter, *Express and Echo*; Harmsworth (30); Associated (36)
Gloucester, *Citizen*; Associated (19); same (40)
Grimsby, *Evening Telegraph*; Associated (25); same (73)
Halifax, *Evening Courier*; Halifax Courier (33); same (37)
Hartlepool, *Mail*; Portsmouth and Sunderland (24); same (29)
Huddersfield, *Daily Examiner*; Woodhead (27); same (43)
Hull, *Daily Mail*; Associated (95); same (105)
Ipswich, *Evening Star*; E. Anglian D. Times (Colman) (30); E.
Counties (Colman) (36)
Kettering, *Evening Telegraph*; East Midlands Allied Press (26);
same (41)
Leeds, *Yorkshire Evening News*; United (122); closed, 1963
Leeds, *Yorkshire Evening Post*; Yorkshire Conservative News-
papers (204); United (143)
Leicester, *Evening Mail*; Hewitt/Associated (40); closed, 1962
Leicester, *Evening Mercury*; Hewitt/Associated (100); Associated
(146)
Lincoln, *Echo*; Daily Mirror (20); Associated (34)
Liverpool, *Echo*; Liverpool Daily Post (284); Trinity Inter-
national (207)
Liverpool, *Evening Express*; Liverpool D. Post (89); closed,
1958
Manchester, *Evening Chronicle*; Kemsley (224); closed, 1963
Manchester, *Evening News*; Guardian and Manchester Evening
News (Scott) (250); same (291)
Middlesbrough, *Evening Gazette*; Kemsley (69); Thomson (75)
Newcastle, *Evening Chronicle*; Kemsley (190); Thomson (145)
Northampton, *Chronicle and Echo*; United (37); same (39)
Norwich, *Eastern Evening News*; Norfolk News (Colman) (38);
E. Counties (Colman) (51)
Nottingham, *Evening News*; Westminster (47); closed, 1963
Nottingham, *Evening Post*; T. Bailey Forman (90); same (131)

Nuneaton, *Evening Tribune*; Leamington Spa Courier (25); EMAP (13)

Oldham, *Evening Chronicle*; Hirst, Kidd and Rennie (25); same (41)

Oxford, *Mail*; Westminster (25); same (41)

Plymouth, *Western Evening Herald*; Harmsworth (62); Associated (59)

Portsmouth, *Evening News*; Portsmouth and Sunderland (81); same (93)

Preston, *Evening Post*; United (88); same (70)

Scarborough, *Evening News*; Whittaker (8); EMAP (19)

Sheffield, *Star*; Kemsley (156); United (138)

Shields (North), *Evening News*; Westminster (11); closed, 1959

Shields (South), *Gazette*; Westminster (24); Northern Press (27)

Southampton, *Evening Echo*; Southern (60); same (85)

Stoke-on-Trent, *Evening Sentinel*; Associated (72); same (107)

Sunderland, *Echo*; Portsmouth and Sunderland (57); same (66)

Swindon, *Evening Advertiser*; Westminster (22); same (37)

Torquay, *Herald Express*; Harmsworth (18); Associated (31)

Weymouth, *Evening Echo*; Southern (20); same (24)

Wolverhampton, *Express and Star*; Graham (149); Claverley (238)

Worcester, *Evening News*; Berrows (30); Reed (28)

York, *Evening Press*; Kemsley (44); Westminster (54)

Wales

Cardiff, *South Wales Echo*; Kemsley (132); Thomson (93)

Newport, *South Wales Argus*; Thomas (32); United (41)

Swansea, *South Wales Evening Post*; Associated (47); same (68)

Scotland

Aberdeen, *Evening Express*; Kemsley (67); Thomson (75)

Dundee, *Evening Telegraph and Post*; D.C. Thomson (48); same (47)

Edinburgh, *Evening News*; United (129); Thomson (114)
Edinburgh, *Evening Dispatch*; Findlay; closed 1963
Glasgow, *Evening Citizen*; Beaverbrook (144); closed, 1973
Glasgow, *Evening News*; Kemsley (99); closed, 1955
Glasgow, *Evening Times*; Outram (293); Lonrho (180)
Greenock, *Telegraph*; Orr (24); United (21)
Paisley, *Daily Express*; Lochhead (19); Lonrho (12)

Northern Ireland

Belfast, *Telegraph*; Baird (120); Thomson (148)

Papers founded after 1945

Burnley, *Evening Star*; Thomson, 1965; closed 1983
Chatham, *Evening Mail*; launched and closed, 1969
Chatham, *Evening Post*; Kent Messenger, 1969; same (27)
Chelmsford, *Evening Herald*; launched 1980, closed 1982
Colchester, *Evening Gazette*; Essex County Newspapers, 1970;
    Reed (31)
Doncaster, *Evening Post*; United, 1966; closed, 1983
Guildford, *Surrey Daily Advertiser*; launched 1974, closed 1980
Hereford, *Evening News*; News of the World, 1959; closed,
    1967
Luton, *Evening Post*; Thomson, 1967; amalgamated Hemel
    Hempstead *Post and Echo*, 1975; closed 1983
Reading, *Evening Post*; Thomson, 1965; same (32)
Slough, *Evening Mail*; Thomson, 1969; closed, 1982
Southend, *Evening Echo*; Westminster, 1969; same (61)
Telford, *Shropshire Star*; Midland News; Claverley (94)
Watford, *Evening Echo*; Thomson, 1967; amalgamated Hemel
    Hempstead *Post and Echo* 1975; closed 1983

Note: This list excludes some 'series titles' (such as in Birmingham Evening Mail group) and some new titles later
amalgamated.
Sources: Camrose (1947); Press Council; Royal Commissions
on the Press.

Outline Chronology

1946   TV service resumes, 7 June.
1947   Royal Commission on the Press (reports 1949).
1948   First TV newsreel (silent), 5 January.
1949   Beveridge Committee on Broadcasting (reports 1951).
1950   First TV coverage of general election results.
1953   Press Council set up.
        Coronation televised.
        First edition of *Panorama*, 11 November.
1954   Television Act establishes ITV (starts, 1955).
        TV licences growing at 800,000 per annum.
1955   Wartime newsprint controls end.
1956   Eden makes first televised ministerial broadcast, 27 April.
1957   Queen's Christmas message broadcast on TV.
1958   TV advertising passes national press advertising.
1959   First TV general election campaign coverage.
        The *Guardian* drops 'Manchester', prints in London.
1960   *News Chronicle* and London Evening *Star* close.
        Pilkington Committee on broadcasting (reports 1962).
1961   Royal Commission on the Press (reports 1962).
        Sunday Times colour magazine starts.
1963   Lay members join Press Council.
1964   BBC 2 starts, 20 April.
        Pirate radio starts (Radio Caroline).
1965   Cigarette advertising banned from TV.

1966   *The Times* puts news on front page.
1967   BBC2 starts regular colour.
        Pirate radio banned; Radio 1 starts.
        BBC local radio starts.
        ITV re-franchises and shake-up.
1969   BBC1 and ITV start regular colour.
        Murdoch buys *Sun* and launches it as tabloid.
1971   Independent Local Radio authorized (starts in 1973).
1974   Annan Committee on broadcasting (reports 1977).
        Royal Commission on the Press (reports 1977).
        First election radio phone-ins.
1975   House of Commons trial radio broadcasts (regular from 1976).
1978   *The Times* and *Sunday Times* suspend publication in industrial dispute, November (till November 1979).
1980   London *Evening News* and *Evening Standard* merge.
1981   Murdoch completes purchase of *Times* newspapers.
1982   ITV re-franchises.
        Channel 4 starts.
        Hunt Report signals cable expansion.
1983   Breakfast time TV (BBC and ITV).
1984   Maxwell buys *Mirror* newspapers.
1985   Peacock Committee on BBC finance (reports 1986).
1986   Murdoch moves *The Times* to Wapping, January.
        Today and *Independent* launched.
1989   Official Secrets Act reformed.
        Regular House of Commons TV starts.

Bibliography

Readers will find further detail and discussion about many features of the period after 1945, including media not discussed here, such as film and magazines, in Jeremy Tunstall, *The Media in Britain* (London, Constable, 1983). James Curran and Jean Seaton, *Power without Responsibility: the Press and Broadcasting in Britain* (London, Routledge, 1988) has become an established text, regularly updated. It has more historical depth than Tunstall but less range and tabular information. Both books have comprehensive bibliographies, and Tunstall's is annotated. Ralph Negrine, *Politics and the Mass Media in Britain* (London, Routledge, 1989), covers comparable ground. An excellent survey of theories and approaches to the study of mass media is Denis McQuail, *Mass Communication Theory* (London, Sage, 2nd edn, 1987).

There are always new books about the press and broadcasting, but, as yet, few general and succinct histories. On the press, see Lee (1976), Smith (1979) and Boyce, et al., (1978). Koss (1981, 1984) is a two-volume study of the press and the party system; Ayerst (1971) is a history of the (Manchester) *Guardian* but its reach in fact is broader. Briggs' monumental history of broadcasting (strictly, of the BBC) already ran to four volumes in 1990 (Briggs, 1961–79). A similar ITV enterprize up to 1982 is in three volumes (Sendall, 1982, 1983; Potter, 1989). Smith (1973) contains a useful historical analysis.

Media people and outsiders regularly publish more or less

ephemeral critiques of the media in general and of particular parts. Good examples are by Wintour (1972), Whale (1980), Jenkins (1979, 1986), Hetherington (1985), Tunstall (1971) and Schlesinger (1978).

Another category includes the relation of media to specific events and issues. Examples include the Glasgow University Media Group (1976), Harrison (1985) and Cumberbatch, et al., (1986) on industrial relations; Morrison and Tumber (1988) on the Falklands War; Golding and Middleton (1980) on welfare policy; Blumler and McQuail (1968) and Seymour-Ure (1974) on politics and elections.

There is a constantly replenished supply of memoirs and biographies (which are often the most enjoyable reading of the lot). Recent examples are Evans (1984) and Milne (1988). For a general discussion of press barons, see Brendon (1982), and for Beaverbrook in particular, see Taylor (1972).

A recent reference bibliography is D. Linton and Ray Boston, *The Newspaper Press in Britain: an annotated bibliography* (London, Mansell, 1987).

The following list includes sources cited in the text and those named above.

Annan, Lord 1977: see Committee on the Future of Broadcasting (1977).

Anon. 1913: *Bohemian Days in Fleet Street*. London: Simpkin, Marshall.

Ayerst, D. 1971: *The Guardian*. London: Collins.

Barwise, A. and Ehrenberg, A. 1988: *Television and its Audience*. London: Sage.

BBC 1946: *BBC Year Book 1946*. London: BBC.

BBC 1952: *BBC Year Book 1952*. London: BBC.

BBC 1966: *BBC Handbook 1966*. London: BBC.

BBC 1976: *Annual Review of BBC Audience Research*, 3. London: BBC.

BBC 1986: *Annual Review of BBC Audience Research*, 12. London: BBC.

Belson, W. A. 1967: *The Impact of Television*. London: Crosby, Lockwood.

Beveridge, Lord 1951: see Broadcasting Committee (1949).

Blumler, J. and McQuail, D. 1968: *Television in Politics*. London: Faber.

Boyce, G., Curran, J. and Wingate, P. (eds) 1978: *Newspaper History*. London: Constable.

Brendon, P. 1982: *The Life and Death of the Press Barons*. London: Secker & Warburg.

Briggs, A. 1961, 1965, 1970: *The History of Broadcasting in the United Kingdom*, vols. 1–3. London: OUP.

Briggs, A. 1979: *History of Broadcasting in the United Kingdom*, vol. 4: *Sound and Vision*. London: OUP.

Broadcasting Committee (1949) 1951: *Report*, cmd. 8116. London: HMSO.

Broadcasting Research Unit 1985: *The Public Service Idea in British Broadcasting*. London: BRU.

Butler, D. and Kavanagh, D. 1984: *The British General Election of 1983*. London: Macmillan.

Butler, D. and Kavanagh, D. 1988: *The British General Election of 1987*. London: Macmillan.

Butler, D. and Stokes, D. 1971: *Political Change in Britain*. Harmondsworth: Penguin.

Clark, P. 1981: *Sixteen Million Readers*. London: Holt, Rhinehart & Winston.

Cockerell, M. 1988: *Live from Number 10*. London: Faber & Faber.

Committee on Broadcasting (1960) 1962: *Report*, cmnd. 1753. London: HMSO.

Committee on Financing the BBC 1986: *Report*, cmnd. 9824. London: HMSO.

Committee on the Future of Broadcasting 1977: *Report*, cmnd. 6753. London: HMSO.

Craik, J. 1987: Elections. In J. Seaton and B. Pimlott, *The Media in British Politics*, Aldershot: Avebury, chapter 4.

Cudlipp, H. 1962: *At Your Peril*. London: Weidenfeld & Nicolson.

Cumberbatch, G. et al. 1986: *Television and the Miners' Strike*. London: BRU.

Curran, J. and Seaton, J. 1988: *Power Without Responsibility*, 3rd edn. London: Routledge.

Docherty, D., Morrison, D. and Tracey, M. 1987: *The Last Picture Show?* London: Broadcasting Research Unit.

Economist Intelligence Unit 1966: *The National Newspaper Industry*. London: EIU.

Evans, H. 1984: *Good Times, Bad Times*. London: Coronet Books.

Glasgow University Media Group 1976: *Bad News*. London: Routledge and Kegan Paul.

Glencross, D. 1985: 30 Years of Independent Television. *Airwaves*, Spring 1985. London: IBA.

Glenton, G. and Pattinson, W. 1963: *The Last Chronicle of Bouverie Street*. London: George Allen & Unwin.

Goldie, G. W. 1977: *Facing the Nation: Television and Politics 1936–1976*. London: Bodley Head.

Golding, P. and Middleton, S. 1980: *Images of Welfare*. London: Macmillan/Martin Robertson.

Harrison, M. 1985: *TV News: Whose Bias?* Hermitage: Policy Journals.

Harrop, M. 1987: Voters. In J. Seaton and B. Pimlott, *The Media in British Politics*, chapter 4.

Hartley, N., Gudgeon, P. and Crafts, C. 1977: *Concentration of Ownership in the Provincial Press*, Royal Commission on the Press, Research Series 5. London: HMSO.

Hetherington, A. 1985: *News, Newspapers and Television*. London: Macmillan.

Hoggart, R. 1957: *The Uses of Literacy*. London: Chatto & Windus.

Howkins, J. 1982: *New Technologies, New Policies?* London: British Film Institute.

Ingrams, R. 1979: *Goldenballs*. London: Private Eye/Andre Deutsch.

ITA 1967: *ITV 1967: A Guide to Independent Television*. London: Independent Television Authority.

Jenkins, S. 1979: *Newspapers: The Power and the Money*. London: Faber & Faber.

Jenkins, S. 1986: *Market for Glory*. London: Faber & Faber.

Koss, S. 1981, 1984: *The Rise and Fall of the Political Press in Britain*, 2 vols. London: Hamish Hamilton.

Lee, A. J. 1976: *The Origins of the Popular Press, 1855–1914*. London: Croom Helm.

McQuail, D. (ed.) 1972: *The Sociology of Mass Communications*. Harmondsworth: Penguin.

McQuail, D. (ed.) 1977: *Analysis of Newspaper Content*, Royal Commission on the Press, Research Series 4, cmnd. 6810–4. London: HMSO.

McQuail, D. 1987: *Mass Communication Theory*, 2nd edn. London: Sage.

Margach, J. 1978: *The Abuse of Power*. London: W. H. Allen.

Milne, A. 1988: *DG: The Memoirs of a British Broadcaster*. London: Hodder & Stoughton.

Morrison, D. and Tumber, H. 1988: *Journalists at War*. London: Sage.

Negrine, R. 1989: *Politics and the Mass Media in Britain*. London: Routledge.

Nicholas, R. 1951: *The British General Election of 1950*. London: Macmillan.

Paulu, B. 1961: *British Broadcasting in Transition*. London: Macmillan.

Peacock, Sir A. 1986: see Committee on Financing the BBC.

Pilkington, Sir H. 1962: see Committee on Broadcasting (1960).

Potter, J. 1989: *Independent Television in Britain*, vol. 3. London: Macmillan.

Royal Commission on the Press (1947–1949) 1949: *Report*, cmd. 7700. London: HMSO.

Royal Commission on the Press (1961–1962) 1962: *Report*, cmnd. 1811. London: HMSO.

Schlesinger, P. 1978: *Putting 'Reality' Together: BBC News*. London: Constable.

Seaton, J. and Pimlott, B. 1987: *The Media in British Politics*. Aldershot: Avebury.

Sendall, B. C. 1982: *Independent Television in Britain*, vol. 1. London: Macmillan.

Sendall, B. C. 1983: *Independent Television in Britain*, vol. 2. London: Macmillan.

Seymour-Ure, C. 1968: *The Press, Politics and the Public*. London: Methuen.

Seymour-Ure, C. 1974: *The Political Impart of Mass Media.* London: Constable.

Seymour-Ure, C. 1977: National Daily Papers and the Party System. In O. Boyd-Barrett, C. Seymour-Ure and J. Tunstall, *Studies on the Press*, Royal Commission on the Press, Working Paper, 3. London: HMSO.

Shawcross, Lord 1962: see Royal Commission on the Press (1961–1962).

Smith, A. 1973: *The Shadow in the Cave.* London: George Allen & Unwin.

Smith, A. 1979: *The Newspaper: an International History.* London: Thames & Hudson.

Taylor, A. J. P. 1972: *Beaverbrook.* London: Hamish Hamilton.

Tunstall, J. 1970: *The Westminster Lobby Correspondents.* London: Routledge & Kegan Paul.

Tunstall, J. 1971: *Journalists At Work.* London: Constable.

Tunstall, J. 1983: *The Media in Britain.* London: Constable.

Whale, J. 1980: *The Politics of the Media.* London: Fontana.

Wintour, C. 1972: *Pressures on the Press.* London: Andre Deutsch.

Index